T0290610

CHRISTOPHE JAUQUET

TRENDS IN THE TRANSFORMATION ECONOMY

Where health,
well-being
& happiness
matter most

Lannoo
Campus

D/2024/45/34 – ISBN 978 94 014 9937 8 – NUR 800

Cover and interior design: Karl Demoen and Joost van Lierop

LannooCampus Publishers is a subsidiary of Lannoo Publishers, the
book and multimedia division of Lannoo Publishers nv.

LannooCampus Publishers
Vaartkom 41 box 01.02
3000 Leuven
Belgium
www.lannoocampus.com

P.O. Box 23202
1100 DS Amsterdam
The Netherlands

Table of Contents

PREFACE

Dear reader,

There is a reason why I do what I do.
There is a reason why, 10 years ago, I became a keynote speaker, author and podcast host. Or at least one reason stands out most, perhaps.

I want to provide people with what I personally did not have the time for as a business leader: *"Making sense of the changes in the world to build a better business for my customers."*

So, I hope this book will bring you precisely that, whatever company or organisation you may work for, whatever function you hold.

What's certain is that you'll discover insights, examples and trends on various topics in this book, ranging from Artificial Intelligence to healthcare, mental health to finance, sustainability to corporate well-being, and from sex to the Metaverse. But more importantly, this book answers three of the most pertinent questions business leaders face today.

1. *How do we benefit from technological innovations?*
2. *How do we contribute to societal and environmental challenges?*
3. *How do we bring what matters most to our customers?*

Whatever industry you are working in, I'm confident you'll discover the answers or related inspiration to these questions while reading the book.

But the main answer to these questions is: *"We are entering The Transformation Economy."*

This is a shift in how value is created for customers. It is driven by the previous questions and results in solutions that go beyond meeting the customer needs and expectations. A great Customer Experience is no longer enough. People seek Customer Transformations that make them *"feel better, healthier and happier"*.

That is what matters most to them.
That is what we all value most in life.

The first of five parts of the book will introduce the importance of these transformations. The second part explains how to create those Customer Transformations.

It may sound easier said than done.
And you'll learn that it is indeed not that difficult.

I've conducted several years of research, experiments and interviews for this book to make Customer Transformation more tangible.
The result is the Life Aspirations Model.
It's a model that makes this "feeling better, healthier and happier" more tangible.
It's a model that is built on universal human values and priorities.
It's a model that helps create Customer Transformations for any business.

As with any model, framework or matrix, it may feel weird at first.
But by the end of the book, it will sound (almost too) obvious.
That's a promise.

Because aspirations are the new needs.

You'll discover the Life Aspirations Model in the second part of the book.
The following sections will then showcase how Life Aspirations are used in Healthcare, Business and Technology. (These are also the three main categories of my keynotes and my newsletter.).

You can always refer back to the Model at any time.

We've even printed coloured pages to help you find the Life Aspirations swiftly.
It serves as a reference, so it might be the least pleasant part to read in one sitting.

Like my first book, that's also how this book is written:
It's a reference guide on the Transformation Economy.

Here's what I would recommend:
- Read Chapters 1 to 5 because they introduce the Transformation Economy.
- Dip in and out of the Life Aspirations Model as needed.
- Consult the chapters 6 to 14 in any order (or read them all in one flow).

The book contains a ton of examples, often separated from the main text by an indent. You can skim over them or discover how it's been done before.

The book also covers various industries.
It can inspire you even if you are not active in a specific industry.
You'll learn from the Life Aspirations applied.
You'll discover how perhaps you can play a role in that industry.
You'll realise yourself how it might enter your sector as well.

But all in all, it will help you understand one thing:
We have indeed entered the Transformation Economy.

This book answers the three questions business leaders ask themselves today about technological innovations, societal and sustainable challenges, and what customers value most. But most of all, I hope this book makes sense of the changes in the world.
I hope it helps you to build a better business for your customers.
If so, I am convinced it can help build a better, healthier, happier world.

And that would then make me happy.
Because that is the reason why I do what I do.

Thank you for picking up this book. I really appreciate the time you invest in it.
Now, sit back, relax and let the inspiration take hold.

-Christophe-

P.S. If this type of content is up your alley, then subscribe to my newsletter on Transformations in Health, Business and Technology.

Subscribe via www.christophejauquet.com.

PART 1

TRANSFORMATIONAL TWENTIES

CHAPTER 1

TRANSFORMATION: THE WORD OF THE DECADE

As we entered the 2020s, I sent out a newsletter to my subscribers stating that 'transformation' would be the most important word of the decade ahead. What I meant by this is that companies and brands would be expected to transform the world, and the customers in it, in order to remain valuable enough for them. How could they do this? By honestly helping people with their Life Aspirations.

If the 2010s were all about 'digital transformation' for businesses, I firmly believe that the 2020s are about customer transformation. I'm not suggesting that digital will become less important. But the impact of applying digital solutions will shift from simply transforming products or services into an enjoyable experience towards transforming customers. Offering satisfying customer experiences (CX) will no longer be enough; brands will have to be aspirational. They will have to be the sustainable, diversity-endorsing, healthy and happy heroes their customers aspire to be themselves.

The Transformation Economy is the economic model centred on offering solutions designed to facilitate personal growth, better health and increased happiness in society and on this planet.

This is the Transformation Economy we will be delving into in this book. It's the economic model centred on offering solutions designed to facilitate personal growth, better health and increased happiness in society and on this planet. It prioritises experiences that lead to positive change in individuals' lives rather than traditional goods and services. The focus is on value creation through transformative experiences that enhance the well-being and overall quality of life for the customer, leading to a more life-aspirational form of commerce.

I alluded to this in my first *Healthusiasm* book, dedicating two segments in the first chapter to the rise of the Transformation Economy and the relevance of transformations themselves. In chapter 5 of this book, I will come back to why the Transformation Economy is so important for all types of businesses today. But first let's pay some attention to why transformations are relevant and in what ways today's society is motivated to transform even the parts of their lives that were previously considered untouchable or taboo. In this segment we'll learn that people today are concerned by three significant types of transformation:

- Transforming ourselves – health and happiness
- Transforming society – inclusion, equity and diversity
- Transforming the planet – sustainability and climate change

We'll delve into these various sought-after transformations and their role in propelling the significance of the Transformation Economy in this first section. The second part will guide you on creating these transformations for your customers, while the following sections explore how healthcare, business, and technologies (will) have to become (more) transformational. But first, let's lay the groundwork by taking a closer look at these transformations.

Transforming ourselves

In today's self-service world, individuals manage their own financial, travel and hospitality needs. This trend is extending into personal development as well. As technology democratises health and self-care, people are seeking ways to gain greater control over their own health and happiness, often from companies not traditionally linked to healthcare and in areas of life that were previously left untouched like science, ageing and death.

People are also enthusiastically adopting the new self-monitoring technologies that give them greater insight into and recommendations about their own health. Activity trackers, pulse metres, and blood pressure monitors, but also genetic and ketone testing are all now available to us as private individuals. We can use the information provided by these technologies to conduct our own personal science projects and improve our overall health.

Because we've started thinking about life differently. We live. We age. We die. But today we don't simply wait for those inevitable stages to occur. We no longer feel 'as old' as previous generations did. We don't want to be limited by age, despite the physical signs of ageing like wrinkles and grey hair. This shift has fuelled a 'Flat Age Society' where lifestyle choices are less age-dependent, where the massive anti-ageing industry is transforming into an ageing-well industry. The scope for transformation lies in the ever-present paradox: we want to grow old without the drawbacks of ageing. The rapidly expanding longevity industry seeks to increase health span, not just life span, exploring everything from traditional pharmaceuticals to life-changing biohacking, with a focus on living well rather than just living longer.

But it doesn't stop there. We aspire to transform death and how we die as well. We don't want to die alone in a cold, sterile environment, but surrounded by our loved ones. We don't want our funeral to be a sad, dark affair, but rather a celebration of a life well lived, filled with love and joy. We want to give back to the living in death by taking care of the planet with more sustainable burial practices. Death has been transformed from something sinister to a moment of healing.

Transforming society

People all over the world want to feel connected with others and be part of a community; it makes them happy and gives them a sense of belonging. However, many people still feel lonely and this has been getting worse year after year, affecting their happiness and health. The COVID-19 pandemic intensified this loneliness because it prevented people from seeing others and doing normal social activities, changing how they live and see themselves. This has led to self-care – where the focus was previously often on 'me-time' – becoming more about caring for ourselves as a social being and coming together with other people in a caring atmosphere, whether online or in person. Society may have become increasingly fragmented, but concepts such as 15-minute cities, urban collective farming and ageing in place aim to rebuild the social cohesion we've lost over the last 100 years.

There's no one type of self-care that works for every individual. We need a blend of activities, alone and together. And when people look for these activities, they have begun looking to others for support or to support them in turn. In doing so, they are breaking the taboos around topics that were previously considered too personal, shameful or different. With a desire to find the best approach to their own physical and mental health, people are finding each other in various ways. This approach far outweighs the few minutes a health professional can devote to it. Mutual support networks are now helping those living with chronic illness to find help, recommendations and a sense of belonging to a community.

We share information, approaches, opinions, techniques, and technologies in these new social networks. And because even the most dedicated medical professional can't possibly keep abreast of developments as well as a whole group of motivated people, such social networks can often enable greater insight into potential therapies than the average general practitioner. Even for those with no specific health concerns, sharing approaches and new technologies has enormous benefits and makes them feel part of a wider community.

CASE IN POINT

BRINGING PATIENTS TOGETHER

Look at how solutions such as **Carenity** *(the first social network for people living with chronic conditions),* **PatientsLikeMe** *(the world's largest personalised health network) or any* **Facebook** *group devoted to a particular condition do just that. They answer patients' needs (for information), meet their expectations (by being convenient) and help them with their life aspirations (ensuring they don't feel alone with their illness). I'm also impressed by the start-up* **Patient Partner** *for the same reason. They bring together patients about to undergo surgery with people who have already had the same operation, thus providing patients with information, relevancy and togetherness. All of these platforms fully engage patients by making them feel they're not alone.*

Meanwhile, social media has enabled voices that were once less heard, including minority groups, to share their stories. Online and local communities are uniting to challenge unfairness and promote social change. Traditional media, including TV and newspapers, are now more inclusive, showing diverse stories and backing important social issues. Workplaces are evolving too, reflecting society's demand for diversity and community support. In politics, we see a trend towards more representation from diverse groups. Education and healthcare are also adapting, to emphasise inclusion and use technology that makes services accessible to all.

Transforming the planet

You might not immediately see how transforming the planet is related to our own personal aspirations, but climate change is having an impact on our mental health and how we lead our lives. A global survey published in *The Lancet* in 2021 showed that almost 60% of 16- to 25-year-olds feel 'very' or 'extremely' worried about climate change, with nearly 4 in 10 asserting that they're 'hesitant to have children' as a result. Our drive to transform our immediate environment and the planet at large overlaps with our own health and happiness. But unlike the past 100 years, now our concern is not about extracting as much of the Earth's resources as possible, but instead about taking our place in an ecosystem that can already support us: transforming the planet into a healthy setting for the human race and all the other species that share it.

Indeed, there's growing evidence that if we don't make major efforts to reverse human impact on the planet, many regions will soon become increasingly hostile to the species currently present there – humanity included. The World Health Organization (WHO) has calculated that climate change could cause an additional 250,000 deaths and cost an extra 2–4 billion US dollars annually around the world. The WHO, therefore, considers climate change to be the single biggest health threat to humanity. In order to protect and preserve human health, we first need to protect and preserve the source of that health – nature.

CHAPTER 2

TYPE OF TRANSFORMATIONS

We've embarked on the transformational decade of the 2020s. In the first chapter, we've briefly discussed the transformations people seek to pursue. Now, we delve deeper into these transformational trends.

In this chapter, we will argue that people want to transform every moment in life, from running and ageing to dying or dealing with death. These Personal Transformations touch on aspects that previously did not receive sufficient attention. But (personal) science, cultural changes and new aspirations are transforming all these moments in our lives.

People also look beyond themselves to make a transformational impact. We live in an increasingly polarised society with not enough (focus on) equity, diversity and inclusion. Meanwhile, loneliness prevails, reality shifts, and change accelerates. Hence, people aspire to change society like never before. Contributing to these *Social Transformations* is becoming crucial for governments and corporations alike. Many social constructs are actively being transformed to achieve more equity, diversity and inclusion. The human aspiration for togetherness drives this. We are social animals, after all. We are stronger together.

Finally, the third transformation is also vital to tackle together. We realised that climate change is a health issue and that no healthy people can exist on a sick planet. Governments, businesses and organisations must aspire to a sustainable strategy that nurtures nature and allows us to nurture in nature.

At the end of these subchapters, you will understand how these three transformations are essential and omnipresent in today's reality. You will comprehend how people are driven to impact moments and parts of their lives that previously were untouched and for which they are looking to every business for help. These transformations are the drivers of the Transformation Economy. Including these transformations (personal, social, planetary) in your strategy will be critical for the near future of your business, whatever industry you are in. Chapter 3 will then explain how you can create value for your customers by focusing on these Transformations.

2.1 Personal transformations

We live in a world where, in many aspects of their lives, people are used to taking matters into their own hands. Think about the self-service solutions in the financial, travel, transportation or hospitality industry that empower their customer to be more efficient and improve customer experience. And this empowerment will soon also become the norm when it comes to our health and happiness, leading to a transformation in health and self-care that will bring empowered, personalised care. From prevention to diagnosis, people will receive more support through tools and solutions they can use themselves. The patient's participation will also radically increase their involvement in treatment and disease management, while earlier hospital discharge will give patients more responsibility. All of these changes will make 'self-care' a more critical aspect in each phase of health management, because people want to become the best version of themselves. More than ever, they want to transform themselves today.

Self-service represents a considerable challenge to the healthcare system, which has traditionally been closed off and protected from outside interference.

This represents a considerable challenge to the healthcare system, which has traditionally been closed off and protected from outside interference. But new and cheaper technologies, new knowledge and – above all – innovative new approaches to how healthcare is accessed are beginning to blur the boundaries between healthcare and self-care. In addition, users – who are more savvy than ever before – are constantly seeking out new, simple ways to access the information and care they need. They are also turning to companies and brands that have no direct affinity with health and self-care for help, because our environment, habits, and the objects we interact with daily can nurture our health and even contribute to our health and happiness.

This focus on Personal Transformations has sparked an interest in parts of our lives that were previously off limits or taboo. Science, ageing and death are great examples of things that people no longer accept as they are. They aspire to transform even these areas to change their lives positively and personally.

The personalisation and scientific revolution

Personalisation is everywhere, from the music you hear in your headphones to the special offers your regular supermarket sends you. Personalisation combined with access to scientific information has enabled people not only to learn about issues relevant to them, but also to set up and understand their own personal science. As patients, we are no longer willing to merely accept the treatment plan laid out by an overworked doctor who has no time to address us as an individual. As humans, we're constantly seeking to improve our health and happiness. And the falling cost of technology enables this quest.

In recent decades, the cost of science has dropped so much that even more advanced scientific techniques have become available to us. The most striking example is, without a doubt, DNA sequencing. In less than 20 years, the cost of DNA sequencing has dropped from $2.7 billion to $300. Biometric sensors and medically approved algorithms have also become cheap enough to be integrated easily into consumer electronics. As a result, almost one in two people use health apps while 30% of people are running around wearing health trackers that provide 'scientific insights' into their health (Morning Consult, 2023).

As science has become cheaper and more accessible, it has become a habit in our daily lives. We read the nutritional labels on food and the ingredient lists of cosmetics. We track the quality of our sleep, our sun exposure and our walking (a) symmetry. The COVID-19 pandemic reinforced this obsession with science as we monitored the levels of CO_2 in our homes. Every day, people want to hear insights and opinions given by medical or health experts, which they listen to critically and from which they form their own opinion. Health experts and medfluencers are some of the most trusted influencers on social media with 40% of patients saying that this information even affects how they cope with a chronic disease (Ogilvy, Influencer trends, 2023). Many brands have seen these changes coming so they try to improve or market their products more intelligently with the help of medical experts or claims. Customers don't want to be bamboozled by slick, obviously fake marketing slogans anymore. They want products that are backed by science and shared by these experts.

Many brands market their products with the help of medical experts or claims.

True personalisation for our health is therefore gaining ground. For example, Nestlé, Campbell Soup and a Japanese sushi restaurant make diet recommendations based on your DNA. This kind of transformation is much anticipated. In 2019, Mintel Research reported that 42% of British consumers are interested in a personalised diet based on their DNA. These kinds of health-related solutions will become as adaptive as your personalised Spotify playlist. In fact, Shiseido already has a dedicated app that analyses the condition of your skin, your sleep quality and data about your environment (such as temperature and humidity) to dispense personal skincare products for you each day. Similar adaptive solutions already exist for hair products, vitamins and replacement meals as well. There's even an artificial intelligence (AI) bot that can act as a mental health companion, growing every day to become your best friend.

Making science more personal

Personalisation and science is something that more and more people are incorporating into their own health management. This began with the launch of consumer wearables incorporating sensors. Initially, the health information provided was minimal, the data quality doubtful and the insights didn't actually generate much value.

Personal science is about people looking for a personally relevant answer to a personal health-related question. It's the scientific truth by and for an individual.

Nowadays devices contain medical-grade sensors and algorithms that provide a whole new set of opportunities to explore personal health topics, questions and problems. You can now observe, measure and learn from more diverse and solid data, allowing you to answer questions about your own personal energy, sleep or pain. As a result, you might discover that low-carb lunches make you more productive in the afternoon, that sleeping 8 hours rather than 7 hours improves your chances of being well-rested by 53% or that a heart rate over 170 BPM when running a 5K will make your joints hurt more. Personal science is about people looking for a personal answer to a personal health-related question. It's no wonder that the future of health and self-care is about true personalisation, with personal health assistance or digital twins powered by artificial intelligence providing the ultimate support (see Chapter 13.1). Companies willing to embrace this can be at the cutting edge of the wave.

PERSONAL SCIENCE USED BY RUNNERS

*Running is arguably the 'simplest' and oldest sport in the world, dating back to 775 BC. You put on a pair of shoes (or not) and go out running. You might take a banana to boost your energy if it's a long run. But that has changed a lot in recent years. Running has transformed into the poster child of Personal Science as technology has started to support people in their running ambitions. Step counters came first. They may have been around since the 1960s, but it wasn't until **Nike** incorporated the Nike+ iPod sensors into one of their shoes that they became popular in sports. Running apps complemented these activity trackers with personal reminders, recommendations and information. Wearable devices then sparked a new wave of personalisation. Smartwatches, rings, bracelets or earplugs contain built-in sensors that keep track of bodily movements, gather biometric data or assist with location tracking. Today, people can analyse their cadence, stability, step width, heartbeat, oxygen, heart rate variability and the volume of oxygen their body consumes. Perhaps they have a motivational coach in their ears who advises them based on these insights. It might be important to them that their clothing be breathable, lightweight and moisture repellent. Some items may provide ultra-precision body zoning or muscle compression, distribute sweat when needed or help prevent blisters. Perhaps their sports apparel helps with cooling or heating. And bras are tailored to any woman personally. All of this is available to improve your personal performance.*

CASE IN POINT

Today, you don't just 'put on your shoes and go running'. You would probably visit a runners lab equipped with the most recent high-tech measuring devices for an accurate analysis of more than 20 parameters that define your running posture and movement. Feet, legs, back, and body composition are evaluated to identify the shoe that best fits you personally.

You can also 'forget' about just taking a banana. Food has become much more personal as well, with personal dietary advice available not just on the day of the run but to build up your nutrition in the months before and to help you recover afterwards. Continuous glucose monitoring and other metabolism tracking devices like Lumen inform you about what your body needs and when. During your training, the Gx Sweat Patch by **Gatorade** *teaches you how much fluid and sodium is lost and how quickly, and compares your numbers to other athletes. That unique sweat profile generates personalised recommendations about hydration and electrolyte zones to optimise your performance. The intake of (simple or complex) carbohydrates, lean proteins, essential vitamins, minerals and antioxidants (like glutamines, probiotics, fish oil, calcium, L-carnitine, magnesium and amino acids) are often calculated to the minute and to the individual's body mass.*

All these personal insights can be complemented with a DNA analysis specifically made for runners, like **ORIG3N**, *to better understand how your genes impact training, nutrition, endurance and recovery. On the day of the big run, these personalised recommendations will be further adapted based on the measured (or expected) humidity, wind speed, temperature and altitude. As such, running has transformed from being the 'simplest sport' to a sport based on the scientific truth by and for an individual.*

Help people make sense of personal science

The personalisation revolution won't just be about companies making products available to customers. It will be about guiding customers through the forest of personalised science.

Until today, the healthcare system too often acted like a know-it-all. It's what I refer to as a system-based approach rather than a client-based approach (see Chapter 6). The system will tell you what to do. The system always knows better. I don't need to spell out the tension that this could create between the healthcare system and patients when personal science becomes even more common.

How can we prepare the healthcare system for the rise of personal science? What will it take for healthcare professionals to be able to accept this change? Will they end up being ignored? Is this the burning platform for healthcare? Maybe it is. Maybe it is not.

But obviously, there is a great danger lurking here. It's something we saw a lot in 2020 in the simple words: 'I've done my own research.' It's easy to laugh at that statement, but a lot more challenging to convince the person otherwise. The mere fact that so many people can no longer be convinced by the evidence provided by professional scientific experts comes with a significant risk. But we can't deny that personal science exists. In fact, this is one of the harshest realities for companies today: a large proportion of their customers are 'confidently stupid' as a result. However, people won't remain stupid as more data and better algorithms will help generate smarter insights.

People may seem confidently stupid today, but they won't remain stupid.

I don't believe personal science will go away. In fact, I am pretty sure it will surge in the next few years. So, how can you deal with it? If I were to launch a start-up today, it would show people how to manage personal science. Ordinary people may not be trained to be scientific researchers but they do want to observe, understand and learn from their own measurements. What we can do is help them with an empirical process and numerical reasoning. We can teach them to establish an outcome and define what should be tracked. We can't swim against the current, so we may as well find a way to go with the flow. More on this in Chapter 8.3 on Decentralised Healthcare.

Ageing

But personalisation and the scientific revolution aren't the only great examples of the focus on personal transformations. Ageing, too, is something we've begun to think about differently. Why would we not want to have an impact there as well? People now desire to transform how they see their age, how they age and even to challenge the concept of ageing in itself.

The changes our bodies go through over the years can change how we feel about ourselves. Lower energy, more curves and saggy skin can all affect our health and happiness. But that's life. At some point, we all reach a peak in our ability. As those humorous birthday cards say, it's all downhill from here. As we get older, our performance steadily declines. As humans, we are uniquely aware of that inevitable fate. Our body doesn't fail to show us that ageing is happening, developing wrinkles, grey hair and weaker muscles as a testament to our ageing bodies. We can see these changes in our parents and grandparents; we can see them in ourselves.

However, there is a transformation happening in society in how we 'undergo' ageing. We don't feel 'as old' as previous generations did at a certain age. It is often proclaimed that 40 is the new 30 or that 60 is the new 40. We feel less limited by our age, even as we grow older and greyer, even though wrinkles start to appear on our formerly smooth faces and even as we experience some frailty or loss of function. But we don't see it as being one step closer to death. Ageing has undergone a transformation of its own, to living well while ageing well. People want to be the best version of themselves, regardless of their age. They aspire to feel as healthy and as happy as possible, regardless of their age. In fact, it's sparked a sort of mantra: 'I'll be old later.'

Whereas a century ago people didn't want to look poor, now they don't want to look old.

Whereas a century ago people didn't want to look poor, now they don't want to *look* old. Today, we don't want to change our clothing, transport or activities to what was once supposed to be suitable for our age. We see older people walking around in the same sneakers, going to the same restaurants, using the same smartphones and enjoying the same leisure activities as 30-year-olds. And, to the dislike of many, we're 'pressured' by those filters on social media to continue looking young and beautiful for longer. I refer to this trend as the 'Flat Age Society'.

This desire to 'not look old' is reinforced by the increasing bias and even discrimination against older people, commonly known as ageism. According to the World Health Organization, half of the world's population is ageist against older people. This fact also tends to affect women more than men. I'm sure you've seen the movement by female actors in Hollywood for better roles for women as they age. Just because they're growing older doesn't mean that people want to be seen or treated as old.

Unsurprisingly, people are spending billions to look younger, stimulating an enormous anti-ageing industry. Whatever your poison – books, supplements, videos, courses, Instagram – there is a resource to support people fighting the signs of ageing. Weight loss clinics, personal coaches, nutritional advisors and other health gurus guide their clients on the best way to preserve their youth for longer. Meanwhile, anti-ageing creams and make-up help users disguise the marks of time. To go further, you can even trim a decade or two off your appearance using cosmetic surgery.

We all want to get old but we don't really want to be old.

But there still is a huge paradox in ageing. We all want to get old but we don't really want to *be* old. We want to see our families grow, the world evolve and to enjoy our lives but we don't want to experience frailty, loss of function or the deterioration of what was. Ageing is therefore a key research focus in the medical and pharmaceutical industries. Clinical trials targeting ageing doubled between 2012 and 2018. We're not just talking about the big players like GSK, Novartis, Celgene and AbbVie; there are many smaller companies also entering the longevity market. In fact, investment in longevity start-ups grew 16-fold in the same period.

INVESTING IN LONGEVITY

Longevity start-ups have become increasingly newsworthy recently. **Biosplice**, *founded in 2008, made up more than 20% of the anti-ageing and longevity industry and was valued at a staggering 11.6 billion dollars in April 2021. Meanwhile, pharmaceutical company* **AbbVie** *has extended its collaboration with Google's* **Calico Life Science** *several times, investing millions of dollars in their research and development on age-related diseases. There are also many stories of famous billionaire investors taking an interest in longevity start-ups, from Bill Gates, Jeff Bezos and Peter Thiel to Michael Bloomberg, Richard Branson, Mark Zuckerberg, Tim Disney and more. There's also the C-suite at* **Altos Labs** *that brings together the most prominent names in life sciences, including top pharmaceutical companies (such as GSK and Genentech), Nobel laureates, genius CRISPR pioneers and renowned health tech founders (such as those at GRAIL and Juno therapeutics). Longevity has become big in the start-up world.*

Different methods are being explored, from older pharmaceuticals like Metformin and Rapamycin to newer classes of medicine like senolytic drugs, that have been shown to prolong the lives of mice. Specific dietary supplements, targeted exercise and specific calorie restrictions have also become a focus in the race for longevity. However, more futuristic-sounding solutions are on the horizon as well. Imagine receiving blood plasma from someone younger than yourself, using printed organs or taking medicines manufactured from stem cells. We are entering a dubious phase of biohacking, human enhancement or even transhumanism, for which society is not yet mentally, ethically or philosophically prepared.

HUMAN ENHANCEMENTS

*Bryan Johnson is an entrepreneur and founder of **Kernel**, a company that develops advanced neural interfaces, and Braintree, a fintech firm that he sold to PayPal in 2013. After his success in technology and business, he shifted his focus to an ambitious personal health project.*

The 45-year-old Johnson embarked on a quest to reverse his biological age through a rigorous and experimental health regimen. He launched 'Project Blueprint' with the goal of achieving the health and body of an 18-year-old. This involves a comprehensive, data-driven approach, incorporating extensive daily monitoring of biometric data, strict dietary restrictions, exercise routines, sleep optimisation, and cutting-edge medical procedures. He's taken over 35,000 images of his bowels, blasts his pelvic floor with electromagnetic pulses, undergoes weekly acid peels and laser therapy, has fat injected into his face, takes two dozen supplements while on a strict vegan diet, and injects himself with his son's plasma... just to name a few.

His regimen is overseen by a team of over 30 medical professionals, including doctors, physiotherapists and nutritionists. They conduct regular tests and make adjustments to his programme, which include interventions at the cellular level and therapies to improve organ function.

Johnson's efforts are part of a broader interest in the field of biohacking, where individuals use a variety of techniques in an attempt to optimise health and extend lifespan. His project is also aligned with the field of rejuvenation biotechnology, which aims to therapeutically reverse the ageing process.

*While society attempts to grasp the consequences of this human enhancement trend, it certainly is rising in popularity considerably. Bryan Johnson even conceived the **Rejuvenation Olympics**, a public website that acts as a forum to share protocols and validated results for age rejuvenation. The platform contains a leadership board where – to date – 1,750 people battle to have the largest relative rejuvenation compared to their 'chronological age' (or what most people call the number of years/months/days since we were born).*

I hope I grow old enough to see it. Or do I?

Of course, all the innovation, progress and success stories delaying ageing aren't without their fair share of controversy. We live on an already overpopulated planet increasingly marred by social inequality, polarisation and the scarcity of basic resources. Rather than working on transforming ageing, surely we should be coming up with a solution to war, poverty, famine and drug addiction? And that's not to mention the risk that ageing solutions could deepen the divide between rich and poor, between those who can afford to live longer, healthier lives and those who can't. And how do we fund the lengthening lifespans of those who have already retired? In 2023, Emmanuel Macron's retirement reform, raising the French state pension age to 64, wasn't met with open arms even though it is still lower than those in surrounding countries. While it can feel morally dubious to invest in solutions to prevent ageing, it will happen regardless. And it will affect every business, no matter the sector.

But there's another troublesome aspect to prolonging life spans. Although many scientists are convinced that ageing will be solved earlier than most diseases, regulatory authorities – such as the US Food and Drug Administration – don't (yet) consider ageing to be a disease. In other words, it isn't yet possible to file a drug that targets ageing. In any case, we're nowhere near creating a drug that is able to rejuvenate people. Understanding the processes of how we age on a physiological level is extremely complex. However, the good news is that the progress being made will help us understand the biological consequences of ageing: age-related diseases.

And this is important, because more than half of people over the age of 65 are living with two or more long-term health conditions. This phenomenon is called multi-morbidity. Although many diseases are typically 'clustered', each disease is treated by different specialists with a particular care pathway and disease-specific medications. Medical research, drug development and healthcare systems are mainly centred on a specific disease, which makes it hard to understand the correlations between those clustered diseases.

Medical research, drug development and healthcare systems are mainly centred on a specific disease, which makes it hard to understand the correlations between clustered diseases.

Conversely, the longevity industry aims to understand the biological causes of ageing so that they can reverse it. In doing so, they are starting to understand the underlying causes of these disease clusters and are making it feasible to prevent these diseases. Understanding how we age will allow us to make ageing healthier. In the short term, we can expect the longevity industry to add health span, rather than life span, to their targets. After all, there's no point in letting people live until they're 140 years old if they *feel* like they're 140 years old.

People don't mind being old as long as they don't feel old. That's why, despite the name, this trend I call 'Ageless Ageing' is not fully about anti-ageing. It's not really about living longer either; it's about living well today. It's also about managing your age more holistically rather than trying to disguise it. The beauty industry was one of the first to embrace this trend, with many products (from Pause, Arbonne, Aurage and Mylène, for example) being (re-)branded from anti-ageing to well-ageing. This may sound like a cheap marketing trick, but the underlying drivers are being conscious of being healthy and an enthusiasm for health as we grow older. That's something every company can and should learn from.

Death

Just because death is one of the few certainties in life doesn't mean it can't be transformed. There's something scary about dying. Often we'd rather not talk about it. Why focus on the end when living is what we're doing right now? Death can often be seen as a failure, the result of our bad habits, one wrong move or a failure within medicine. In recent decades, dying has become a hidden, lonely and more sterile event. Rather than dying in their own homes, people are dying more and more often in a clinical environment like a hospital, hospice or retirement home.

During the COVID-19 pandemic, the dying process became even less human. Rather than the warmth of a family circle, 'lucky' patients died with only an unrecognisable, masked, overworked caregiver by their side. The 'unlucky' died alone. Instead of a funeral where friends and family gathered to remember a life well lived and pay their respects, loved ones were forced to watch proceedings on Zoom or even not join in at all. We weren't only scared to death of catching the virus, we were scared of ending up alone at the end. Protective measures meant that saying our goodbyes was largely impossible. We were informed of the death of our loved ones by phone. The physical and psychological toll on the population, but especially on healthcare workers, was huge.

We struggle to discuss dying, but conversations about death are often just as meaningful as conversations about life itself. Fortunately, the taboo around death is beginning to crumble. Now more than ever before, there are places where people can gather to talk about death. What used to be considered a little sinister is now seen as a form of healing. Numerous blogs, Instagram accounts, podcasts and YouTube channels offer insights and support on a topic that was previously not widely discussed. Death is, more than ever, alive.

IN DEATH AS IN LIFE

Funeral director Caitlin Doughty has more than 2 million subscribers on YouTube, while a global chain of **'death cafes'** *even brings people together to talk about dying in more than 15,000 locations across 85 countries.*

In 2016, deputy head teacher Deborah James was diagnosed with bowel cancer. After a 6-year battle, she died in June 2022 surrounded by her friends and family and beloved by many members of the British public. She had refused to sit around and wait for the cancer to take her life, and worked tirelessly throughout her treatment and after entering palliative care to fundraise and raise awareness about the disease. Even with all the tubes and the clinical settings, she was determined to enjoy life to the end, even publishing dances on social media dressed in a hospital gown.

CASE IN POINT

Just as birth has become a beautiful, conscious moment, dying is also becoming a human experience. The University of Vermont's College of Medicine now offers a programme that allows you to graduate as a Death Doula, poetically translated as a 'midwife of death'. Death Doulas deal with the welfare of the dying person and those around them, to ensure a meaningful and peaceful death. I expect we will see more of these kinds of wellness coaches in the future.

Just as birth has turned into a beautiful, conscious moment, dying is also becoming a human experience.

Funerals are also gradually becoming something that can be fun. Dying people have started organising their own ceremonies. Surfers go out to sea together. Some people decorate their own house. Others ask for colourful clothes only, no black. Solemn commemorations have become personal festivals, which are increasingly being held while the person is still alive, as a celebration where creativity, intimacy and humanity are lived to the full.

What's essential in life is also essential when life ends. People no longer want to be buried encased in hardwood that will take hundreds of years to break down. Our environmental footprint is just as important when we're dead. That's where offerings like Recompose, which uses a patented system to convert human remains into soil to nourish new life after we die, flourish.

Fun funerals are also a lively start to a shared grieving process. Sorrow shared is sorrow halved. Previous generations may have learned not to talk about grief, but that's no longer the case. Mourning is no longer taboo. Mourning is very much alive. This new grief also breathes new life into the way in which we commemorate people. Ashes are pressed into diamonds, bodies are planted under trees, seeds are grown in ashes, vessels glow with the organic energy of the deceased body's biomass. Commemoration has become a new part of life.

MOURNING AS PART OF LIFE'S FABRIC

Modern Mourning *is a social platform in the Netherlands where people talk to each other about grief and goodbyes. Meanwhile, burial places, like the* **Greenwood Cemetery** *in Brooklyn, have become meeting places for cocktail parties, yoga sessions and art exhibitions.*

My best friend at university recently lost the battle against cancer. Having been a very passionate person who loved life, he wanted to leave a meaningful legacy born from his passions and values. He said the last three years became the most meaningful of his life: He founded **'Lust For Life'**, *a non-profit that aims to emotionally and creatively support his loved ones in their mourning process. With exhibitions and online sales of pictures from his travels, he also wants to continuously contribute to* **Kom Op Tegen Kanker**, *a non-governmental organisation that stands up for the right of (former) patients to the best treatment and care. This initiative (and name) could not showcase his own lust for life better.*

Transforming ourselves through how we live, age and die

The desire to transform is entering all parts and moments of our lives, from before we're born to how we age to after we're gone. Ageing and dying are (still) two of the few certainties in our lives. We all increasingly want to do what we can to live a happy and healthy life, and we're beginning to realise that ageing and dying well is part of this too. If we want to lead harmonious lives, we need to be 'happy' with the fact that we will age and die someday, as well as with *how* we will age and die. This should serve as inspiration to business and healthcare leaders to reflect upon their role in this trend. The beauty, finance and real-estate industries have already understood this and adapted their customer strategies. The question is: how will you, as a business or healthcare organisation, adapt to this major transformation in how we live, age and die?

2.2 Social transformations

There has been a visible transformation in social attitudes towards equity, diversity and inclusivity in recent years. Across various domains, from media to workplaces, from healthcare to political arenas, we notice more efforts being made to redefine and reshape the age-old social constructs that were rooted in very unequal practices for too long. This transformation is largely driven by the fact that humans are social animals: We are stronger together, we want to feel like we belong and we need to have meaningful and loving relationships. As these are absolutely essential aspects of our lives, this social transformation is receiving greater attention than ever in today's society. And it won't go away anytime soon; there are many challenges still ahead of us.

Equity, diversity, and inclusion

Social media has played a pivotal role in this transformation in social attitudes. It provides a space for less-heard minorities and other marginalised voices to share their stories and perspectives. The awareness and empathy they raised brought global attention that has helped create a more inclusive social fabric. Look at how #BlackLivesMatter and the #MeToo movement sparked widespread discussions and action to further social justice and equality (see Chapter 10.5 on Sexual Wellness). Additionally, social media platforms bring people from diverse backgrounds together. They can create communities to connect, learn, and advocate together for deep societal change. Online, but also local, communities are calling for changes. Groups and movements are working hard to raise awareness about unfairness in society and to make real changes in local areas, countries and even the world. These groups help people understand the existence of substantial problems.

Social media played a pivotal role in creating a new social fabric.

As a result, traditional media, advertising and entertainment industries that produce television programmes, movies and newspapers often (have had to) follow suit to meet these social norms as well. They have started showing more stories and characters from different backgrounds. Important issues like, for example, the rights of LGBTQ+ people and equality for people of all backgrounds have become more regular parts of the news stream, making people more aware of topics that were too often neglected in the past. While there is still room for improvement, the necessity to challenge existing stereotypes, promote diversity and contribute to a more inclusive cultural narrative has become more pronounced than ever before.

Part of this change was reinforced by increased diversity in media rooms. More diverse people making and deciding what goes in the media means we get to see and hear more different opinions than in the past. This is a positive change we've also seen take shape in the corporate world as more formal commitments are made to foster an inclusive workplace.

But businesses are not only diversifying their workforce by prioritising representation from different racial, ethnic, gender and ability minorities. They're also tailoring workplace policies (and metrics) to meet the unique needs of their diverse employees. And it does not stop there. Nowadays, companies are expected to be sustainable not just in their offices but also in how they interact with people and the environment outside. They need to consider where they get their materials (ethical sourcing), take care of the environment (environmental stewardship), and actively help and work with the communities around them. This is a big change from before, as companies now have to show they care about more than just making money. More on this in Chapter 2.3 Planetary Transformations.

BENEFIT-FOR-ALL CORPORATIONS (B CORPS)

B Corp *represents a global movement of businesses that are dedicated to social and environmental sustainability. Founded in 2006, this non-profit organisation provides certifications to companies that meet rigorous standards of social and environmental performance, accountability and transparency. The early B Corps were predominantly US-based, small and medium-sized companies in food and energy. But in recent years, larger and publicly traded companies from a wide range of industries and regions have pursued B Corp certification as well, reflecting the growing importance of this social transformation. Some countries like the US, Italy, Canada, Colombia and Ecuador have established legal frameworks for B Corps that want to balance making a profit with social and environmental goals.*

CASE IN POINT

As in corporations, political representation is becoming more diverse as well. More women, as well as people from ethnic, racial, and LGBTQ+ communities, are stepping into political roles. There are still significant challenges and sometimes systemic barriers, which make the pace of change very different across countries. However, there is a clear move towards greater inclusion and diversity in the political landscape. We can slowly see policies and laws being revised to reflect a more equitable and just society. Some policies have started supporting gender equity in all facets of life, such as equal pay, reproductive rights, and gender expression. Unfortunately, this is not without some major exceptions in many parts of the world. Nevertheless, these topics are so important and loud today that further social transformations will come.

Other institutions like schools, universities and healthcare are focused on social transformations as well. Schools and universities are actively working to decolonise and diversify their curricula. This involves introducing content that embraces a broad spectrum of cultures, histories and perspectives, ensuring every student feels a sense of belonging and validation in their educational journey.

Meanwhile, the social transformation in healthcare tends to focus on 'access'. While healthcare budgets are increasingly limited, the goal remains – perhaps even more than before – to create a healthcare system that is equitable and accessible to everyone, where providers are culturally diverse, have the necessary cultural competence and understand how different groups are affected by various health issues. This is vital to treat different people adequately. For example, it has been proven that women don't necessarily experience the same heart attack symptoms as men. Whereas we might expect chest pain to be the telltale sign, many women are more likely to experience nausea, sweating, vomiting and pain in the neck, jaw, throat, abdomen or back. Raising awareness of these kinds of differences across backgrounds also helps address the root causes of the current inequities in healthcare.

THE SOCIAL DETERMINANTS OF HEALTH

*The **Social Determinants of Health** or, in other words, the social factors that affect people's health, are a significant social transformation that has been driven by the **World Health Organization** and several action groups. They define it as the non-medical factors that influence health outcomes like the conditions in which people are born, grow, work, live and age, and the wider set of forces and systems shaping the conditions of daily life. These also include economic policies and systems, development agendas, social norms, social policies and political systems. The unfair and avoidable variations in these conditions, policies and systems show a consistent pattern within and across different countries: the lower a person's socioeconomic status, the poorer their health tends to be. That's why it is vital to tackle these influential factors and provide everyone with an equal chance at good health.*

*Several companies, most often based in the US, are focused on these social determinants as well. **IBM** and **Philips** use data analytics and AI to identify at-risk populations and to design interventions that address these underlying social factors. The American integrated managed care consortium **Kaiser Permanente** launched a multichannel support centre in 2023 to screen and better address the social needs of 3 million members and non-members. Health insurance company **Humana** offers healthcare providers tools and resources to identify and address social determinants. Additional compensation will also be provided for enhanced care coordination centred on three components – patient screenings; documentation of assessment; and connecting the patient to appropriate resources.*

Alongside these social factors, one of healthcare's major concerns for the future is technology. Technology should make information and services easier to access for all, no matter their abilities. This is especially important in healthcare of course. Technological solutions in the field of telemedicine and digital health, which are expected to be a significant step toward increasing healthcare equity, should be designed to be useful for everyone, including the elderly or people with disabilities. However, technology usually generates a faster pace that conflicts with the slower pace of older people. This conflict requires special attention in the design process of technologies as we transform society. Because technology should be transformational for everyone, as we will see in Chapter 12.

Humans are social animals

The focus on equity, diversity and inclusion is driven by universal human aspirations like Solidarity, Kindness, Meaning, Belonging, Relationships and Love. The second part of this book will highlight each of these aspirations in more detail. But at the core of these aspirations and this social transformation lies the simple fact that humans are social animals.

Today's society, however, doesn't always feel social. In 2018, research by the Kaiser Family Foundation revealed that 20% of the global population felt lonely. In 2021, the World Happiness Report identified loneliness as one of the predominant reasons for unhappiness, and a cause that's increasing every year. We want to spend time with and talk to other people. We need to feel like we belong. Because if we don't feel like we belong, we risk feeling lonely, socially anxious or clinically depressed.

CASE IN POINT

THE MODERN SOCIAL DISEASE – LONELINESS

When **Apple** noticed that more and more of their 500 million users were talking to Siri about their feelings, they hired over a dozen psychologists to optimise the chatbot. Meanwhile, an artificial intelligence (AI) companion has even been specifically created to help people with their loneliness. It's called **Replika**, the AI companion who cares. Many others have followed suit since or will come to the market in the following years (see Chapter 14.1).

Because loneliness is a major issue that places a heavy burden on society, governments are taking action as well. In 2018, the **United Kingdom** created the position of Loneliness Minister, a response to what former Prime Minister Theresa May called the "sad reality of modern life". Seeing the effectiveness of this approach, Japan also established a similar role in 2021 to address growing concerns of social isolation as roughly 15% of the population never has contact with anyone outside their family. The UK also became the first government in the world to publish a loneliness reduction strategy which included a recommendation for 'social prescribing, Front-line doctors can refer patients suffering from loneliness to local group activities. The UK government has invested over £20 million in various initiatives to reduce loneliness.

If humanity was lonely before 2020, there's no doubt that COVID-19 made the situation much worse for around 8 billion people around the world who were prevented from meeting anyone outside of their immediate family. Although this often had a greater impact on those living alone, even people surrounded by their families experienced the effect on their mental health. Not only did the measures taken to combat the pandemic disrupt the normal processes of human interaction, such as the start and end of romantic relationships, births and deaths, it also forced us into patterns few of us have ever before experienced.

We're different people at home than in other areas of our lives.

This can be explained by the fact that we're different people at home than in other areas of our lives. Not only do we do things differently at home, such as wearing more informal clothing, we also adopt different roles and attitudes. As a result of social distancing measures, we found that a large part of our identity had suddenly disappeared – or rather, had been reduced to the size of a window in a virtual meeting. We were no longer able to walk around the office as the boss, the project manager or team leader. We were no longer able to show who we were when we went out shopping, as our identity was hidden behind our face mask. Bars, restaurants, gyms, sports clubs – places that allow us to be someone – were closed. Our identity, which since childhood has been shaped by interacting with others, was suddenly taken away.

BEING APART, TOGETHER

To help amend this sudden enforced loneliness, the **World Health Organization (WHO)** asked the gaming industry to set up a campaign called #PlayApartTogether. The aim of the campaign was to encourage healthy physical distancing by offering special events, exclusives, activities, rewards and inspiration – through the medium of some of the most popular games in the world. As a result, the popularity of gaming grew by 45%. But the gaming industry didn't stop there. The game **Fortnite** organised a live concert by **Travis Scott** that attracted 12.3 million people, all online. Online game platform **Roblox** followed suit, live-streaming concerts for 33 million people in their virtual world. And needless to say the players themselves weren't slow with creative collaborations. In Japan and the USA, some youngsters built replicas of their schools, allowing graduations to take place in the virtual world with teachers and school principals present, developing a new form of educational togetherness. In the Netherlands, **Bianca Carague** even made a space where people could virtually meet with mental health therapists from around the world, all in the game **Minecraft**.

CASE IN POINT

A polarised world

Social platforms gave a voice to the minorities whose voices had previously gone unheard and ignited a social transformation. They were able to do this because humans are social animals. But there is still a growing danger lurking in society that will make social transformation even more important: polarisation. And I think it's fair to state we live in a society that's becoming ever more polarised.

We want to belong to a group that acts and thinks like us because we know that together we're stronger.

We live in a confusing world where it's often hard to know what information is true (if there actually is such a thing) and what is false. The algorithms used by social media are a big part of this, effectively putting you in an echo chamber that provides you with more of the same and reinforcing, rather than challenging, your beliefs. The likes that we give or receive trigger the social media algorithms to provide you with more of the same, showing content that aligns with our existing views. This amplifies, reinforces or echoes our own opinions. In these echo chambers, differing views are underrepresented or totally absent. Moreover, the popularity of social media feeds on that human desire for togetherness because we need to feel that others share our beliefs, that they are endorsed. We want to belong to a group that acts and thinks like us because we know that together we're stronger. We want confirmation that our wants, needs and beliefs are important. Obviously, this caters perfectly to our innate aspiration for connection, validating our need to be part of a group with shared beliefs.

FACT-LITE MEDIA PLATFORMS

In 2021, after he was banned from Facebook and Twitter following the 2021 attack on the Capitol, former US president **Donald Trump** *launched a new social media platform called* **Truth Social**. *This alt-tech social network was, similar to* **Parler** *and* **Grab**, *built as an 'uncensored' alternative to (then) Twitter and Facebook, allowing conservatives and far-right activists to speak freely – and feel stronger together. John McEntee, Director of the White House Presidential Personnel Office during the Trump Administration, even created a dating app for conservatives, claiming that other dating apps exclude "people who aren't offended by everything".*

Recently, big social media companies have reduced their teams that check for misinformation. **X** *(formerly known as* **Twitter***) started this when Elon Musk took over. He cut down the team and allowed some accounts that were previously blocked, including Donald Trump's, to return. Later,* **Meta** *(the company that owns Facebook, Instagram and Threads) also reduced its team that handles false information. These layoffs in social media disinformation teams can only serve to make social media as a whole a more dangerously fact-lite experience. This is a concern because about 70% of people consume news from these platforms. Meanwhile, new technologies like artificially generated images or deep fakes are making fake things seem very real. It is becoming ever harder to know what's true or not.*

Through a combination of fear, fake news, peer pressure and social media influence, people's opinions, feelings and beliefs can easily split into (at least) two very different groups. This often leads to deep disagreements between the two groups as they have become strongly divided on topics that are essential to our society, such as political preference, abortion, vaccinations and even the war in Palestine, to name but a few. As a result, their views become more extreme and they are less open to listening and more likely to argue or misunderstand each other because they see things so differently. In this polarised situation, it's rare to find opinions that are in the middle rather than the extremes.

The growing popularity of generative artificial intelligence and large language models risks adding fuel to this fire as will be explained in Chapter 13.1. At the time of writing, these models had little to no transparency making it hard to understand what the automatically formulated answers were based on. If the training data of these models is not known, it's also hard to prevent biases or misinformation. But what's more dangerous is the power that these automated tools have to convince. On Google it's easy to scrutinise certain websites, but when a decent-looking answer is directed at you with conviction it will be harder not to be influenced, even if the information is wrong. I'll elaborate on these and other challenges in the final part of this book: Transformational Technologies. In the meantime, let me draw your attention to why these social transformations are so important for companies.

Companies need to be socially stronger together

Even though this polarisation makes groups of people feel stronger and more certain about their own beliefs, it's not necessarily the best way to move forward as a society. I'm not saying that opposing thoughts or beliefs are not valuable. But when false, incorrect or incomplete information is shared so easily that it ruptures the social construct of our society then one could argue that we could have a far greater impact if everyone were fully aligned. We saw this tension in its purest form during the COVID-19 pandemic. Vax or anti-vax. Mask or no mask. COVID pass or not. Research findings came and went. Information and communication were also (mis)leading. Opinions were based on sentiment and personality. Never ever has society been so split on such important topics.

Without elaborating further or sharing too much of an opinion on these discussions, I did like how Danish Prime Minister Mette Frederiksen approached this polarising situation. She resurrected a word that hadn't been used since the Second World War. To achieve greater solidarity amongst Danes, Frederiksen brought back the word *samfundssind*. There's no direct English translation of the word; it's a combination of the words 'samfund' (meaning 'society') and 'sind' (meaning 'mind'), to describe a feeling of collective responsibility and community spirit. In other words, it means Solidarity. And that's precisely what the world did on many occasions. The pandemic showed us how social we are as humans. But it also showed how much stronger we are when we work together towards the same goal.

WORKING TOGETHER, WE STAND STRONGER

The development, production and distribution of vaccines was successfully achieved together. Data was openly shared. Collaborations were set up. Fierce competitors like **Apple** *and* **Google** *developed a protocol together to facilitate digital contact tracing during the COVID-19 pandemic. Belgian supermarket competitors* **Ahold Delhaize** *and* **Colruyt** *set up a collaboration to provide healthcare workers with essentials. In the Netherlands,* **Help 'n Appie** *facilitated donations to (closed) restaurants. With the money, they cooked for healthcare workers and the lonesome elderly. There were millions of similar initiatives, big or small, where people helped each other cope with this situation together.*

In France, we saw an impressive ecosystem unfold during the first wave of COVID-19. **Coalition Innovation Santé**, *uniting more than 20 pharma companies and over 40 hospitals, was set up to tackle the lack of continuous patient care. Within no more than four months, the coalition selected 30 start-ups from 600 different projects. They also enabled 2.5 million euros in private funding to support the deployment of these start-ups across 40 hospitals. The approach was so successful it continues its approach in France and is being exported to other countries under the name Coalition Next.*

CASE IN POINT

I believe companies should reflect on what they learned from that situation and take those lessons with them in future endeavours. Even if we don't face as immediate a threat as during the pandemic, we have to expect that the polarisation of society will continue to require more togetherness from companies – and indeed societies – to function properly. But there are two more reasons to argue in favour of deeper collaboration between companies to achieve this social transformation.

The fluid reality we live in today requires more collaboration.

The first reason to collaborate more is the 'fluid reality' we live in today. The world has changed a great deal in recent years and it's continuing to change at an ever-increasing pace. We are living in precarious times, in conditions of constant uncertainty. We can no longer rely on past experiences to prepare for or navigate the future. We've moved away from the relative stability, permanence and weight of the 'solid' modern era and now live in an unstable, fleeting period where constant change and instant obsolescence are the 'fluid' reality. You only have to look at things like how quickly artificial intelligence became omnipresent in boardrooms, how fuel prices skyrocketed as Russia invaded Ukraine and how the Taliban was able to take back control of Afghanistan. These were situations that (almost) no one could have predicted. Meanwhile, new technologies are surfacing faster and faster, reaching a very high level of adoption throughout society in no time. No company can master all of these changes alone. They need to work with others.

Another reason to collaborate is the increasing complexity in society. Peter Hinssen elaborated on this in his book *The Network Always Wins*, stating that that businesses must evolve into network-centric, collaborative organisations to survive and thrive. The boundaries that once sharply distinguished one industry from another are fading. Industries are looking at their customers more holistically and matching broader consumer needs with their broader social ambitions. Companies are making much-needed innovative sidesteps in sectors they have never set foot in before, which is creating more complexity as a result. It's not possible to do it alone. We need to collaborate and build partnerships together.

SPEEDING UP THROUGH PARTNERSHIPS

Nike *was one of the first companies to bring an activity tracking bracelet to the market, but they quite quickly chose to stop production. Instead, they decided to partner with* **Apple**, *who were better placed to deal with the changes in technology.* **Mercedes-Benz** *and* **Garmin** *developed a partnership in the area of sensors for bio-markers for the same reason. Similarly,* **Eli Lilly** *created an ecosystem for the smart insulin pen to include different diabetes platforms, including one from a rival pharma company, to cover a wider range of users. They were convinced it would only be possible for them to achieve improved decision-making for patients if they worked together. The ecosystem optimises accurate, real-time data collection that would never have been possible for them to achieve alone.*

The **Global Wellness Institute** *is bringing together 4,500 different organisations worldwide to eradicate preventable lifestyle diseases. What an amazing project!* **Future4care** *in Paris is a collaboration between an insurance company (***Generali***), an IT service provider (***Capgemini***), a telecoms company (***Orange***) and a pharmaceutical company (***Sanofi***) to accelerate the scaling of European health start-ups that might interest more parties than traditional medical companies.* **Headspace**, *the digital well-being platform has joined forces with* **Ginger** *to provide behavioural health coaching by therapists and psychiatrists. This shook up the wellness world, because Headspace was already collaborating with* **Netflix, Sesame Street, Nike, Weight-Watchers** *and multiple airlines to provide solutions beyond the boundaries of their own industry. And finally,* **Novo Nordisk** *partnered with more than 30 cities to tackle factors that can increase the risk of type-2 diabetes among people living in urban environments.*

Future social transformation

The ongoing social transformation is largely being accelerated by our ability to share our opinions on different social platforms. It includes people in the conversation that previously were not, it generates diversity that in the past was less prevalent and it brings attention to equality like never before. This social transformation is happening because humans are social animals. We want to feel solidarity or belonging and have meaningful, loving connections. But this transformation is not easy in a society where often false, incorrect or incomplete information is shared. People then form certain opinions for themselves and look for others with similar thoughts and that is what happens in the echo chambers of social media platforms. We want to feel together, but in doing so we are digging a deeper gulf between us and others. This polarisation will be critical to the future of society. And it's only the beginning. But the human aspirations that are driving these behaviours are not going away. I see a role for companies and brands to get together and tackle polarisation in the complex and fluid reality we're living in today. Because that is what social transformation is, or will be (even more), about.

2.3 Planetary transformations

Today, we live in a world where people want to transform their personal lives and the society they live in. But when it comes to our planet, we know that there is no plan(et) B. Not yet, at least. People are well aware that changes in the environment have a great impact on them. It can even influence their current and future health. And this in turn sparks the third transformation we are seeing taking place: the planetary transformation.

Humans and nature are highly dependent and interlinked. As such, climate change is the greatest threat to human health. Making climate change about health also promotes more sustainable behaviour among consumers. Meanwhile, we're actively seeking to make the environments we're in, whether external or internal, greener and more sustainable. We know, more than ever, that we need nature to relax, to return to our origins and recharge our batteries.

Climate change is the greatest threat to human health.

For companies, there is no magic solution to becoming greener, more sustainable and more aligned with the needs of the planet. There are only steps in the right direction and the will to truly do one's best. You don't need to act like you have the answers. In fact, it's preferable if you don't. Instead, acknowledge that you don't know everything and be humble and down-to-earth about how you are trying your best to make a difference. After all, perfect is unattainable and better is better than nothing. The focus on planetary transformations, on sustainability, is here to stay. We all need to do our part and customers will start seeking out that intention more and more often. Because they know that there can be no healthy people on a sick planet.

Back to nature

We take refuge in nature to unwind, recharge and exercise. This was particularly apparent during the various COVID lockdowns, with nature often the only authorised escape from our homes. Gardening, walking and fresh air became an essential getaway for many of us. Meanwhile, the planet was taking a (much-needed) break thanks to the pause in our hectic lifestyles. We were able to hear birdsong we had never heard before, observe a sky that seemed clearer and bluer, watch waterways become cleaner. We read about how air quality had improved everywhere. What we have been doing to our planet for decades suddenly became strikingly obvious. This, in turn, confirmed something that, fundamentally, we already know: Mother Earth needs nurturing so that we can continue to nurture ourselves in nature.

Mother Earth needs nurturing so that we can continue to nurture ourselves in nature.

By walking outside and enjoying nature, rather than rushing past it on the way to the office, we rediscovered this symbiotic relationship for ourselves. But perhaps it shouldn't have come as a surprise. People who report stronger connections with nature generally report higher levels of well-being, understood as being happier with more meaning and satisfaction in life. This tendency to reconnect with nature is also a counter-reaction to the omnipresence of the digital world. People are becoming more and more conscious of the damaging effects all our digital devices and screens have on our health by capturing our attention for so much of the day. We want to get away from our screens, so we leave the house. The idea of the digital detox has been around for over a decade now but it hasn't yet reached its peak. As technology's grip on our society tightens, you can expect many more people will want to escape to the reality and familiarity of nature.

This form of ecotherapy, which encourages humans to connect with nature again, is ubiquitous. It is not limited to the healthcare industry as described in the NHS example below. It's also easy to spot the indoor greenery revolution in contemporary interior design and architectural trends.

NATURE ON PRESCRIPTION

In recent years, major healthcare institutions, like the UK's **NHS** *(National Health Service), have ramped up their investment in green prescriptions. This initiative encourages healthcare practitioners to prescribe walks in nature or community gardening for their patients, for the positive influence on their physical and mental health.*

The popularity of biophilic design is deeply rooted in our desire to reconnect with nature. Patios are seeing a revival and nature-facing windows are more popular than ever. Interior design also aims to provide us with the relaxing feel of nature. Green walls are 'on trend' and bring a touch of nature. Many paints are also chemical-free today. Wooden structures and other natural elements bring that touch of nature to our homes while unnatural, often unsustainable, materials are rejected. Meanwhile, ventilation systems help diffuse natural microorganisms throughout the air and sales of houseplants have skyrocketed. They remove harmful pollutants from the air, stabilise humidity levels, reduce the symptoms of 'sick building syndrome' and can give that jungle feeling to a space. Workplaces are following suit by decorating entrances and meeting rooms with vertical gardens.

Climate change impacts human health

The presumed origin of the COVID-19 virus also highlighted the close links between humans, animals and the environment. Of course, this SARS variant was not the first infectious disease to spread from animals to humans. We actually share two-thirds of known human infectious diseases with animals. Many diseases, including malaria, Ebola and HIV/AIDS, have jumped from wildlife to humans. It's expected that ongoing climate change will aggravate the severity and danger of this evolution, for example when melting glaciers risk release 'zombie' viruses that have lain dormant for thousands of years.

In August 2022, the journal *Nature Climate Change* published one of the most extensive meta-analyses pooling research data on the impact of climate change on human health. The objective of the research was to fully quantify the global threat of pathogenic diseases and their relationship with climate change. It included the previously mentioned two-thirds of infectious diseases and some 40 conditions that are overlooked in most research on the correlation between climate change and human health. Respiratory, cardiovascular, neurological, gastrointestinal and skin problems are aggravated by extreme heat, rising sea levels, wildfires, drought, air pollution and severe weather events.

Climate change exacerbates so many illnesses that it's difficult to evaluate its true magnitude.

Climate change exacerbates so many illnesses that it's difficult to evaluate its true magnitude. However, it also has an indirect impact on our overall health. It endangers health and happiness on every continent by jeopardising our living conditions. Extreme temperatures, poor air quality and heavy or scarce precipitation (from severe storms to droughts) also threaten food security, housing, the labour market, employment, regional wealth, local economies, healthcare deliveries and even our mental health (partly due to climate anxiety). The environment has a massive impact on our health. In fact, health inequality is primarily attributed to the differences in climate. While we've worked hard to superficially minimise these differences, climate change has entrenched health inequality once again. It's a vicious circle. Regions that are the most vulnerable to the effects of a changing climate tend to be the ones least equipped to manage and recover from it. Climate change now risks nullifying any progress we've achieved in the last 50 years in the development of global health and health equality.

Climate change is the greatest threat to humanity

The World Health Organization has calculated that between 2030 and 2050 climate change will cause approximately 250,000 additional deaths per year from malnutrition, malaria, diarrhoea and heat stress alone. It will also cost an extra 2–4 billion US dollars annually around the world. WHO, therefore, considers climate change to be the single biggest health threat to humanity. In order to protect and preserve human health, we first need to protect and preserve the source of that health – nature. The medical research community fully recognises this daunting perspective. In 2021, more than 200 medical journals joined together to release an unprecedented statement citing climate change as the "greatest threat" to global public health. In an open letter to G20 leaders, more than 40 million health professionals urged political leaders to engage in a healthy recovery from COVID-19 in which nature can thrive. A healthy recovery, the letter states, should bolster efforts to fight pollution, climate change and deforestation. This will be critical to prevent "new health threats from emerging for vulnerable populations".

However, the relationship between climate and the healthcare industry is complex because it is considered to be one of the biggest polluters, even exceeding aviation. Ironically enough, the sector's damage to the climate affects our health considerably, potentially even worsening a vast range of diseases and increasing mortality rates due to rising temperatures.

CASE IN POINT

HEALTHCARE'S FOOTPRINT

Hospitals use a lot more energy than other buildings – more than double per room every day in fact. Per day, they also use a lot of water, up to 568 litres, and generate around 1.5 kilograms of medical waste, such as used bandages and needles. Things like cleaning chemicals, medicines, disposable items, moving patients and workers, handling waste, and preparing food all harm our environment.

*The **Global Green and Healthy Hospitals** is an association with over 1,600 health organisations from 78 countries. They work to make hospitals better for the environment by using less water and energy, making it easier to get to and from the hospital, building healthier buildings, buying things that are better for the environment, and managing waste well. Meanwhile, some countries are starting their own projects like the **KLIK** green project in Germany. This project is helping 250 hospitals and clinics to eliminate 100,000 tonnes of carbon dioxide equivalents in the next three years.*

The pharmaceutical industry is also making changes. Every year, 4.5 trillion medicines are produced but many are not used. The **Sustainable Medicines Partnership***, made up of 30 groups, wants to improve the way we get medicines. Meanwhile, companies like ten23 health are creating new ways to make medicines that are good for our planet.*

Climate change is a health issue

Climate change activists have been around for decades and many people dismiss them as they would religious prophets, shouting about how the world will end if we don't change our ways. However, a relatively new phenomenon is the medical prophet. In 2021, at COP26 in Glasgow, the healthcare community had its very own pavilion for the first time at a UN climate conference. Over 60 events were organised in the span of two weeks to showcase the health arguments that support ambitious climate action across many different sectors and topics. Professor David Pencheon, a UK doctor leading the NHS Sustainable Development Unit, urged leaders to treat climate change as a health issue as well as an environmental issue. "It makes it much more immediate to everybody."

Treating climate change as a health issue makes it much more relatable for everybody.

In fact, consumers already agree with Pencheon's point of view. Research by Nielsen in 2021 showed that 61% of consumers strongly agree that environmental issues harm our current and future health. And as businesses, we can use this opinion to make a real difference. Because the problem with sustainability is that it often suffers from the attitude that it's someone else's problem (commonly known as the freebooter problem): "Let somebody else do the work. I'm just going to continue doing what I always have." However, when it becomes personal, people change their behaviour. So 'climate change as a health issue' might be the greatest opportunity we have to successfully fight climate change. This message has already been shown to have an impact. When asked why they eat organic food, people cite health benefits more often than benefits for the planet. Growth in the consumption of organic foods has come about more due to people's aspirations for their personal health than for sustainability reasons.

By demonstrating how climate change is a health issue, we can make people realise to what extent our personal health is dependent on the planet's health. The more facts we read, the more we understand this symbiotic relationship. Microplastic pollution can now be found deep in the lungs of humans, as well as in fish living 100 metres below the surface of the ocean. As Patrick Hanaway, Medical Director at the Institute of Functional Medicine, wrote in his article *Diversity: From Diet to Flora to Life*: "The unique microhabitats and geologic stability have given way to modernity, and we have seen more than 80% of the habitat in this ecosystem [in the Blue Ridge Mountains of western North Carolina] diminished over the past 100 years. So too we have seen similar alterations in the diversity of the gut microflora within the human inhabitants over the same period of time".

Treat the planet like we treat ourselves

There is a growing understanding of how our health is linked to the health of our planet. Consequently, there is a growing belief that the way we treat the planet should be no different from the way we treat our own bodies. The Healthusiasm trend means that we no longer accept a 'silver bullet' approach to our health, a single solution that will help us manage it. When we're sick, for example, we aren't just prescribed antibiotics. Instead, people adapt their nutrition, sleep patterns, physical and mental exercise to better manage their health. Technology also often helps us fight disease and optimise our health. How we treat the planet should be no different. We're slowly abandoning the idea of single solutions, like pesticides in agriculture. Meanwhile, just as they do for our personal health, science and technology are playing an increasing role in the fight against climate change. The potential of science and technology has grown and is growing exponentially, from ocean-cleaning devices to plastic-eating enzymes.

Sustainable business strategy

Such genius innovations often make us feel as if the solution that will save us is just around the corner. The story spun by these 'wizards' is confusing, almost the opposite of the prophets we mentioned earlier, and thus they make it hard for us to understand the reality. Is the end near? Or have we found a solution? The plethora of opposing voices makes it difficult for the average person to understand the situation, let alone take a position. And if people are confused, businesses are as well.

It is hard for us to understand the reality. Is the end near? Or have we found a solution?

Such confusion makes it challenging to build a future business strategy in this new reality. Whatever action you take to tackle climate change never feels good enough. It certainly can't be anything like as ground-breaking as the 'wizards' claim to have achieved, so surely it would simply vanish into thin air. You worry that it won't be enough for the 'prophets' either and may expose you to a backlash. All this fear and uncertainty about the risks means many companies don't dare to take any action at all.

CLIMATE DOOM OR CLIMATE OPTIMISM?

Extinction Rebellion *is a global environmental movement that uses nonviolent civil disobedience, such as occupying sites, blocking roads and mass protests, to compel governmental action. The stylised, encircled hourglass, known as the extinction symbol, is characteristic of the movement's pessimistic vision of the future.*

Meanwhile, the **Solarpunk** *literary and artistic movement rejects climate despair and insists on reclaiming optimism, envisioning and working towards a sustainable future interconnected with nature and community. Adherents seek to answer and embody the question "What does a sustainable civilisation look like, and how can we get there?"*

extinction rebellion

solarpunk

But these wizards and prophets aren't (yet) representative of your customer base. While it's difficult to alleviate all those daunting fears at once, it isn't necessary to perform magic in one fell swoop. What is important is realising that, although your business might be doing well today, it can do still better tomorrow (by focusing on these planetary transformations). Move forward consistently, confidently and with pride about some progress. That's how you do better. Amplify, with modesty, the positive changes you bring to the health of your customer and this planet. Because this is where the unique opportunity lies for businesses.

Amplify, with modesty, the positive changes you bring to the health of your customer and this planet. This is where the unique opportunity lies for businesses.

Integrate sustainability and health jointly into your business strategy. The link to health makes sustainability much more tangible and recognisable for your customers. Design Customer Transformations that help the planet in such a way that they also protect, help and improve your customers' health and happiness – and those of your employees, too. Don't oversell your progress but translate it into what matters most for your customers: their health and happiness. In the next chapter, I'll elaborate more on the value of such Customer Transformations.

CHAPTER 3

CUSTOMER TRANSFORMATIONS

More than ever, people are conscious of what is happening in the world and realise that some situations are neither optimal nor good: from the climate crisis to social inequalities, from a polarised society to the overworked healthcare industry, from the mental health emergency to digital overload. But many understand that this can be improved. Today, even 'less urgent' matters can be improved like one's running performance or how we talk about death, sex or money. People want to see these things change for the better. And they are motivated to do good themselves. Or at least, they want to do better than before or than others. This desire for transformation has been one of the most significant trends in society.

Customers want you to help them with these transformations. This is the value they expect from you.

Sometimes, people feel empowered to impact or even change elements themselves. On other fronts, they acknowledge that they can't do it alone. They are demanding change, or transformation, as I call it. That's when they turn to you, the business owner, healthcare provider or governmental body. They want you to help them with these transformations. This is the value they expect from you.

And it's not easy. What people value changes over time. *Possessing things* has already become less valuable than *experiencing things*. I wrote about that in the first *Healthusiasm* book. But today, it's indeed about *transforming things*. It's about transforming ourselves, society and the planet. We value this in every part of our lives and, consequently, from every business. In this chapter, we will explore more in-depth how this evolution impacts what you provide for your customers, patients, consumers, drivers, visitors, etc... I will explain how the Experience Economy has evolved into the Transformation Economy. The following chapters will then provide you with tools that you can use to achieve this as well.

The Experience Economy

Every business starts by understanding what it is that their potential customers, specifically *need*. Using that insight, they can define a market and competitors, establish the resources and capabilities they need, plan their communications and so forth. But it always starts with meeting a specific *need*. That is how you create products or services for a specific group of customers. That's how you start creating the value customers want to pay for or engage with. Somebody might need electricity, insulin or a credit card. If they need this product or service, it is valuable to them.

CUSTOMER
NEEDS

= products or services

Over time, more companies may join the market, offering similar products or services. If there is little difference between the various options, customers tend to opt for the cheapest one. This forces companies to lower their prices to remain competitive. But there is an obvious way out of this downward price spiral. Companies can still differentiate their products and services from the competition and remain valuable to their customers, as Joseph Pine II and James Gilmore explained in their book *The Experience Economy*. They wrote that when goods and services alone no longer create enough value for customers, companies should provide better experiences.

Value creation

Source: Joseph Pine II and James H. gilmore, The Experience Economy, 2011 Strategic Horizons LPP.

EXPERIENCES CREATE MORE VALUE

I might need electricity and so choose the cheapest supplier. But if one supplier is known for its customer friendliness, quick reaction time, online dashboard and problem-solving approach, then I might be willing to pay more for that particular supplier. After all, that might be the experience that I prefer because it meets my expectations better. If I need a new credit card after losing one, I expect a new card to be delivered to my door the next day. I'd prefer a bank that can provide me with the experience that I appreciate so much when shopping online where next-day delivery has become so ubiquitous.

In the Experience Economy, simply meeting customers' needs will no longer suffice. You have to meet their expectations as well. These expectations are the result of the amazing experiences that customers have appreciated and grown accustomed to in other parts of their lives. By meeting those expectations you can differentiate yourself from the competition. That's how companies can create value for their customers once again.

CUSTOMER   CUSTOMER
NEEDS * EXPECTATIONS

= customer experience

The last chapter of my first *Healthusiasm* book elaborated on creating better customer experiences by focusing on the 12 recurring expectations that people have. Each of these expectations is a result of experiences in parts of our lives that may have nothing to do with your business. However, they are experiences that we have grown accustomed to and that we expect from products or services in all parts of our lives. Meeting those expectations will undoubtedly improve the overall experience and, thus, engagement with the solutions you provide them. These expectations can be applied to any business but are even more relevant when providing health-related products and services.

EXPECTING A SIMILAR EXPERIENCE

I might need insulin, but I expect my insulin delivery system to be as intuitive as my smart phone and as personal as my Netflix account. Whatever the experience I appreciated while using those products and services, I expect the same from my insulin delivery system. Such experiences remove friction and increase my engagement with my own health management.

This focus on experience-driven solutions will even be vital in a value-based healthcare system. In such a system – which is considered the only sustainable healthcare system for the future – healthcare providers (hospitals, physicians etc.) and perhaps even patients would be reimbursed based on health outcomes. Solutions will need to provide enough value for patients to get them engaged with the solution. This will only be possible if health and self-care solutions are truly engaging or, in other words, if they provide experiences that people are ready to engage with. These solutions must meet the needs and recurring expectations of the ones that are supposed to use them. I'll elaborate more on why that is essential for patients in Chapter 6.

Companies already mastering customer experience, like tech and retail companies, currently have an edge over providers in industries like healthcare, education, or finance.

Experience-driven solutions that meet these expectations have already been vital to businesses in most other industries. For over a decade, they've been focused on differentiating from competitors by providing the best possible customer experience. That's why I believe companies already mastering customer experience, like tech and retail companies, currently have an edge over providers in industries like healthcare, education, or finance, to name a few. As a result, many of these companies are extending their offering towards these other industries. Part 4 on Transformational Business will provide many examples of this shift.

But that is why many non-healthcare companies are trying to solve a health need today. These companies know how to meet the customers' expectations and create better experiences than those provided by the healthcare system. What's more, these companies also realise that health and happiness matter most in the lives of their customers. What better way to create a deeper connection and more value for customers than helping them with what matters most? As we will see in the next paragraph, that is a crucial driver for this shift towards the Transformation Economy.

The Transformation Economy

In the Experience Economy, companies focus on creating better experiences to help products and services stand out from the competition, because alone those products and services are no longer enough. But what if every company starts offering similar customer experiences? It will, again, become too difficult to differentiate between them. After all, the expertise and technology needed to create great customer experiences is becoming widespread and many companies are better organised around this digital transformation. Creating great experiences to stand out will become more difficult and customers will once again opt for the cheaper experiences. Pine and Gilmore explain that the market will then evolve towards Customer Transformations. These are experiences that also make people feel better, healthier and happier.

Value creation

CUSTOMER VALUE

Transformations

Experiences

Services

Products

Commodities

CUSTOMER DIFFERENTIATION

Source: Joseph Pine II and James H. gilmore, The Experience Economy, 2011 Strategic Horizons LPP.

CASE IN POINT

TRANSFORMATIONS IN THE ENERGY MARKET

Let's have a look at how the Energy market evolved. It's a fair statement to say that there is no real difference between suppliers in the electricity they provide. People choose one electricity supplier over another simply because they offer exemplary service (e.g. help desk) or experience (e.g. installation or repairs). Today, however, we see more and more people choosing green electricity providers, specialising in renewable or sustainable energy. Even in a market with skyrocketing prices, many people would still prefer green energy providers because it makes them feel better about their choice. They feel better because they know that it has an impact on the health of our planet as well as our own health and happiness. Choosing green electricity providers even makes customers more engaged with the company or brand.

This evolution makes perfect sense in the light of the many transformations that people are focused on (see Chapter 2). People want to transform those parts of their lives they've never had any ambition to transform before, like the environment, society or even ageing and dying. This evolution is not a coincidence. It shows that we all want to become the best version of ourselves. It makes us feel better, healthier and even happier. Companies that aspire to be more transformational will be the ones to create these Customer Transformations. They will be the ones to make people feel better, healthier and happier. They will be the ones that differentiate themselves from their competitors. As a result, they will thrive in the Transformation Economy.

HOW TO BE MOST VALUED

CASE IN POINT

Why is **Apple** *the highest valued company in the world? It's clear that their product – the iPhone – is valued more than a phone from several decades ago, but it is also valued more than a phone by Huawei, Google and even Samsung, because they provide better services and experiences. By adding exceptional privacy and security features and making the overall technical experience automagical, they help their customers achieve their aspirations of having less hassle and stress. But the health focus that Tim Cook installed when he took over from Steve Jobs is the value people seek. The Apple watch is a great example. Turning a watch into a health and self-care device means more Apple watches are sold than in the entire watch industry. The watch can be transformational for those wearing them.*

Tesla *became valued 2.5 times higher than any other car manufacturer with a similar strategy. The company provides mobility (their product) with good services (maintenance, insurance, assistance) and even greater experience (superchargers, Tesla app, software updates, self-driving features). But many people choose Tesla because of their transformational impact (sustainability, power walls, energy plans).*

In turn, **Nike** *is the highest valued sports business for similar reasons. Their shoes (product) may no longer stand out and perhaps the Nike Training app (service) doesn't differentiate them much either from apps by other sports brands. But their collaborations with Apple Watch (experience) and additional solutions (free classes, exclusive products, health expert advice etc.) provided to those who work out a lot turn the entire experience into transformations.*

> *Nike helps their customers to 'Just Do it' even more. In Chapter 10.3 I'll elaborate on how Nike make their customers feel transformed.*
>
> *Marketing guru Seth Godin said it best: "If **Nike** created a hotel tomorrow, you would know what value to expect. If **Marriott** made sports shoes, you would simply have no clue what to expect." The same can be said for Apple and Tesla. They create a recognisable value that makes people feel better, healthier and happier. And people value this more than brands that don't make them feel transformed.*

In my first book, I successfully tackled the 12 recurring customer expectations that create better customer experiences. In this book, my ambition is to help you design Customer Transformations that make people feel better, healthier and happier. In the next section, Aspiring to Transformations, you'll be presented with a model you can apply to build Customer Transformations in your everyday business, whatever industry you are active in. The model is centred around people's Life Aspirations, universal human desires and values or, in other words, motivation to transform themselves, society and the world. Helping them with these is presenting them with what I call Customer Transformations. This makes the Transformation Economy.

CUSTOMER   CUSTOMER   LIFE

NEEDS * EXPECTATIONS * ASPIRATIONS

= customer transformations

PART 2

ASPIRING TO TRANSFORMATIONS

CHAPTER 4

HEALTH AND HAPPINESS MATTER MOST

In previous chapters, we've covered how people are looking for transformations at three levels today: themselves, their immediate environment (society) and the planet as a whole. They want to do better or make things better. They feel empowered. But at the core of their drive lies one particular desire or value. Ask people repeatedly why something is important to them, and you'll come to the core value of that person. You'll understand why it is essential to them. From the type of transformations in the world today, health and happiness could be considered the ultimate aspiration. It's also the most common answer to the question: "What matters most to you in life?" Any other answer to that question could always be brought to being healthy and happy (by asking them why). Health and happiness are the single most essential elements in our lives.

Health and happiness are the single most essential elements in our lives.

Making a healthier planet will positively impact our health. Fighting for inclusion will positively impact our health. Improving how we age will positively impact our health. There are, in fact, only a few things we do in life that negatively affect our health. Often, these actions are related to some form of addiction, or we are seldom happy with them. Health & happiness is the core of our lives, or life in general. It's what matters most to us. So, when people want to do good or focus on transformations, it will always influence our health & happiness.

Companies in the Transformation Economy that want to consider what matters for their customers will focus on Customer Transformations, as we've seen in the previous chapter. They're looking at their customers more holistically, searching to meet what goes beyond the immediate customer needs and expectations. In that exercise, brands and companies realise that what matters most for everybody is their health and happiness. The first *Healthusiasm* book was dedicated to this: people don't just think about their health when sick; health isn't restricted to a few medical decisions. Taking care of oneself is vital for every one of your customers. As a result, in the Transformation Economy, the boundaries that once sharply divided one industry from another are fading. Companies are taking innovative steps sideways into sectors they've never previously explored, with the (in)direct objective of "making customers healthy & happy". Every business transforms into a health business.

EVERY BUSINESS IS A HEALTH BUSINESS

In Belgium, telecom operator **Proximus** *launched a telehealth solution called Doktr during the COVID-19 pandemic.* **Black+Decker**, *the American manufacturer known for their power tools, also joined the health movement and launched a smart health companion called Pria. The companion not only dispenses medicine but also serves as a telehealth solution.* **Hyundai Motors** *has introduced a new car interior concept focused on the health of drivers during trips. This cockpit uses technology to sense the driver's health and aims to keep the driver in a good mood while driving.* **Mitsubishi Electric** *released an air conditioner that can adjust to people's moods (relaxed, tense or distracted) in a room, automatically helping people with their well-being. 'Pokémon Sleep' is a* **Nintendo** *game that tracks your sleep with your phone and rewards good sleep with new Pokémon to discover. This isn't Nintendo's first health-related venture; they've previously released games like 'Captain Novolin' and 'Wii Fit', and launched health-focused projects like the 'Quality of Life' initiative and 'Ring Fit Adventure'. These efforts show Nintendo's ongoing interest in combining gaming with health and wellness.* **Hy-Vee**, *a supermarket chain in the Midwest and South of the USA, has started a health programme where customers can get nutrition advice, health checks, and online fitness classes. This programme is designed to help people stay healthy and fit.* **Dove** *created a short film showing how social media can hurt young people's mental health. Their new campaign focuses on this problem, continuing their work on encouraging positive self-image and real beauty online.*

What does 'healthy & happy' mean?

In my first *Healthusiasm* book, I laid out that health and happiness are the two most important aspects in the lives of every human being. In order to connect with their customers, companies should find ways to make their customers healthy and happy. After the book came out, 92% of readers and clients from different industries confirmed the importance of making their customers healthy and happy (proprietary market research via MonkeySurvey, 2021), but many asked me the same question. What does health and happiness really mean for their customers? Health and happiness all sounds so 'fluffy'.

This question was a direct result of the difficulties that companies and organisations have when trying to implement a successful health or wellness strategy. I noticed that initiatives taken by my clients were all centred around the same four pillars of health and wellness: physical activity, nutrition, mental health and sleep. These pillars are well known; whenever a person wants to influence their own health or happiness, they increase their physical activity, improve their eating habits, enhance their sleep or take better care of their mental health. Surely such a strategy must work because improving one of these four aspects is what we all do when we want to be(come) healthier and happier. But it doesn't.

The Wellness Bingo is rarely a successful health strategy because you start with the tactics.

I call this approach 'The Wellness Bingo': to win, you need to get all four. But the reality is that by taking this approach, every company was launching similar strategies with hardly anything to differentiate themselves from their competitors. Moreover, all these initiatives were too far removed from their core business, making it hard for their customers to relate. The initiatives were generic, not relevant to their customers, and achieved very limited business results or health improvements.

| exercise | food | sleep | mental health |

I quickly realised that this was not a formula for success. Imagine setting up a digital strategy by launching a website, a mobile application, a chatbot and an e-commerce platform. It wouldn't work either. You cannot start with the tactics if you don't know what your objective is. Which customer needs do you want to meet? And how does that help your own business? These are the essential questions to answer before deciding upon a digital strategy.

Companies must first define the customer needs they want to meet with a health strategy.

A health strategy is no different. Companies must first define the customer needs they want to meet. Therefore, they have to understand what health and happiness mean for their customers. The question that readers and clients asked me was thus very valid: "How can we make health and happiness less fluffy? How can we make it concrete?" This is what I've been working on for this book: a framework that makes 'health and happiness' more tangible by describing what customers actually need.

Trendwatching.com – one of the world's leading consumer trend firms – predicted in 2015 that aspirational needs would become the driver of consumer behaviour. People would purchase the products, services and experiences that helped them achieve their aspirations. **Therefore, I believe that aspirations are the foundation for designing Customer Transformations, much like expectations were the foundation for customer experiences**. What's more, aspirations can also make health and happiness more tangible for my clients and readers. So let's have a look at what aspirations are, how they've evolved recently, and what they mean for marketing and health.

Aspirations

Aspirations are used in different contexts, such as work, sports, relationships and school. The concept of aspirations is even commonly used in scientific fields like psychology, sociology, economics and biology. Although you can easily find a variety of definitions and examples, they're often not coherent in meaning or relevance across the board. Nevertheless, 'an aspiration' always tends to refer to something one hopes to achieve in life. It's a positive word that uplifts our motivation (or Healthusiasm) and therefore gives us reason to live, fight or keep trying. But aspirations differ from 'ambitions' in that ambitions tend to be related to career, power or success. Aspirations also differ from 'dreams' in that they are more structured than 'mere' dreams.

Aspirations show where our priorities and values lie at that point in our lives.

Our aspirations are often inspired by the most important areas of our lives. They lay out what we want to achieve in those areas. Although these aspirations are rather general and future-focused, they show where our priorities and values lie at that point in our lives. While most people have aspirations, not all will work towards them in the same manner. In some cases, of course, aspirations will remain vague and won't be achieved at all. There will always be more people with aspirations than people actively doing something about it. However, aspirations can be a driver for behavioural changes, motivating people to set goals that help them achieve those aspirations. These goals are specific, time-bound, and backed by real actions. They represent what we need to do to get to that place we aspire to reach.

Aspiration moderation

Our basic and social needs are essential to our survival. Once they are largely fulfilled, people start wanting things that often they don't really need. But as these wants increase, the satisfaction that comes with wanting decreases. That's when people become aspirational, hoping that achieving aspirations will provide satisfaction again. We want to be the best version of ourselves. However, unrealistic aspirations lead to even greater dissatisfaction or even bigger psychological issues. We have seen this happening in the last decade, especially in the Western world. People from most parts of the developed world are trying to become more moderate, more realistic, with their aspirations.

For a long time, our aspirations – or aspirational needs – were about becoming better, smarter, healthier, stronger, more eco-conscious, and so on. It was all about improvement. Our aspirations made wellness, coaching, fitness and educational businesses more successful than ever before. But they even determined consumer behaviours. We bought products that supported us with our aspirational needs, that made us (feel like) a better person or that shared the same values.

In today's society, aspirations no longer necessarily refer to 'improving' yourself or something, at least not in the literal meaning of the word. Like with many shifts, this became apparent in the wellness and self-care industry first. We saw people starting to feel guilty for not exercising as much as possible or ashamed if they weren't always that happy. As a result, they felt like they weren't living up to their aspiration of becoming the BEST version of themselves. This is a phenomenon that André Spicer and Carl Cederström called 'the wellness syndrome'. In their book of the same name (2015), Spicer and Cederström argued that the ever-present pressure to maximise our wellness has started to work against us. The World Happiness Report (2019) confirms this by stating for the first time that 5% of the population are unhealthily addicted to working out and exercising.

In our quest to become the best version of ourselves, we have forgotten to do best for ourselves. Therefore, Aspirations are no longer only about 'improving'.

Aspirations are no longer about perfection; we are exhausted as a result of impossible standards and bored of perfection. Aspirations have become more moderate. "It's ok to be ok, and it's ok not to be ok." Growing as a person can be about not being focused on growing. Quitting can sometimes be better than not quitting. Because we aren't all warriors all the time, right? "Living a balanced life" sounds aspirational enough today. And so, sometimes the best thing for us can be to *accept* things the way they are. Also, *enjoyment* can sometimes be better than focusing on improvement. And sometimes, the best thing could be to *prevent* something from happening. Aspirations are no longer only about *improving*; they're about being the best version of yourself. It's about taking care of ourselves to live life to fullest of our potential.

prevent · accept · enjoy · improve

DIFFERENT TYPES OF ASPIRATIONS

Patients might need to accept their disease first before they can feel healthy and happy. Elderly people might want to enjoy life while they still can. During COVID, we were focused on preventing our health from worsening.

However, that doesn't yet help businesses that are trying to answer specific aspirations. Thus the question still remains: how can we define specific aspirations for those 4 types? I'll explain this in the next chapter, when I explore how I discovered a series of recognisable Life Aspirations.

CHAPTER 5

ASPIRATIONS ARE THE NEW NEEDS

Aspirations, moderate or not, function as a driver for change. Aspirational people will look for ways to make that change happen. And that's when they might be looking your way for help. Whatever business you are in, your mission will always be to help your customers with the change they desire (or should desire according to you). Whether you are a start-up founder, a healthcare professional, a brand manager, an innovation lead, a hospital manager, a pharmacist or a product designer, the solutions you offer to your client will always be about change.

According to Seth Godin – global marketing guru and author of numerous books on the subject – marketers are in the business of making change happen. It could be to change the perception of a brand, to convince people about the importance of ecology or to increase patient engagement with a health solution. Every message conveying a solution contains a promise made to someone who has a particular desire or problem. "If this works for you, you are going to discover…"

Marketers bring betterment to people who look for better.

What makes marketers successful in making change happen is that they don't start with a solution. Marketers empathise with and are curious about other people. They wonder what people are struggling with and are fascinated by their dreams and desires. Marketers bring betterment to people who look for better, first by inventing and designing the right solution for a group of people with particular dreams and desires, then by communicating the promise of change as a step closer to the dreams and desires of their customers.

In his book *This is Marketing*, Seth Godin laid out a fundamental list of **dreams and desires** that all people share: from adventure and affection to respect and safety; from friendship and looking good to romance and sex. He called these the universal fundamentals for the change that people are seeking. They form the basis of the promise that marketers should be making. Marketers change people by taking them on a journey to become the person they've dreamt of or desired to become.

"Marketing is about aspirations, about making people healthy."

Diane Young, CEO of The Drum (leading global publisher in the marketing industry)

In my quest to make 'health and happiness' less fluffy, I was trying to identify exactly which aspirations make people want to be healthy and happy. It's no wonder that I was so intrigued by Seth Godin's list of human dreams and desires. For several weeks, I worked with that list and conducted a series of exercises: identifying opposing fears (reliability vs falsehood), complementing them with related words (eg. fake news), mapping health and self-care products (eg. fact checking, labels) and linking them with health and wellness trends (eg. medfluencers, health washing). Through these exercises, I was able to describe what these fundamental dreams and desires mean for one's health and happiness. It became the first version of the Life Aspirations I've centred this book on.

Life Aspirations

Godin's list of human dreams and desires translated well into universal aspirations that are tied to health and happiness. While there is no precedent for a list of health-related aspirations, it became clear in my research on the psychology of aspirational living and life goals that these Life Aspirations make perfect sense. This was also confirmed by the psychologists I invited to challenge the different Life Aspirations. But perhaps the biggest confirmation came from analysing the behaviour of health consumers.

The Global Consumer Health and Wellness survey by Nielsen IQ (2021) highlighted that health and wellness is the single most important consumer force. A vast majority (64%) of consumers are interested in products and services that are customised to meet their specific health needs. According to the research, this cohort of consumers has considered aspirational needs to be super vital for them. The report also reinforced the importance of specific aspirational consumer priorities like performance, looking good and strength. It also mentioned how mindfulness (avoiding stress), community interactions, prevention and protection are essential for health and happiness. All of these are in line with the Life Aspirations that I translated from Seth Godin's list of dreams and desires.

Specific aspirations that lead to a healthier and happier life for one person may vary depending on individual preferences, values and circumstances. I realised that companies selling nutritional supplements, in particular, are already using health aspirations very well in that regard. Today, you can find supplements to look good, be more relaxed, find strength, gain energy, boost your immunity or protect yourself (from hair loss for example). Supplement companies have already managed to translate their customers' dreams and desires to be healthy and happy into tangible Life Aspirations.

Life aspirations are the needs that your customers have to be(come) healthy & happy.

When I developed the Life Aspirations model, it became clear to me that this would provide companies with more opportunities than the aforementioned 'wellness bingo'. Life aspirations are the aspirational needs that your customers may have, so starting a health strategy based on these needs will undoubtedly be more successful than diving straight in with the tactics (exercise, nutrition, sleep and mental health). But this model also allows companies to identify the Life Aspirations that fit their company's DNA more easily. Instead of helping customers with generic recommendations – eat better, move more – companies can now select the Life Aspirations that fit their company's mission, business objective or product line.

Companies can now select the Life Aspirations that fit their company's mission, business objective or product line.

This book is all about showcasing how these Life Aspirations help to design the Customer Transformations your organisation needs to be able thrive in the Transformation Economy. Products and services are based on customer needs. They are turned into great experiences if they meet the customer expectations. By considering relevant Life Aspirations as well, you design experiences that make people feel better, healthier and happier. Customer transformations are indeed the combination of meeting the needs, expectations and aspirations of your customers. In the remaining chapters of this book, we'll explore how different industries are already focused on Customer Transformations. But first, let's finish this chapter with the Life Aspirations model.

CUSTOMER
NEEDS * EXPECTATIONS * ASPIRATIONS

CUSTOMER

LIFE

= customer transformations

The Life Aspirations model

Making customers healthy and happy may sound fluffy. It doesn't sound tangible either when people say they want to be or remain healthy and happy (or become healthier and happier). When we try to make health and happiness more tangible, it's important to remember that we should not only try to remediate some physical or mental ailment. Even for patients with a debilitating disease or an urgent medical need, health and happiness means much more than just solving that basic need. The Life Aspirations I've set out in this book will help you to identify the most important areas of their lives and what they want to achieve in those areas. When addressing Life Aspirations, you promise a change to your customer that is important to them. "If this works well for you, I promise you will discover..." And that promise goes beyond solving a medical need or meeting a specific health-related target but helps with their dreams and desires that feed their overall health & happiness.

HEALTH & HAPPINESS IS MORE THAN SOLVING A MEDICAL NEED

When diabetes patients want to be healthy and happy, they don't just need an insulin delivery system that provides a great experience. They actually aspire to have enough energy throughout the day while being protected from the risk of hypoglycaemia. When patients with Crohn's disease want to be healthy and happy, they actually aspire to go out and have meaningful connections without stress. Elderly people may aspire to be careful and live autonomously, while youngsters may aspire to look beautiful and feel accepted. A marathon runner aspires to boost his performance and recover well in between. An epilepsy patient aspires to accept her progressive disease and feel safe.

The Life Aspirations described in the next part could be considered 'one level' below health and happiness. They translate what is meant by it into something more concrete. They make it more tangible. They can even turn 'making customers healthy & happy' into something more achievable for companies. If you understand what health & happiness means for your customers, you can help them pursue their Life Aspirations. If you know what Life Aspirations they pursue, you help them be(come) healthy & happy.

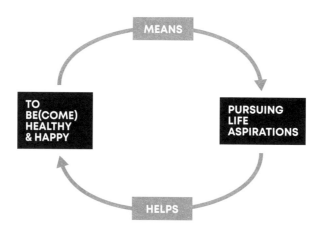

As highlighted in previous segments, aspirations have become more moderate. The Life Aspirations model has been created to reflect these evolutions as well. After all, not all Life Aspirations are about 'improving' one's health in the literal sense of the word. My research on Life Aspirations uncovered several universal aspirations that could be grouped under the three additional overarching categories related to health: prevent, accept and enjoy. Beyond improving their health and happiness, people also want to *prevent* their health from worsening, *accept* their current situation and *enjoy* life as much as possible. From the research mentioned earlier, I've identified 24 different Life Aspirations that can be categorised into these 4 types. Together, these 24 Life Aspirations explain very well what a person can aspire to and help organisations to balance their communications and optimise their solutions.

In the coloured part of this book, I go into more detail about each individual Life Aspiration and how you can use it. There's no need to read through all 24 aspirations in one sitting; in fact, I recommend you don't. Treat it more like a reference guide that you pop back to when you're working on a new communications plan, a fresh aspect for your product or service, or a health-related angle to your business model. The first few pages outline how you can use this part on aspirations and the structure of each aspiration. After that, I go into detail about each one. But for now, you may wish to skim through just a couple of them before flicking through to part three, four and five, where we look at how these Life Aspirations are applied in Healthcare, Business and Technology.

The Life Aspirations Model

In this segment of the book, I'll elaborate on each of the 24 Life Aspirations: what they mean, why they're important for your health and happiness and how organisations, companies and brands are already trying to support their customers with these aspirations.

Just like the last chapter of the first *Healthusiasm* book – on Expectations – this segment is intended as a reference you can fall back on at any time. It serves as an inspiration for different use cases and situations. So reading it all in one go won't particularly make it interesting or useful. Instead, I suggest you read the examples in the following parts of the book and look up the relevant Life Aspiration to get more information or a better understanding.

For this purpose, each Life Aspiration on the next few pages will be presented similarly. This structure is deliberately designed as a manual to facilitate immediate and complete understanding. It is also crafted to allow you to create a persona, do additional research, or launch queries in Large Language models, as discussed next.

How to use the Life Aspirations

I explained how these Life Aspirations are rooted in our universal human dreams and desires. They are the drivers shaping personal motivations for centuries if not millennia. This statement may sound bold now or when discovering these Life Aspirations, but I promise you'll confirm this by the end of this book. You'll realise that these Life Aspirations are universally relevant and timelines. But you will also understand the wide application of these in your work. Here are a couple of ways you can do so:

1. **Primary Research**: Qualifying or quantifying certain Life Aspirations in market research will help you understand what they mean for your customers or how important they are to one another over time.
   - *(For example, in-depth interviews with diabetic patients on the specific Life Aspiration of **Energy** make it very insightful and help to assess the potential of Customer Transformations focused on Energy.)*

2. **Secondary Research**: The use or mention of Life Aspirations (and of their related words) can be analysed in documents, websites, social media, customer testimonials, or feedback to understand their relevance better for specific target groups.
   - *(For example, if social media listening indicates no **Joy** in eating hospital food while eating is a joyful event in other parts of their lives, then it could be worthwhile to tackle that situation.)*

3. **Trendwatching:** Societal, technological, cultural or economic trends make some Life Aspirations become more important over time. This helps to understand why and how some aspirations need to receive some additional attention.

> (For example, during COVID there was an increased aspirational need to feel **Safeness** when going outside. What did/does this change mean for your business?)

4. **Generative AI**: Large Language models can be prompted with specific Life Aspirations (and their related words), allowing you to understand better what they could mean to you or your business.

    > (For example, PROMPT: *We are a food brand with a creative image. We manufacture and sell healthy and trendy snacks. Provide some ideas on how we can, with our portfolio of products, also spark or motivate **Creativity** within our customers?*)

5. **Innovations**: Life Aspirations are universal. Innovations help pursue these Life Aspirations differently. It can predict whether your customers will want that innovation if it helps to pursue their aspirations better.

    > (For example, can ChatGPT help the desired **Autonomy** of people when looking for recipes or is the difference with our current websites with recipes too small?)

6. **Existing Offering**: Your current products and services provide a great experience that meets the needs and expectations of your customers. You can turn this into a Customer Transformation by taking into account particular Life Aspirations.

    > (For example, a car manufacturer may already provide a great driving experience, but by helping drivers maintain or improve their **Energy**, they offer a transformational experience.)

7. **Communication**: By including recognisable and relevant Life Aspirations in your communication, you can stress the transformational impact of your solutions.

    > (For example, communications by a pharmaceutical company towards patients with Crohn's disease could highlight how its medication helps to go out and have **meaningful relationships.**)

Now, before you get started, here are a couple of remarks as you discover these Life Aspirations:

In researching and drawing up this model, I've tried to be as complete as possible. But I don't think it's actually feasible to be exhaustive. As Seth Godin said about his fundamental list of dreams and desires: "You might perhaps discover a couple more that I have omitted, but you won't find ten more dreams and desires." Similarly, it's possible you will think of particular nuances that aren't mentioned in this model (in which case I'd love to hear them), but there won't be another dozen that are missing.

You'll also quickly realise that most Life Aspirations are interlinked and can even reinforce each other in attaining similar health and well-being outcomes. But I'm convinced that separating them specifically into this model helps to name and pinpoint what you really want to achieve or help your customers with. It emphasises a narrower focus and puts a recognisable common name on it, which will yield more success in defining how you want your customers to feel healthy and happy. But never hesitate to combine Life Aspirations that are complementary to what you want to achieve. This can help define and even reinforce the unique value proposition you provide to your customer.

Finally, addressing the elephant in the (board) room is necessary: the Sustainable Development Goals and how they relate to Life Aspirations.

As you may know, the Sustainable Development Goals (SDGs) are a collection of 17 global goals set by the United Nations in 2015 that aim to tackle global challenges such as poverty, inequality, climate change, environmental degradation, peace and health. The aim is to get all countries working towards a more sustainable and prosperous future for the planet and its inhabitants. These goals are a call to action. Countries and regions are expected to integrate them into their regulations so that companies and brands contribute by, in turn, incorporating these goals into their business strategies, activities and initiatives. By doing this, companies help tackle the global challenges and build long-term trust with their customers.

Sustainable Development Goals, therefore, also contribute to a better and healthier world like Life Aspirations do. The Sustainable Development Goals are also expected to respond to what should ultimately be important to customers. Furthermore, there are mutual links between SDGs and Life Aspirations: For example, Quality Education (SDG Goal 4) contributes to more **Consciousness**; Gender Equality (SDG

Goal 5) generates a sense of **Belonging**; and Partnerships (SDG Goal 17) is closely related to the concept of **Solidarity**; to name just a few. The most significant difference is that policy institutions impose the SDGs onto companies through hard metrics, reporting and consequences. The Life Aspirations, on the other hand, are bottom-up. It is a translation of what is essential in your customers' lives. They are universal human dreams and desires that arise from their values and priorities.

But of course, they work together really well and can even reinforce each other. You can make official SDG projects more valuable to your customers by communicating about them via recognisable Life Aspirations. On the other hand, by understanding the Life Aspirations that closely match your customer priorities (and your company's DNA), you will also select the right SDGs for your company to work on.

With that said, I guess you are ready to discover the great realm of Life Aspirations.

Remember, this section is not designed to be read in one sitting. It is a complete reference work that you can easily refer to later to find the right aspiration for your project or offering.

THE LIFE
ASPIRATIONS
MODEL

The Life Aspirations Model

PREVENT	ACCEPT	ENJOY	IMPROVE
Solidarity	Kindness	Nothingness	Healing
Caring	Gratitude	Spontaneity	Strength
Safeness	Belonging	Autonomy	Energy
Calmness	Realness	Relationships	Self-development
Clarity	Meaning	Loving	Creativity
Consciousness	Self-worth	Joy	Looking good

1.1 Solidarity – *(feeling stronger united)*

1.2 Caring – *(being careful with myself and others)*

1.3 Safeness – *(feeling safe and protected)*

1.4 Calmness – *(avoiding stress and anxiety)*

1.5 Clarity – *(being mindful and focused)*

1.6 Consciousness – *(being aware and comprehending)*

2.1 Kindness – *(being kind to myself and others)*

2.2 Gratitude – *(having appreciation and being thankful)*

2.3 Belonging – *(feeling accepted and included)*

2.4 Realness – *(being genuine and true to myself and others)*

2.5 Meaning – *(living life with a meaningful purpose)*

2.6 Self-worth – *(feeling good about myself)*

3.1 Nothingness – *(doing, feeling, seeing or hearing nothing)*

3.2 Spontaneity – *(acting spontaneously)*

3.3 Autonomy – *(living independently and autonomously)*

3.4 Relationships – *(having meaningful connections)*

3.5 Loving – *(loving or being loved)*

3.6 Joy – *(having amazing experiences)*

4.1 Healing – *(recovering and restoring)*

4.2 Strength – *(having power and resilience)*

4.3 Energy – *(having vitality and stamina)*

4.4 Self-development – *(growing and cultivating oneself)*

4.5 Creativity – *(imagining and inventing)*

4.6 Looking good – *(being attractive)*

PREVENT

Beginning with a sense of solidarity, individuals cultivate caring relationships that pro-vide a foundation of emotional security. This security fosters inner calmness, enabling clarity of thought and a heightened state of consciousness, collectively forming a proac-tive path to prevent the decline of both health and happiness.

1.1 Solidarity – *(feeling stronger united)*

The participation in a larger group fosters collective strength to face a situation or prevent a condition from worsening.

1.2 Caring – *(being careful with myself and others)*

The active, responsible engagement in nurturing and tending to someone or some-thing in order to avoid decay or deterioration.

1.3 Safeness – *(feeling safe and protected)*

The behaviour of keeping someone or something free from harm, injury, damage, danger or loss.

1.4 Calmness – *(avoiding stress and anxiety)*

The deep sense of peace achieved by limiting exposure to external events or situa-tions that create undue pressure or cause exceptional, prolonged concern and fear.

1.5 Clarity – *(Be mindful and focused)*

The desirable state of mind, free from the constant stream of thoughts, emotions and external stimuli, allowing us to gain perspective and make better decisions.

1.6 Consciousness – *(being aware and comprehending)*

The innate desire to be aware and understand things to serve a variety of cognitive, emotional and practical purposes.

SOLIDARITY – feeling stronger united

*For some people, feeling healthy and happy implies being **stronger when united.***
*Likewise, this **solidarity** contributes to feeling and being healthier and happier.*

Solidarity means being part of a larger group to foster collective strength and prevent a situation or condition from worsening. It embodies the sense of unity and mutual support within a community or group, creating a bedrock of shared values and goals. It manifests as a collective spirit where individual self-interest is often transcended for the community's well-being. This sense of unity extends to standing up against unfair treatment, sharing resources and rallying together for collective action, often in the context of social justice initiatives. Particularly significant is the self-sacrifice that solidarity may demand – whether in terms of time, resources or emotional support – prioritising the group's collective well-being over individual gains. As a powerful social tool, solidarity also serves as a defence mechanism against worsening conditions, fostering collective strength and resilience.

Solidarity not only reaffirms the notion that there is strength in numbers but also provides a comprehensive range of resources that contribute to the group's overall well-being. Within a framework of shared responsibility, group members actively participate in problem-solving endeavours, pooling together their unique skills, knowledge and perspectives to address challenges. This leads to enhanced decision-making capabilities and the prevention of deteriorating situations. Furthermore, the emotional and practical support within such groups contributes to individual resilience, providing a buffer against mental and emotional strain. The sense of accountability instilled by solidarity motivates proactive efforts to prevent further deterioration, while the collective voice amplifies advocacy and influence, effectively challenging external negative forces.

Solidarity takes tangible form in various settings and is especially evident in initiatives aimed at improving the health and well-being of a community. In European healthcare systems, where healthcare is largely publicly funded, solidarity comes to life through a collective agreement among citizens to pool their resources, usually via taxation, to ensure equal healthcare access for everyone, irrespective of their economic status. Support groups for mental health disorders or substance addiction provide an essential emotional lifeline, operating on mutual aid and solidarity. Community initiatives like food drives, neighbourly check-ins and crisis response teams offer practical examples of solidarity. The concept also manifests in advocacy efforts, including anti-stigma campaigns and protests against detrimental healthcare policies. In all these forms, solidarity is a potent force for collective good, driving meaningful change and fortifying communal well-being.

Related words:

unity, camaraderie, togetherness, fellowship, mutual support, cooperation, cohesion, alliance, harmony, consensus, fraternity, esprit de corps, collaboration, team spirit

CARING – Being careful with myself and others

*For some people, feeling healthy and happy implies being **careful with myself and others**.*
*Likewise, this **Caring** contributes to feeling and being healthier and happier.*

Caring is the active, responsible engagement in nurturing and tending to someone or something in order to avoid decay or deterioration. The concept of 'care' transcends various aspects of life, including self-care, interpersonal relationships and even brand-to-customer interactions. Care involves a complex blend of empathy, understanding and compassion, coupled with action to nurture well-being and overall health. This could mean prioritising your own physical and mental well-being, lending emotional support to loved ones or taking steps to preserve and protect the environment. The term equally applies to businesses or organisations aiming to create a positive impact in the lives of their consumers. Care, in each of these instances, signifies a level of responsibility, commitment and dedication to ensure better conditions for whoever or whatever is at the focus.

The idea of care serves as an ethical principle and has palpable positive effects on individual and collective well-being. For individuals, self-care strategies – whether physical, emotional or mental – enhance life quality, resilience and interpersonal relationships. Similarly, caring for others generates a sense of purpose, fortifies social bonds and even provides health benefits like stress reduction. In a broader context, businesses and organisations often incorporate care into their brand ethos, committing to customer well-being, sustainability and community support. Such commitments aren't just ethical choices; they have real-world impacts, bolstering brand image and customer loyalty.

Notable examples bring this concept to life. Pharmaceutical giant **Novartis** encapsulates its mission in the slogan 'Caring and curing', a nod to its commitment to both patient well-being and medical innovation. **Johnson and Johnson**'s CARE INSPIRES CARE® platform, initiated during their 2014 FIFA World Cup™ sponsorship, encouraged over 25 million acts of care, showcasing that mass mobilisation of care can enact global change. **Volvo**'s Care programme simplifies car ownership with an all-inclusive subscription service, 'taking care' of maintenance, insurance and basic wear and tear for you. This programme represents an evolution in customer care, making vehicle ownership stress-free so the customer can focus on what really matters: the journey ahead. These examples affirm that care remains a powerful catalyst for positive change in personal life, community interactions or consumer relations.

Related words:
thoughtful, benevolent, solicitous, protective, comforting

SAFENESS – feeling safe and protected

*For some people, feeling healthy and happy implies feeling **safe and protected.***
*Likewise, this **Safeness** contributes to feeling and being healthier and happier.*

Safety encompasses behaviours to keep oneself or others free from harm, injury, damage, danger or loss. A state of good health is a vital component of this safety as it minimises the risks of illnesses and strengthens the body's defences against health issues. When individuals feel safe and secure, their bodies and minds can relax, reducing stress and anxiety levels and fostering positive emotions and a more optimistic outlook on life. Thus, achieving a state of health and safety is interconnected, forming a cycle where each positively influences the other, elevating one's quality of life. The interrelation of health and safety creates an environment where individuals can confidently navigate their worlds, with decreased stress levels and an increased likelihood to participate in health-promoting behaviours.

Feeling safe and protected is fundamental to our physical and psychological well-being, establishing the base for happiness. This feeling of safety curtails the production of stress hormones, paving the way for quality sleep, emotional stability and many healthy behaviours. It is the catalyst for a more active lifestyle and fosters a secure social environment, providing critical emotional support. Additionally, it motivates individuals to adopt long-term health-promoting behaviours such as regular medical check-ups, acting as a protective barrier and allowing for fuller, more enriched engagement with life. In essence, the feelings of safety and protection are quintessential to human flourishing, integrating health benefits and a more profound sense of happiness and fulfilment.

Real-world examples highlight the implementation of safety innovations and modifications. Volvo exemplify this by introducing advanced safety features in their vehicles, such as collision avoidance systems and initiating the **Volvo** Lifesaver project, equipping cars with an AED linked to a national call system for resuscitation by civil aid workers. The automotive industry, in general, has evolved by incorporating female crash test dummies, allowing for enhancements in vehicle safety features like seat belts and airbags. Additionally, products like **Athena** by ROAR for Good and protective clothing by Dainese have been developed with a focus on women's safety, addressing specific needs and anatomical differences. These examples delineate the multi-faceted approach to safety, illustrating the continual advancements and adaptations across different industries and aiming to cultivate an environment where everyone can feel protected and secure.

Related words:
security, protection, safety, secureness, assurance, certainty, guard, defence, precaution, safeguard

CALMNESS – being free from stress and anxiety

For some people, feeling healthy and happy implies being **free from stress and anxiety.**
Likewise, this **Calmness** contributes to feeling and being healthier and happier.

Calmness is the deep sense of peace achieved by limiting exposure to external events or situations that create undue pressure or cause exceptional, prolonged concern and fear. It's achieved by countering or mitigating stress and anxiety. Stress and anxiety, while closely related, are distinct psychological reactions. Stress typically arises from external pressures or challenges, such as work deadlines or family conflicts. Its effects, ranging from headaches to difficulty concentrating, tend to recede once the stressor is addressed. On the other hand, anxiety is characterised by an internal sense of excessive worry or fear, often not linked to specific events. This can be more persistent, affecting individuals even without immediate stressors with symptoms like rapid heartbeat and restlessness. Recognising that the two can influence each other is crucial: enduring stress may lead to anxiety, and existing anxiety can exacerbate stress. For both, calmness proves beneficial.

Calmness, a state of mental and physical relaxation, is cultivated through activities or techniques designed to alleviate stress and tension. It brings many health benefits, including reducing harmful stress hormones, lowering blood pressure, enhancing sleep quality and easing muscle tension. Apart from physical advantages, calmness significantly contributes to happiness. It boosts mood by elevating mood-enhancing hormones, sharpening focus, fostering emotional resilience and supporting overall mental well-being. Practices emphasising clearness and self-awareness are pivotal to relaxation, enabling individuals to understand better and control their emotions promoting holistic wellness.

Calm has emerged as a front-runner in digital wellness, resonating deeply with users with an aspiration of calmness. However, several other businesses have also initiated strategies to promote relaxation and reduce anxiety. **TUI Group**, a prominent European travel agency, has introduced a 'Stress-Free Package' for travellers aimed at minimising travel-induced stress through flexible booking and complimentary services. **Rituals**, a cosmetics and home fragrance firm, produces products like scented candles and essential oils, all curated to foster relaxation. Recognising the stress related to financial wellness, financial institutions have taken steps to aid customers in managing their financial health. **Bank of America**, for instance, offers 'Better Money Habits', a financial wellness programme providing a suite of educational resources. Similarly, **BBVA** emphasises financial education, offering many resources through its Centre for Financial Education and Capability.

Related words:
clarity, focus, serenity, tranquillity, peace, composure, repose, poise, equanimity, relaxation, ease, harmony, restfulness, coolness, undisturbedness

CLARITY – be mindful and focused

*For some people, feeling healthy and happy implies **being mindful and focused.*** *Likewise, this **Clarity** contributes to feeling and being healthier and happier.*

Clarity is the desirable state of mind, free from the constant stream of thoughts, emotions and external stimuli, allowing us to gain perspective and make better decisions. It is a foundational pillar for personal well-being, improving stress management and augmenting productivity. Mindfulness stands out as a prominent technique for cultivating this invaluable mental state. Rooted in the philosophy of living in the present, mindfulness encourages an individual to embrace the current moment with a non-judgmental and curious lens. This trait, often honed through mindfulness meditation and other related activities, is a strategic avenue to achieve the coveted mental tranquillity and clarity.

Maintaining clearness, such as through mental headspace and mindfulness, can profoundly impact one's holistic well-being. A focused presence helps shift attention away from past regrets and future anxieties and facilitates better mental clarity. It also acts as a catalyst for deeper interpersonal connections by fostering attentive communication. Evidence suggests that mindfulness bolsters immune function, potentially serving as a defence against illnesses. Additionally, cognitive faculties like memory, attention and focus are heightened, which is particularly beneficial as one navigates the challenges of ageing. Moreover, genuinely immersing oneself in life's moments can lead to amplified joy, whether this is in the company of loved ones, relishing a delectable dish or admiring the intricacies of nature. Ultimately, such practices, emphasising the 'now', offer an enriched physical and emotional life.

Several enterprises have discerned the invaluable role of mental headspace and have woven it into their brand ethos and services. **Headspace**, a leading name in digital wellness, provides meditation resources via its app and has formed synergies with carmakers, hotels and airlines to promote on-the-go relaxation. A notable alliance is with **General Motors**, aiming to infuse serenity into vehicular travel. Concurrently, **Marriott** and **Headspace** have curated mindfulness content for guests. **Headspace** has even united with **Nike**, merging physical training with mental fortitude. **Lululemon**, a prominent name in athletic wear, champions a balanced lifestyle and incorporates mindfulness resources for its community. Meanwhile, **MUJI**, the Japanese minimalist retail brand, translates its product philosophy into life values, underlining the tenets of simplicity and mindfulness. This has been further amplified by hosting meditation events. Moreover, global hospitality entities progressively integrate mindfulness into their travel experiences, highlighting the ever-growing appetite for balanced, mindful excursions.

Related words:
clarity, focus, lucidity, limpidity, sharpness, lucidness, crispness

CONSCIOUSNESS – being aware and comprehending

*For some people, feeling healthy and happy implies being **aware and comprehending.***
*Likewise, this **Consciousness** contributes to feeling and being healthier and happier.*

Consciousness is the innate desire to be aware and understand things for various cognitive, emotional and practical purposes. People continually aspire to comprehend the myriad facets of their health and happiness, enabling them to elevate their overall well-being and make informed decisions. The quest for knowledge spans several domains, including the essence of a balanced diet, the vitality of regular exercise, the significance of restful sleep and techniques for effective stress management. The pursuit of consciousness also encompasses understanding mental health, fostering robust relationships, achieving work-life balance and exploring self-awareness. Additionally, the role of environmental factors is not to be ignored. Individuals can craft strategies that amplify their holistic well-being by delving deep into these spheres.

Indeed, cultivating an understanding of life bears fruit in the form of enhanced health. This enlightenment emerges in multiple facets: health literacy empowers individuals with the knowledge to establish healthier lifestyles; emotional intelligence nurtures mental well-being by fostering sound interpersonal relationships; self-awareness paves the way for personal growth and optimal decision-making; and grasping the broader societal and environmental contexts influences informed decisions and advocacy for health-centric policies. This pursuit of knowledge, encompassing oneself, others and the wider world, is instrumental in fostering well-rounded health and happiness.

Various enterprises, including pharmaceutical companies and patient associations, champion health awareness campaigns, emphasising many conditions, ranging from physical ailments to mental well-being. In the consumer world, **Nestlé**'s 'Nestlé for Healthier Kids' initiative, originating from the Swiss multinational's commitment to nutrition literacy, endeavours to usher in healthier lives for 50 million children by 2030. Their approach hinges on the pillars of nutritional education, enhanced product recipes and physical activity advocacy. Similarly, through its brand '**Knorr**', Unilever unveiled the 'Knorr Future 50 Foods' initiative in alliance with **WWF**. It champions diverse and sustainable foods that are nutritious and environmentally benign. The project underscores the dual benefits of these 50 foods – promoting human health and fostering a sustainable planet. These corporate initiatives exemplify the collective stride towards a healthier, more informed global populace.

Related words:

awareness, wakefulness, alertness, understanding, insight, knowledge, sentience, apprehension, self-awareness, enlightenment, comprehension

ACCEPT

Beginning with practising kindness and gratitude, individuals cultivate a sense of belonging and connection. As they embrace their authentic selves and find meaning in their actions, a deep sense of self-worth blossoms, leading to a fulfilling journey of enjoying life to the fullest.

2.1 Kindness – *(being kind to myself and others)*
The act of being empathic, compassionate and understanding towards oneself and others.

2.2 Gratitude – *(having appreciation and being thankful)*
The practice of recognising good things, events, people and circumstances, and expressing appreciation for them.

2.3 Belonging – *(feeling accepted and included)*
The human emotional wish to be accepted by a group and to feel included and valued within a social context.

2.4 Realness – *(being genuine and true to myself and others)*
A more colloquial term that conveys a sense of genuineness or truthfulness without hiding behind masks or false personas.

2.5 Meaning – *(living life with a meaningful purpose)*
The significance, purpose, worth or value that we attach to our life, our experiences or certain aspects of our existence.

2.6 Self-worth – *(feeling good about myself)*
The positive evaluation of oneself and the belief in one's own worthiness of love, respect and care.

KINDNESS – being kind to myself and others

*For some people, feeling healthy and happy implies being **kind to myself and others**. Likewise, this **Kindness** contributes to feeling and being healthier and happier.*

Kindness is the act of being empathic, compassionate and understanding towards oneself and others. It's not limited to understanding someone's emotional state but when we comprehend the feelings of others, our inclination to extend supportive actions increases. It involves offering support, help or consideration. Acts like holding a door, assisting someone or giving a compliment are simple yet potent gestures of kindness.

Engaging in kindness has cascading effects on individual and collective well-being. Kindness uplifts the recipient and confers physiological and psychological benefits to the giver. It triggers a 'helper's high' through endorphin release, diminishes stress and bolsters feelings of connection, reducing feelings of isolation. Physiologically, kindness can bolster immune system functioning, lower blood pressure courtesy of oxytocin and possibly extend lifespan through consistent positive emotions. From a mental health perspective, kindness is a bulwark against depression, elevates self-worth and builds self-esteem. These myriad benefits underscore how integral kindness is to our well-being.

Several companies integrate kindness into their business ethos and practices. **Dove** champions self-esteem with their 'Real Beauty' campaign, challenging conventional beauty norms and advocating kindness to oneself and others. **KIND Snacks** intertwines its product line with a mission to make the world kinder, supporting charitable endeavours with their KIND Foundation and fostering a culture of kindness with the KIND movement. Kindness is a cornerstone for **Starbucks**, emphasising their belief in being a 'people business serving coffee'. They amplified this philosophy through an augmented reality experience that facilitates sending virtual kind messages anywhere in the world. Further endorsing this mission, Starbucks collaborated with **Lady Gaga**'s Born This Way Foundation, supporting the #BeKind365 initiative and partnered with **Headspace** to offer kindness-themed meditations. These companies showcase how integrating kindness into business practices resonates with customers and strengthens brand identity.

Related words:
warmth, empathy, sympathy, consideration, compassion, goodwill, benevolence, altruism, humanity, gentleness, goodness, thoughtfulness

GRATITUDE – being thankful and having appreciation

*For some people, feeling healthy and happy implies being **thankful and having appreciation**. Likewise, this **Gratitude** contributes to feeling and being healthier and happier.*

Gratitude is a profound recognition of the positive aspects of life. It encompasses acknowledging and appreciating the good deeds, events and experiences in our lives. This sentiment can be directed toward others for their acts of kindness, towards oneself for personal milestones or just an appreciation for the joys of daily life. When people experience gratitude, they often feel a natural inclination to reciprocate the kindness they've received. This concept is inherently tied to 'giving back', which refers to contributing to society or individuals in recognition of the good fortune one has received. It manifests gratitude in action, translating feelings of thankfulness into tangible activities like volunteering and charitable donations.

From a health perspective, gratitude plays a pivotal role in mental and physical well-being. Psychologically, gratitude fosters positive emotions, increases happiness, reduces stress, enhances relationships and boosts sense of self-worth. It also acts as a bulwark against adversities, promoting resilience. In terms of physical health, consistent gratitude has been correlated with various benefits. Studies have indicated improved sleep quality, better heart health and even enhanced immune function among those who practice gratitude. This isn't to suggest that gratitude is a panacea. Still, it forms a vital component of a holistic approach to health, complemented by other essential factors like diet, exercise and medical care.

Numerous entities stand out when it comes to real-world applications of gratitude and giving back. **Interflora**, a leading flower delivery service, and **ThankU.io**, a digital platform, are companies built around expressing gratitude. Cosmetics company **Lush** is known for its 'Charity Pot' programme, which donates 100% of the purchase price of certain products to grassroots organisations. **TOMS Shoes'** One for One programme donates a pair of shoes to a child in need for every pair sold. **Salesforce** implements a 1-1-1 philanthropic model that gives back 1% of its equity, 1% of its product and 1% of employee hours to charitable causes and community work. In sports, the **NBA** is a testament to the power of giving back. The league emphasises community outreach and empowerment with initiatives like NBA Cares, Basketball Without Borders and the NBA Foundation. These myriad efforts exemplify the profound impact of recognising and acting upon the blessings in our lives.

Related words:

thankfulness, appreciation, gratefulness, recognition, acknowledgment, appreciative, humility, respect, compliment, courtesy

BELONGING – being accepted and included

*For some people, feeling healthy and happy implies being **accepted and included.***
*Likewise, this **Belonging** contributes to feeling and being healthier and happier.*

Belonging is a deep-seated emotional desire to be accepted and valued within a group or social context. It embodies the idea of ensuring everyone feels respected and included, irrespective of race, gender, age, religion, disability or any distinguishing trait. The essence of belonging goes beyond individual contexts, permeating societal structures such as ensuring equal access to resources, fostering diverse workplaces and maintaining equity in personal relationships. At its core, belonging champions the celebration of diversity, the equitable treatment of all and the creation of inclusive spaces where everyone is empowered to participate fully.

The instinct to belong has its roots in our evolutionary history. As social beings, our mental and physical health is intrinsically tied to our social connections. Socially integrated individuals tend to exhibit boosted self-esteem, reduced stress and an enhanced sense of happiness. A robust sense of belonging fosters validation and acceptance, enriches relationships, provides purpose and magnifies shared experiences. On the other hand, loneliness has been equated to risks like obesity and smoking. For instance, a study titled 'Loneliness and Social Isolation as Risk Factors for Mortality' underscored the risks of social isolation, equating its adverse effects with established health hazards. In sum, belonging to something – be it a family, friend group, team, community or organisation – is crucial for our mental and physical well-being.

The quest for belonging is evident across various spheres. Religious practices, political affiliations, sports fandom and social justice movements illustrate humanity's innate yearning to belong. Businesses, too, play a pivotal role. Inclusive marketing, for instance, can elevate customer loyalty and satisfaction. Companies such as **Unilever**, with its 'Unstereotype Alliance', have championed diverse representations in advertising. **Sodexo** prioritises services catering to varied client needs, **Lloyds Bank** offers an array of accessibility services and **Deutsche Telekom** ardently promotes digital inclusion. Each of these initiatives underscores the universal essence of belonging, reinforcing the importance of inclusivity and respect in today's interconnected world.

Related words:

accepted, valued, respected, welcomed, affirmed, embraced, recognised, included, acknowledged

REALNESS – being genuine and true to myself and others

*For some people, feeling healthy and happy implies being **genuine and true to themselves and others**. Likewise, this **Realness** contributes to feeling and being healthier and happier.*

Realness is a more colloquial term that conveys a sense of genuineness or truthfulness without hiding behind masks or false personas. It means a raw sense of honesty, going beyond the often hollow claims of authenticity. While authenticity might originate from individuality or a focus on one's own interest, realness encompasses the genuine, two-way dynamics of a relationship. It's about honest, direct interactions without the barriers of deceit or pretence, ensuring both sides of the relationship are genuine and transparent.

Fostering a genuine environment has a profound impact on individuals, directly correlating with their health and happiness. Genuine interactions alleviate stress, as people aren't mentally burdened with discerning truth from falsehood. Such interactions foster a deep sense of belonging, making individuals feel valued and connected. Stating from this realness, trustworthiness establishes emotional security, allowing deeper, sincere connections. Clear, honest communication minimises misunderstandings, bolstering mental health. Such environments also encourage authentic self-expression, increasing happiness and reinforcing self-worth. Emotionally, the benefits spill over into physical fitness, from better immunity to enhanced longevity.

The current era's turbulence intensifies the collective yearning for authenticity. With rampant misinformation, there's a heightened demand for brands to be ethical, sincere and honest. **IDEO**, during the BlackLivesMatter movement in 2020, embraced feedback, admitting to their shortcomings and vowing to be more socially responsible. After the 2011 Japan earthquake, **Toyota** transparently communicated production disruptions but diligently worked to uphold customer commitments, solidifying its bond with the community. **IKEA**'s open discourse about the challenges of sustainable production and its community-driven actions, like aiding refugee camps, exemplifies its dedication to realness, reliability and genuine care for its customers.

Related words:
authenticity, genuineness, truth, sincerity, truthfulness, veracity, credibility, reliability

MEANING – having a life with a meaningful purpose

*For some people, feeling healthy and happy implies having **a life with a meaningful purpose**. Likewise, this **Meaning** contributes to feeling and being healthier and happier.*

Meaning is the significance and value we assign to our existence, experiences and the world around us. It's the essence of comprehending the broader context of our lives and acknowledging that our actions possess relevance beyond mere superficiality. While many sources, including relationships, work and spirituality, can impart meaning, a profound sense of purpose is often the primary cornerstone of a meaningful life or work.

Embracing a purposeful meaning transcends mere philosophical contemplation; it bears tangible health benefits. A robust sense of purpose fosters psychological well-being, translating to increased life satisfaction, happiness and reduced stress. Such a mindset often motivates individuals towards healthier behaviours like regular exercise and a balanced diet. Consequently, this can bolster social connections, enriching mental and physical health. An insightful study from the Boston University School of Public Health underlined these findings, indicating that purpose correlates to a reduced mortality risk. The research, which assessed over 13,000 adults, found that people with the highest sense of purpose showed the lowest risk of death (15.2% mortality risk) compared to people with the lowest sense of purpose (36.5% mortality risk)

In the corporate realm, meaningful purpose transcends mere marketing rhetoric; it's about resonating and connecting authentically with consumers. **Patagonia**, an exemplary manifestation of this ethos, has continually pivoted its business model to emphasise environmental responsibility and align with the values of its customer base in doing so. In an unprecedented move in September 2022, they moved the company's voting stock to the Patagonia Trust and gave the nonvoting stock to the environmental non-profit Holdfast Collective. On the same note but with a health-focused purpose, **Nike** has launched the 'Well Collective', a strategic shift that extends beyond its primary sports purpose to encompass holistic health and wellness by including aspects like movement, nutrition and mindfulness. This change aligns with the findings from the **Havas Media Group**'s Meaningful Brands report (2023), which states that 71% of people want companies and brands to support and improve their overall health and well-being. In essence, brands that genuinely infuse meaning into their daily business foster deeper customer connections and drive impactful change for people, society and the environment.

Related words:
significance, essence, intention, objective, aim, mission, direction, motivation, value, role

SELF-WORTH – having a good feeling about myself

*For some people, feeling healthy and happy implies having **a good feeling about themselves.** Likewise, this **Self-worth** contributes to feeling and being healthier and happier.*

Self-worth denotes the positive evaluation of oneself and the belief in one's own worthiness of love, respect and care. It's an umbrella term encompassing self-esteem, concentrating on an individual's self-perception. This valuation persists regardless of external achievements or validations. At its core, self-worth forms the bedrock of one's perception of oneself in the broader world.

The profound impact of self-worth on a person's life can't be understated. It is a linchpin for mental and physical health, overall contentment, interpersonal relationships and resilience. Individuals with robust self-worth tend to have fewer mental health issues such as depression, and exhibit greater optimism. This positive self-image often spills over into physical care, promoting better dietary habits, sleep and avoidance of detrimental behaviours. Furthermore, higher self-worth has been correlated with elevated levels of happiness, success and improved relationship quality. Studies such as those conducted by psychologists Ed Diener and Carol Diener (2015) reveal a significant connection between self-worth and happiness across various cultures. Furthermore, the ability to rebound from setbacks, known as resilience, is heightened with increased self-worth, enabling people to navigate challenges with less stress.

Several campaigns and trends underscore the importance of self-worth in society. **Dove**'s 'Real Beauty' campaign stands as a hallmark, advocating for genuine representations of women and combatting conventional beauty ideals. Their global studies, like the 2016 Beauty and Confidence Report, spotlight the ripple effects of self-esteem on happiness, health and opportunities. Another trend, **Barbiecore**, inspired by the iconic doll and the recent popularity of the Barbie movie, has swept the internet (1 billion views on TikTok), emphasising body positivity and self-expression. The Barbie brand, in response, has diversified its dolls, leading to a broader acceptance of varied appearances. Meanwhile, **L'Oréal Paris**, with its legendary slogan 'Because You're Worth It', has consistently echoed the sentiments of self-worth and universal beauty. Their continuous efforts to present diverse representations in their campaigns have made them pioneers in prioritising individual worth over standardised beauty norms.

Related words:

self-esteem, self-value, self-respect, self-regard, self-love, self-confidence, self-belief, self-assurance, self-appreciation, self-acceptance, dignity, pride, self-affirmation, self-trust, self-admiration

ENJOY

Starting from a foundation of autonomy and embracing the spontaneity of life, individuals form deep and meaningful relationships. Through these connections, they learn to love both themselves and others, experiencing profound joy.

3.1 Nothingness – *(doing, feeling, seeing or hearing nothing)*
The absence of attention, distraction, stimulation, satiations or even purpose as an antidote to the 'noise' in the external world.

3.2 Spontaneity – *(acting spontaneously)*
The ability to act in a natural, unplanned and unrestrained manner, with little premeditation or deliberation.

3.3 Autonomy – *(living independently and autonomously)*
The freedom and capacity to make decisions based on one's values, goals and beliefs.

3.4 Relationships – *(having meaningful connections)*
The quality or state of having meaningful connections or social interactions with others.

3.5 Loving – *(loving or being loved)*
The emotional, physical and psychological expressions and experiences that fulfil an intrinsic human desire for mutual caring, intimacy and deep connection.

3.6 Joy – *(having amazing experiences)*
The state of feeling extremely good, often accompanied by a sense of excitement, admiration and a strong positive impression.

NOTHINGNESS – doing, feeling, seeing or hearing nothing

*For some people, feeling healthy and happy implies **doing, feeling, seeing or hearing nothing.** Likewise, this **Nothingness** contributes to feeling and being healthier and happier.*

The absence of attention, distraction, stimulation, satiations or even purpose as an antidote to the 'noise' in the external world. In the cacophonous world we inhabit, it's an inward escapism and/or an external withdrawal that functions as a potential antidote to all the 'noise' in the world. This allows people to disconnect, rest or focus on one thing at a time. With silence becoming a treasured rarity, we're undergoing a cultural shift where absence is being celebrated.

The modern ethos, with its relentless stimuli, has left us feeling burned out and estranged from our very essence. Amidst this turbulence, nothingness serves as a refreshing pause button, bringing a myriad of health benefits in its wake. For instance, cutting down on digital distractions can lead to rejuvenating sleep and overall wellness. Prioritising inattention can hone focus, boost productivity and invoke a profound sense of achievement. Furthermore, this state of nothingness accentuates mindfulness, a practice linked to an array of positive health outcomes. Such periods of disengagement provide room for deep introspection, creativity and personal growth. This mental spaciousness, which allows us to view the bigger picture, is becoming an ever-growing necessity.

While the idea of nothingness might seem avant-garde, it is rooted in ancient practices of retreat and refuge. Today, we see this through the rise of meditation apps or in the popularity of silent retreats attended by many seeking mental deconditioning. Consider the Dutch concept of 'niksen' which translates to 'doing nothing', an act of doing nothing and simply being without an end goal in mind. It signifies the global acknowledgment of the value of nothingness. Even established brands like **Facebook** and **Netflix**, traditionally feeding off the Attention Economy, are recalibrating to this 'Nothingness Economy'. We now also see premium-priced silent **Ubers** or initiatives like **Selfridges** partnering with **Headspace** for a 'No Noise' campaign. The evolving marketplace shows a clear inclination towards products and experiences that let individuals disconnect and immerse in the moment. It's a sign that brands aiming to have minimal mental and environmental footprints, with characteristics such as zero waste, veganism, nonownership and non-alcoholic products are on the right track.

Related words:

absence, omission, nonattendance, absenteeism, unavailability, disappearance, neglect, non-presence, emptiness, vacuity, blank, nihilism, voidness, oblivion, lack, nonexistence, nonmissing

SPONTANEITY – acting spontaneously

*For some people, feeling healthy and happy implies being able to **act spontaneously.***
*Likewise, this **Spontaneity** contributes to feeling and being healthier and happier.*

Spontaneity is the ability to act in a natural, unplanned and unrestrained manner, with little premeditation or deliberation. It manifests as a blend of impulsiveness, creativity and liberation from traditional constraints. Such spontaneous actions can lead to moments of deep engagement, ushering in heightened positive emotions and fostering a mindset that thrives on optimism.

Dr Stuart Brown is a renowned psychiatrist and clinical researcher who has extensively studied the role of play in humans. In his research, Dr Brown discovered that consistent engagement in play, even into adulthood, enhances creativity, improves brain function and escalates energy levels. These activities, enveloped in spontaneity, can bolster relationships, reduce stress and develop confidence in individuals, making them adept at handling unexpected outcomes. Embracing spontaneity can even be therapeutic, offering diverse benefits to holistic health. It presents a respite from daily pressures, enhancing life satisfaction by bringing forth unforeseen joys and memories. Breaking the routine rejuvenates the spirit, facilitating a fresh perspective on everyday challenges. This surprise element can therapeutically activate the brain, triggering positive emotions like trust, love and joy, subsequently releasing 'happy hormones'. A judicious balance of spontaneity can contribute to overall well-being, supporting both mental and physical health. By fostering resilience and adaptability, spontaneity can be a significant tool in navigating life's myriad challenges.

Several European enterprises, spanning sectors such as consumer, retail, tech and travel, ingeniously incorporate spontaneity into their offerings. **Booking.com**, based in the Netherlands, facilitates spontaneous travel through its last-minute deals. Meanwhile, Denmark's **Too Good To Go** curbs food wastage while endorsing unplanned meals. **Klarna**, a Swedish fintech, permits spontaneous shopping by deferring immediate payments. Similarly, **Spotify** spontaneously introduces users to fresh music. In parallel, in healthcare, companies like **Medtronic** and **Dexcom** offer devices that allow diabetics to lead a more spontaneous life, while apps like **mySugr** gamify their health management. Through their innovative services, these companies lower barriers and bolster spontaneity, enriching patient's lives.

Related words:
uninhibited, freedom, unplanned, last-minute, unrestrained, without premeditation

AUTONOMY – living independently and autonomously

*For some people, feeling healthy and happy implies being able to **live independently and autonomously**. Likewise, this **Autonomy** contributes to feeling and being healthier and happier.*

Autonomy signifies the freedom and capacity to make decisions based on one's values, goals and beliefs. It encapsulates the essence of self-governance and determination, enabling individuals to oversee their choices without undue external pressures. At its core, autonomy champions the idea of taking charge of one's life and actions.

The significance of autonomy spans more than mere self-governance – it's a cornerstone for optimal well-being and health. Deci and Ryan's Self-Determination Theory (SDT) underscores autonomy as one of the fundamental psychological needs, complemented by relatedness (see aspiration: Relationships), which when met fosters human growth. This autonomy enhances intrinsic motivation, steering individuals towards healthier behavioural choices. Furthermore, it's pivotal in the healthcare sector. When patients have a voice in their medical decisions, it often culminates in better health outcomes, greater treatment adherence and heightened satisfaction. For the ageing demographic, the role of autonomy is even more pronounced. While many seniors grapple with diminished autonomy due to various constraints, preserving their decision-making ability can bolster psychological well-being, life contentment and cognitive vitality.

In a bygone era, consumer choices were largely dictated by local availability and limited information channels. As such, consumers' autonomy was often compromised. However, the digital revolution has dramatically redressed this balance, positioning the consumer in a dominant role. The proliferation of technology has not only democratised information access but also amplified consumers' demands for autonomy. Companies are responding by innovatively tailoring solutions to cater to this empowered consumer base, with the elderly being a notable focus. Companies like **Best Buy**, through its acquisition of **GreatCall**, are pioneering this change. They're designing products like the Jitterbug phone or other tailored devices and services with seniors' autonomy and safety in mind, ensuring they remain independent, secure and fulfilled as they age. Similarly, **Whirlpool**'s senior-friendly appliances, be it auto-shutoff ovens or user-friendly washing machines, underscore the market's trajectory: prioritising and amplifying consumer autonomy.

Related words:

freedom, independency, self-governance, self-rule, sovereignty, freedom, self-determination, self-sufficiency, self-reliance, self-direction, self-management

RELATIONSHIPS – having meaningful connections

*For some people, feeling healthy and happy implies having **meaningful connections.***
*Likewise, **Relationships** contribute to feeling and being healthier and happier.*

The quality or state of having meaningful connections or social relationships with others. This aspiration encapsulates the essence of being social and establishing significant relationships. At its core, it indicates a person's natural tendency to engage in and form meaningful social bonds. This isn't merely about being active socially, but about having interactions that leave lasting, genuine impacts on both parties. A survey by the German Zukunftsinstitut highlighted that a significant majority of people value relationships, family ties and close friendships. Such connections are two-sided: they provide both support in trying times and joy in celebratory ones, proving their importance in our lives. It's the act of sharing vulnerabilities, interests and values that makes them profound.

Being social isn't just about feeling good; it's about holistic well-being. We thrive in community settings, finding purpose, inspiration and a deeper sense of self when surrounded by meaningful relationships. This sense of shared experience directly affects our mental, emotional and physical health. Surrounding ourselves with positive influences fosters healthier habits, shared activities and mutual support, all of which boost our resilience and overall well-being. Studies further reinforce this, showing that peers influence academic achievements and even decisions about habits like drug use. In essence, who we choose to connect with has tangible effects on our well-being and life choices.

Several companies have recognised the significance of meaningful connections and have tailored their initiatives accordingly. **Lidl** Ireland introduced 'The Bakery', not just as a place to savour baked goods but as a platform for mental health awareness events in collaboration with **Jigsaw**. Similarly, in **Saga City**, a dedicated space caters to dementia patients and their families, emphasising connection over direct treatment. Brands like **Airbnb** and **Starbucks** are renowned for fostering genuine connections – **Airbnb** through cultural exchanges with hosts and **Starbucks** by creating a 'third place' between work and home. **WW**, formerly WeightWatchers, builds communities around health, while platforms like **Meetup** allow people to bond over shared interests. Through tools like **Webex**'s Collaboration Insights, individuals can foster inclusive collaboration, further underscoring the broad range of ways companies can nurture sociableness.

Related words:

sociable, relations, camaraderie, close connections, friends, family, neighbours, close collaborators, frolleagues, social interactions

LOVING – loving or being loved

For some people, feeling healthy and happy implies **loving or being loved.**
Likewise, this **Loving** contributes to feeling and being healthier and happier.

Love, both in giving and receiving, is the emotional, physical and psychological expressions and experiences that fulfil an intrinsic human desire for mutual caring, intimacy and deeper connection. Whether it's through words of affirmation, empathetic listening, acts of service or physical touch including sexual intercourse, love manifests in ways that are deeply personal and culturally influenced. This dynamic interplay often serves as a mutual exchange, wherein both parties contribute to each other's overall well-being and happiness.

The scientific community overwhelmingly supports the notion that love has profound psychological and physiological benefits. Research has linked loving relationships to improved cardiovascular health, enhanced immune function and mental well-being. Love also plays a role in stress reduction through the release of the hormone oxytocin and has been found to positively influence pain management. Moreover, when people feel loved and supported, they are more likely to engage in health-promoting behaviours like exercise and proper nutrition. While this correlation between love and health outcomes is strong, it's important to note that quality over quantity of loving relationships makes a difference.

The universal theme of love has also been leveraged in various marketing campaigns by brands globally, even those not traditionally associated with love or sexual wellness. For example, **CVS Pharmacy** has expanded its range to include sexual wellness products, aligning them with their mission of overall health. Similarly, eco-friendly brand **Sustain** has moved beyond period products to offer organic lubricants, emphasising natural, ethical choices in their product line. Companies like **Durex** have also transitioned from being solely associated with protection to championing a full spectrum of sexual wellness through inclusive and educational campaigns. Thus, love and its diverse expressions, including sexual wellness, are increasingly recognised for their intrinsic value to human well-being and are becoming more mainstream in both scientific discourse and brand marketing.

Related words:
love, relationship, couples, affection, romance, intimacy, tenderness, attachment, cherished, treasured

JOY – having amazing experiences

*For some people, feeling healthy and happy implies having **amazing experiences.***
*Likewise, this **Joy** contributes to feeling and being healthier and happier.*

Joy is the state of feeling extremely good, often accompanied by a sense of enjoyment, excitement, admiration and a strong positive impression. It characterises the sensation of remarkable experiences and sheer delight. Joy denotes an extreme level of excellence or impressiveness, accompanied by feelings of excitement and admiration. It captures moments that are not only memorable but also deeply satisfying, leaving a potent positive mark on the beholder.

Evidence strongly supports the idea that joyful or amazing experiences can bolster one's health and overall well-being. Positive psychology and well-being research has illuminated the myriad ways such experiences and emotions can influence both our mental and physical states. For instance, positive emotions have been found to expand our cognitive, emotional and social capacities, fostering resilience and happiness. These positive states of mind can even buffer against stress and promote psychological resilience. Additionally, they can lower risks associated with cardiovascular diseases, reduce inflammation and bolster immune responses. Simple activities like social interactions, outdoor pursuits or immersing oneself in hobbies can foster these positive emotions and contribute to a healthier lifestyle.

Real-world examples elucidate the effects of such positive experiences. For instance, the **SilverFit** system, tailored for senior citizens, employs games to catalyse both cognitive and physical activities. These games, grounded in safety and therapeutic benefits, encourage the elderly to engage more in physiotherapy and exercise. Such engagement indirectly contributes to their overall health, enhancing mobility and mental well-being. Meanwhile, global giant **Disney** underscores the potential for entertainment-focused enterprises to indirectly impact health and happiness. Through initiatives like 'Disney's Magic of Healthy Living', Disney has striven to motivate children and families to choose healthier lifestyles, blending fun content with essential advice on nutrition and physical activity. Through such endeavours, Disney emphasises that the joy and happiness they provide can seamlessly translate into tangible well-being.

Related words:

experiences, enjoyment, excitement, positivity, delight, pleasure, bliss, jubilation, elation, ecstasy, euphoria, glee, exuberance, cheerfulness, merriment, contentment, exhilaration

IMPROVE

Beginning with healing, people address physical and emotional wounds, paving the way for renewed strength and energy. With newfound vitality, they embrace personal growth, nurturing creativity along the way, ultimately culminating in an empowered self that radiates confidence and a genuine sense of looking good.

4.1 Healing – *(recovering and restoring)*
The process of restoration and recovery aimed at alleviating or eliminating physical, emotional, psychological or spiritual distress

4.2 Strength – *(having power and resilience)*
The capacity to exert force against resistance, whether it's physical, emotional or mental

4.3 Energy – *(having vitality and stamina)*
The quest for vitality, enthusiasm, stamina and the vigour to carry out daily activities or pursue goals

4.4 Self-development – *(growing and cultivating oneself)*
The deliberate and conscious actions an individual takes to improve their knowledge, skills, capabilities and overall character

4.5 Creativity – *(imagining and inventing)*
The ability to generate something novel or unique, whether it be an idea, a piece of art, a solution to a problem or a new way of approaching a challenge

4.6 Looking good – *(being attractive)*
The desire to present oneself in a manner that is aesthetically pleasing or attractive, both to oneself and to others

HEALING – recovering and restoring

*For some people, feeling healthy and happy implies **recovering and restoring.***
*Likewise, this **Healing** contributes to feeling and being healthier and happier.*

Healing is the process of restoration and recovery aimed at alleviating or eliminating physical, emotional, psychological or spiritual distress. In the medical realm, healing often centres on bodily recovery, such as tissue repair or infection control. However, psychological and emotional healing is equally crucial, addressing traumas, emotional wounds or mental health challenges through various means like therapy or self-care. Healing is not confined to just restoring a previous state or recovering from an illness; it also includes rehabilitating lost skills or mental states and reconciling emotional or relational issues. For patients and individuals, this holistic approach is a basic human aspiration that transcends mere symptom relief to address the complete state of well-being.

The anticipation of healing serves as a driving force for various groups of people. For patients undergoing medical treatments, it sustains them through challenging therapies and fosters a collaborative relationship with healthcare providers. Athletes view the anticipation of recovery and rehabilitation as crucial, reducing anxiety about potential injuries and helping them maintain focus and performance. For those coping with trauma, the expectation of healing becomes a vital source of hope, motivating them to engage in therapeutic processes and treatments with a more positive and receptive mindset. This anticipation resonates across emotional and psychological domains, making healing a holistic goal that meets the needs of the physical, emotional and sometimes spiritual aspects of individuals.

This holistic view of healing – encompassing not just recovery but also restoration and rehabilitation – has reverberated across multiple industries, spurring growth and innovation. In the health and fitness sector, brands like **Theragun** have popularised recovery tools like percussion massagers. The food and beverage industry has seen a surge in functional drinks like kombucha and protein shakes that aid recovery. The medical and pharmaceutical industries are increasingly focusing on holistic and preventative care, including both physical and mental rehabilitation centres. Meanwhile, the technology sector has given rise to fitness trackers like **Oura Ring** and **Whoop**, which monitor not just physical activity but also rest, sleep and recovery. In the realm of travel and tourism, wellness retreats focusing on holistic recovery are increasingly popular. Overall, the comprehensive understanding of healing has fostered a multi-industry impact, emphasising the interconnectedness of physical, emotional and psychological well-being.

Related words:
healing, recovery, restore, rehabilitation, rest, renewal, revitalisation, regeneration, recuperation, restoration, mending, rejuvenation, cure, remedy, repair, restoration

STRENGTH – having power and resilience

*For some people, feeling healthy and happy implies having **power and resilience.**
Likewise, this **Strength** contributes to feeling and being healthier and happier.*

Strength is the capacity to exert force against resistance, whether it's physical, emotional or mental. Physically, it's about the physical strength and willpower to push one's boundaries in terms of muscle strength, bone density or endurance. Emotionally and mentally, it translates to resilience – the capacity to overcome stress, adversity or any other challenges without succumbing. The ultimate aspiration for strength is multi-faceted, encompassing enhanced physical capabilities, mental toughness and the power to overcome personal and external obstacles.

Aspiring to strength positively impacts both health and overall well-being. Physically, it has a ripple effect and can even reduce the risk of chronic diseases. According to a meta-analysis in the *British Journal of Sports Medicine* (Feb 2022), just 30 to 60 minutes of strength training per week can reduce mortality risk by 10 to 20 per cent, alongside lowering the chances of cardiovascular disease and cancer. On the emotional and mental fronts, this aspiration nurtures resilience. It aids in recovering from setbacks and effectively managing stress. Over time, the journey to strength, whether physical or psychological, fosters a sense of achievement, boosting self-confidence, life satisfaction and overall happiness.

Some brands, even when not inherently linked to health and fitness, are innovatively supporting their consumers in this quest for strength. **Delta Airlines** is a prime example. Beyond their core aviation offerings, they're prioritising passenger health across all fronts. But their in-flight exercise tips cater to comfort, circulation and maintaining strength. Hotels are following suit; many now provide fitness centres since studies indicate that such amenities are a top consideration for guests. Moreover, innovative platforms like **ClassPass** highlight the surging popularity of strength training, with a notable 94% increase in such classes in 2022. For specialised groups, tools like the **SilverFit Newton** provide engaging training for patients by adding game to strength exercises, while organisations like the **WHO** and the **Australian Cancer Council** emphasise and support the crucial role of strength training for both older adults and cancer patients.

Related words:
resilience, willpower, power, force, might, potency, toughness, durability, muscle

ENERGY – having vitality and stamina

For some people, feeling healthy and happy implies having **vitality and stamina.**
Likewise, this **Energy** *contributes to feeling and being healthier and happier.*

Aspiring to energy encompasses the quest for vitality, enthusiasm, stamina and the vigour to carry out daily activities or pursue goals. The desire for energy extends beyond mere physical endurance – it is also about enthusiasm. The goal is not just to be able to do more but to engage more fully in life, whether that's through physical tasks, intellectual pursuits or social interactions. Ultimately, the aspiration for energy aims to enhance endurance, active lifestyles, positive moods and overall zeal for life.

Having increased energy levels has a holistic positive impact on health and happiness. A 2012 study in the *Journal of Positive Psychology* found that higher energy levels are associated with greater overall happiness and well-being. Physically, increased energy often leads to more activity, which in turn reduces the risk of chronic diseases like diabetes and heart disease. According to a 2018 study in *JAMA Psychiatry*, even low-intensity exercise can improve mood disorders, further indicating the link between energy and emotional well-being. Nonetheless, energy deficits are a widespread issue; the World Health Organization estimates that about 35% of adults in Europe are insufficiently active, and energy can be sapped by various factors ranging from medical conditions to lifestyle stressors.

Companies from diverse sectors are recognising the importance of helping people build or preserve energy. From home appliances like smart thermostats and ambient lights promoting relaxation, and hotels enhancing sleep quality with circadian lighting and blackout curtains, to vehicle industries integrating ergonomic designs and ambient solutions for reduced stress, each plays its part. Nutrition giants like **Nestlé** and **Unilever** focus on products offering sustained energy, prioritising reduced sugars and enhanced fibre and protein. Financial giants like **Chase** and **Wells Fargo** have introduced wellness programmes, integrating budgeting tools and counselling to alleviate financial strains, thus conserving mental energy. Even companies outside the healthcare realm are helping with energy regulation for diabetic patients. **Starbucks** and **Nestlé** present sugar-free options and nutritious products, respectively, to stabilise sugar levels. Meal services like **Blue Apron** deliver diabetic-friendly meals, while the rising popularity of continuous glucose monitors aids both diabetics and non-diabetics in energy management.

Related words:
zest, vitality, vigour, liveliness, dynamism, stamina, passion, endurance

SELF-DEVELOPMENT – learning and cultivating oneself

*For some people, feeling healthy and happy implies **learning and cultivating oneself.***
*Likewise, this **self-development** contributes to feeling and being healthier and happier.*

Self-development refers to the deliberate and conscious actions an individual takes to improve their knowledge, skills, capabilities and overall character. It involves recognising one's strengths and weaknesses, setting personal and professional goals and devising strategies to achieve them. Rooted in introspection and self-awareness, self-development is a lifelong process that fosters growth, resilience and a greater sense of purpose and fulfilment. It often encompasses a range of activities such as reading, attending seminars, acquiring new skills and seeking mentorship. Through consistent self-development, individuals can expand their horizons, adapt to changes and realise their fullest potential.

In that regard, growth is also a holistic investment in well-being, offering pathways to a healthier and happier life. On a direct level, learning can lead to better job opportunities and income, thus influencing lifestyle choices that affect physical and mental health. Additionally, acquiring skills like sports or dance enhances physical wellness. On top of that, health education can directly empower individuals to make informed choices that lead to preventative healthcare and an improved quality of life. The indirect benefits of learning and cultivating oneself include the adaptability to handle new situations, reducing stress and enhancing emotional well-being. Continued learning also promotes brain plasticity, which is crucial for cognitive health, particularly in combatting age-related cognitive decline.

Several organisations underscore the aspiration to learn. **Duolingo** has revolutionised language learning, tapping into the universal desire for growth and self-improvement. With its repertoire of over 100 language courses, including whimsical ones from shows such as Star Trek, it has amassed 500 million active users while growing at a 43% year-on-year rate (2022). Similarly, companies outside the education sector are weaving learning into their core offerings: **Fitbit** educates about health beyond just tracking, **Noom** delves deep into the psychology of eating, **Prudential Financial** provides education about investments indirectly affecting stress levels of those investing, **Cigna** champions mental well-being and **Seed** ensures its influencers are well-versed in the science of their probiotic products through their Influencer Academy. Furthermore, initiatives like 'Cities Changing Diabetes' by **Novo Nordisk** epitomise how global collaborations are harnessing education to tackle critical health challenges in urban centres. These examples reflect the pervasive influence of learning in various aspects of life, affirming its role as a catalyst for better health and happiness.

Related words:
grow, cultivate, develop, educate, training, mastery, mature, evolve, foster

CREATIVITY – imagining and inventing

*For some people, feeling healthy and happy implies being able to **utilise their brain fully.** Likewise, this **Creativity** contributes to feeling and being healthier and happier.*

Creativity is the ability of the brain to generate something novel or unique, whether that's an idea, a piece of art, a solution to a problem or a new way of approaching a challenge. It doesn't strictly rely on expertise or proficiency but flourishes on imagination, inventiveness and the capability to form unanticipated connections. At its core, creativity involves the brain's capacity to think outside conventional parameters and discover new ways to navigate problems, convey feelings or interact with our surroundings.

The aspiration to be 'creative' extends beyond self-expression; it aids one's health and emotional well-being. Creative activities offer an outlet for emotional exploration, effectively reducing stress and elevating the sense of accomplishment and happiness. Such activities can induce a state of 'flow', a focused immersion that has been shown to improve cognitive functions and overall mental health. Creativity even has physiological impacts – it can lower levels of cortisol, the stress hormone, and boost dopamine, a neurotransmitter linked with pleasure. Moreover, some studies have linked creative pursuits like music and art therapy to decreased inflammation, potentially reducing the impact of chronic illnesses and enhancing the body's immune system. Thus, creativity is increasingly recognised as a form of wellness, even being dubbed 'the new Vitamin C' for its broad-spectrum benefits.

To make creativity accessible to various age groups, especially the elderly, many organisations offer workshops and courses. For example, **AARP** and **Age UK** provide seniors with an array of creative classes, from arts and crafts to music. Healthcare settings are also catching on; the **Cleveland Clinic Arts and Medicine Institute** integrates arts into patient care, focusing on the well-being and cognitive functions of seniors and patients. **Alzheimer Europe** offers resources on art therapy for dementia patients, underscoring the positive impact of creativity on cognitive decline. In a novel approach, **Medtronic** collaborated with European Parkinson's associations to develop a set of cards featuring quotes and life hacks to infuse creativity and positivity into the lives of Parkinson's patients. These efforts underline the growing recognition of creativity not just as a hobby but also as a vital component of a fulfilling, healthy life. This health trend is further evidenced by the nootropics market, which is growing at an annual rate of 8%. These 'smart drugs' are designed to enhance cognitive functions such as memory, creativity, focus and problem-solving.

Related words:
innovation, imagination, originality, inventiveness, ideation, invention, smart

LOOKING GOOD – feeling attractive

*For some people, feeling healthy and happy implies **feeling attractive.***
*Likewise, this **looking good** contributes to feeling and being healthier and happier.*

The aspiration to look good is a desire to present oneself in a manner that is aesthetically pleasing or attractive, both to oneself and to others. It's influenced by culture, personal preferences and societal expectations and encompasses more than just clothing and grooming; it extends to one's physique, posture and even demeanour. While this quest for physical attractiveness can empower self-esteem and goal attainment, when taken to extremes it can also lead to negative outcomes such as obsessive behaviours and health risks.

A medley of psychological, physiological and social factors substantiates this notion that looking good contributes to feeling good and healthy. Psychologically, a positive self-image can boost self-esteem, thereby enhancing mood and emotional well-being. Physiologically, activities like exercise not only improve appearance but also release endorphins, lifting mood and improving health. Socially, feeling attractive can ease social interactions, leading to benefits like reduced stress and anxiety. Feeling good about one's appearance can also have a ripple effect on professional success and interpersonal relationships, both crucial components for long-term happiness.

Various companies across different sectors offer products and services designed to make people feel more attractive in a healthy way. Body positivity campaigns like **Glossier**'s skincare-over-makeup approach emphasise holistic beauty. In sports, brands like **Adidas** also use various models and collaborate with body-positive activists to show that athleticism is for everyone. In the medical realm, **Tommy Adaptive by Tommy Hilfiger** offers adaptive clothing for those with disabilities. Nonprofits like **Look Good Feel Better** offer beauty sessions for cancer patients and **Freedom Wigs** provides natural-looking options for those dealing with medical-related hair loss. For skin conditions, brands like **CeraVe** and **Eucerin** offer specialised skincare products that make patients with skin conditions feel more confident. These brands offer products and foster a culture of wellness, self-care and body positivity, supporting the psychological, physiological and social benefits of looking good.

Related words:

attractive, stylish, chic, elegant, handsome, pretty, dashing, well-groomed, polished, appealing, charming, dapper, radiant, sleek, well-dressed, stunning, fetching, gorgeous, glamorous, sharp, refined

PART 3

TRANSFORMATIONAL HEALTHCARE

CHAPTER 6

PATIENTS WANT TRANSFORMATIONS IN HEALTHCARE

Transformations have an increasingly more significant impact on people and our world at large. We live in a time when people feel that something needs to change within themselves and in the broader world. So, people have become more aspirational than before. They are actively looking to realise their specific aspirations. As we saw in the previous section, these aspirations are based on universal dreams, desires and values. They contribute to feeling better, healthier and happier. Meanwhile, this is a unique opportunity for companies to establish meaningful relationships, create value, and achieve greater engagement with their products and services. It has brought a new form of competition where those who offer the most relevant transformational experience are more valuable and have customer engagement.

In this piece, we will look at the impact of the Transformation Economy on the healthcare sector, which already seems to be very focused on making its 'customers' feel better, healthier, or happier. I start with this sector because transformations seem logical here, although it may not always be the case, as we will see. Three clear segments of the industry are already becoming quite transformational and will, therefore, also drag the rest of the healthcare sector along with it. But the fact is that patients themselves, just like other customers, expect transformations from suppliers in this sector. Let's first look at patient relationships here to see how this manifests itself.

Patients are in need of a health solution for the acute or chronic condition they are dealing with. However, all too often, they don't comply with or adhere to the solution when it's offered. It seems that lack of engagement is the most logical reason behind this. They are not motivated, not literate enough or simply unwilling to do it. Healthcare providers may think: "Well, we've done what we can. Now it's up to them." After all, somebody better educated on the subject – a healthcare professional – clearly told them what to do and why. That should be enough, right? Well, not necessarily.

I've noticed this train of thought, or even belief, dominating the healthcare system. Physicians seem to think that the healthcare system does what it can, but that patients are often not engaged.

Physicians seem to think that the healthcare system does what it can, but that patients are simply not engaged.

I beg to differ. Patients are more engaged in their health than ever before. However, whether they are engaged with *your* solutions to their health problems is entirely up to you. Rather than seeing healthcare through the lens of a system-based approach that primarily focuses on the needs of patients, we should take their expectations and Life Aspirations into consideration. The good news is that getting patients engaged should not be that hard. It requires the same three components: needs, expectations and aspirations.

Patients are enthusiastic about their health

People are more engaged in their health than ever before, as confirmed by plenty of studies on health behaviours. Regardless of the specific focus of the study – from patients managing diseases or their own health to people leading a healthy lifestyle – any study from the past 15 years on behavioural segmentation will tell you that at least half of participants were proactively involved in their health. They are most inclined to adopt the behaviours that I like to call Healthusiasm (see my first book *Healthusiasm*).

It is remarkable how present these behaviours are today. Two millennia ago, we sought to protect our health by making offerings to the gods. But today we live in a health-conscious world, with information, insights and tools allowing us to have an impact on our health. Healthusiasm is the trend that describes people's increasing engagement in managing their health.

Although the healthcare system has long been the centre of the health sphere, it is no longer the case. As I described in my first book, we're experiencing a Copernican Health Revolution that flips this idea on its head. A plethora of different health and self-care solutions are being offered and provided outside the healthcare system. We are seeing the decentralisation of healthcare as I will explain in Chapter 8.3. This is a paradigm shift.

Patients are (not?) consumers

This change in attitudes and behaviour has reinvigorated the discussion on whether or not patients are consumers. For many years, this (b)old question has polarised the healthcare industry. However, in my view this difference of opinion is useless because neither side is right or wrong. Each party is looking at a different part of the equation, but it's the whole – the ensemble of all elements – that's essential.

First, let's establish the differences between patients and consumers:

We are all consumers or patients at one time or another. The difference is that consumers and patients don't find themselves in the same situation. Whichever situation we're in, our needs will be completely different. While this sounds like the best argument to close the debate and claim that patients are not consumers, it isn't. Both patients and consumers have more than just needs. This is best demonstrated by looking at the experience had in these different situations patients and consumers find themselves in.

Patients typically find themselves in uncomfortable or anxiety-inducing situations where they must decide between (or accept someone else's decision on) very few options with limited information available to them. The outcome of the decision is often unclear and there is no 'after-sales service' offered. If things go wrong, or not as hoped, they may have to live with the consequences.

Consumers don't tend to find themselves in this type of situation. They have the freedom to choose from a wide range of options and are excited to do so. Plenty of transparent information is given about the options and their outcome. Afterwards, if they aren't satisfied, they can always return the goods, get their money back or ask for someone's assistance to help them solve the issue.

Expecting good experiences

Although we may find ourselves in different situations with different needs at different times, we remain the same person with the same expectations. The 12 recurring expectations I wrote about in my first book remain valid, regardless of the situation we're in, whether as a consumer or a patient.

These recurring expectations were created by experiences that we have particularly appreciated or valued throughout our lives. Perhaps something was delivered very quickly or fixed very efficiently or made personally for you. The more we have this kind of experience, the more we expect the same speed, convenience and personalisation in other parts of our lives. All of these positive experiences have shaped our expectations. If I can order something online to be delivered within 24 hours, I don't expect to have to wait seven days for a new credit card. That kind of experience is no longer 'expected'.

Patients are not like consumers in that they have different needs. But patients are like consumers because they have the same expectations towards solutions.

Patients *are not* like consumers in that they have different needs. But patients *are* like consumers because they have the same expectations towards solutions. They want the same experience as if they were consumers. Therefore, it's essential for healthcare providers to understand that they must unbundle the needs and expectations. Only then can they design more engaging health solutions that meet both needs and expectations. Only then can they design better experiences. Unfortunately, that's exactly what the healthcare system has been struggling to comprehend.

The 'System-Based' approach

The healthcare system has always been rather paternalistic. The patient is in need and the healthcare professional tells them what product to take or service to use. The healthcare system ensures functional elements like efficacy, safety and tolerability, which it assumes will suffice to help the patient and solve their problem. These solutions have been carefully studied, tested and proven by some of the best scientists and are then recommended by specialists with multiple university degrees and years of study behind them. It's assumed that the patient in need will comply with the solution, whether that means cholesterol medication for a patient at risk of a heart attack, insulin for diabetic patients who need to improve their energy levels or support to quit smoking due to the risk of lung cancer. The patient is in need and the system tells them what to do. Simple, isn't it? However, in my opinion, this paternalistic approach relies too heavily on meeting only medical needs and thus fails to engage with people's expectations behind those needs. This approach fails to provide a great experience.

The fact that health products and services fail to provide an optimal experience is more problematic than we may realise.

The fact that health products and services fail to provide an optimal experience is more problematic than we may realise. If these solutions don't reflect the experiences patients are accustomed to in other areas of their life, they can't easily engage with the solutions, which then fail to meet their goals, leading to reduced engagements with the solution provided by the healthcare professional.

A system that merely dictates the patient's action will fail to engage patients. It's vital to move away from this paternalistic approach and to create better experiences that fit the expectations of patients as whole humans. People are fuelled by Healthusiasm and are at the centre of their health universe. That solution must adapt to the customer – not the other way around.

The 'Client-Based' approach

On the whole, people are no longer happy to just be told what to do. This is something personal trainers started to realise a long time ago, when they shifted from the 'drill sergeant' method to compassionate and empathetic coaching. A client-based approach starts with the client: what's their reality? What are their *expectations*? What do they *aspire to* in their life? This has modified how personal trainers approach their sessions. First, they need to understand the expectations and aspirations of their clients, asking them how they feel and what they desire to achieve that day. Instead of ordering their clients to do hundreds of push-ups, they support them to do as little or as much as fits their aspirations. This approach involves the client and ensures they can keep going for longer, thus making them more likely to achieve their goals – and solve their needs.

Personal trainers shifted from the 'drill sergeant' method to compassionate and empathetic coaching focused on aspirations in life.

This is not the case in healthcare and it's fair to say that the profession has lost touch with its customers to a far greater extent than it would like to admit. The local village physician was once part of the community, they knew their patients personally and were able to take their reality into account. But scientific progress, underfunding and the drive for growth and scaling has pulled healthcare away from the village community and into the walls of ever-expanding hospitals. What used to be a person-based process has turned into a 'one size fits all' system. Processes, workflows and governance now define how we manage health. (In Chapter 14, I explain how some transformational technologies might help bring back the 'local village physician').

Within the healthcare system, digital transformation has mainly served to optimise processes, leaving the patient as almost irrelevant. In the consumer world, on the other hand, digital transformations start with consumer expectations to create better experiences for them. This fundamental difference showcases how healthcare all too often remains a paternalistic approach trying to meet the medical needs of patients, while the world has shifted toward an approach that aims to meet expectations as well.

Patient transformations

The healthcare industry is by definition the place where people want to be(come) healthy and happy. In Chapter 4, I elaborated on how our Life Aspirations are actually the driving force behind being healthy and happy. We all have such aspirations in life, regardless of whether we are dealing with an illness or not. Today, everyone is actively looking for solutions that help them achieve one or more of those essential aspirations in their lives. This means that solutions need to be valued enough by patients for them to engage with them.

ASPIRATIONS ARE UNIVERSAL AND UNIQUE AT ONCE

*A teenager might desire to **Look good (be attractive)**; a working mom with a new promotion and 2 young kids might dream of **Energy (have vitality and stamina)**; a grandmother perhaps just wants to live with **Autonomy (live independently and autonomously)**. An epilepsy patient hopes to show **Kindness (be kind to myself and others)** towards the progression of their disease; a patient with Crohn's disease wants to feel **Safeness (feel safe and protected)** to go out and foster **Relationships (have meaningful connections)**; a marathon runner desires to optimise her **Strength (have power and resilience)**.*

What these examples illustrate is how simple these Life Aspirations can be. It's about human dreams and desires that are very mundane. And that's what our lives are all about, right? But that's also what it's all about when we're sick. People don't want to be sick. People definitely do not want 'the disease' to take away these everyday, simple desires. Therefore, some patients sometimes tend to ignore their illness or ignore recommended prescriptions altogether. Additionally, some diseases come with stigmas people don't like to face. That is precisely why it is essential to include those Life Aspirations in the solution you offer. And then show your patients how you can help them pursue these aspirations. They will value this more than anything. In the Transformation Economy, people will look for solutions that allow them to grow into their best possible version or, in other words, help them with their Life Aspirations.

EVOLVING TOWARDS CUSTOMER TRANSFORMATIONS IN HEALTH

People need to eat. It's a nice service if food is made available to you (in a supermarket, for example). It's a better experience if it is delivered to your door. But it feels great if that food, delivered to your door, can keep you healthy, independent and energetic.

*Energy (**having vitality and stamina**) and **Autonomy (living independently and***
***autonomously**) are aspirations that offer relevant value. That value is more likely to*
help you persevere in eating healthily.

People sometimes need to undergo surgery. It's a welcome service if this surgery is made
available to you (in a hospital, for example). It's a better experience if a company (e.g.
Medbelle) guides you through the process with appropriate answers to any question
you might have. But it feels great when former surgery patients talk to you about every
(human) aspect of the surgery and how they dealt with it (e.g. Patient Partner). This
*offers more value because it meets aspirations like **Calmness (avoiding stress and***
anxiety)**, **Consciousness (being aware and comprehending)** and **Solidarity (feeling
***stronger united**). As a result, patients are more likely to engage better during the entire*
procedure.

Medical Needs, Customer Expectations and Life Aspirations are three building
blocks that guarantee more patient engagement with your health solution. That's
what will make healthcare solutions become Customer Transformations that will
really engage patients and make them healthy and happy.

In the following chapters, we will look at how we are already actively working on
transformations for some parts of our health. We will discuss the specific needs of
women, the urgent need for better mental health and the scientific insights into
metabolic health. We will also indicate how these transformations respond to specific life aspirations in these segments.

These developments will further influence the rest of healthcare in the coming
years to become more transformational. We will then also look at the further consequences of these developments in the longer term. This chapter will put forward
a number of possible future scenarios that will, therefore, not necessarily materialise as such. Nevertheless, they are worth considering because the actual future
truth may lie along these lines.

CHAPTER 7

THREE MAJOR TRANSFORMATIONS IN HEALTHCARE

Transformations, driven by our Aspirations in life, are changing our near and distant world. No sector will be 'spared' from this meaningful social change. And definitely not the healthcare sector because, ultimately, this sector is all about making people better, healthier and happier. Patients, therefore, desire these transformations. We talked about this in Chapter 6: patients want their important aspirations in life to be considered so that the medical solutions become a more transformational experience that goes beyond meeting a medical need. This type of transformation is not often the case today. Healthcare can rarely be called a pleasant experience, nor does it consider patients' dreams and desires. There is undoubtedly work to be done here.

But positive change is gradually emerging on several fronts. First and foremost, it is driven by people who notice that little account is taken of their Life Aspirations. We mainly see this in *specific groups* of people who take matters into their own hands and make changes. Women's health is the leading example for me. But there are certainly others, of course. Actually, we have seen this happen with various diseases, each time driven by active patients or their friends and family. In addition, we also see that Life Aspirations play a significant role when the need is *urgent*. Mental health is the example here we will treat in the second subchapter (7.2). It is one of the most socially impactful health crises. This crisis requires more and different solutions. But especially with mental conditions, this also requires solutions that take into account what is important to people. Here, too, we are seeing more and more transformations. Finally, technological and scientific progress also brings new momentum in some domains. In the third subchapter here (7.3), we will see how innovations, as well as macro trends, have brought about a transformation in metabolic health.

In Chapter 8, we will attempt to foresee these changes in the future. We look at several scenarios that indicate what it could be like. But even if it doesn't have to be exactly like I'll present it here, it might still turn out like this to some extent. But first, let's tackle the three significant transformations already visible in healthcare today.

7.1 Meeting the Life Aspirations of women

Historically, women have often been pushed to the sidelines in a male-dominated society. The roles and contributions of women were, therefore, often undervalued or overshadowed. This systematic marginalisation focused too much on the 'male' story, which is something I also will refer to in Chapter 10.5 on Sexual Wellness. As a result of this male focus, what women considered essential and valuable was ignored, and their unique experiences and insights were not sufficiently considered. It deprived society of various insights. These long-standing prejudices have hindered progress towards a more inclusive societal framework. It also hindered the creation of solutions specifically for women (like female crash-test dummies, for example). This lack of female-oriented solutions was also the case in healthcare.

In fact, women's health has long been a taboo topic, one that no one was able to talk about – not even women. For centuries, the pain experienced by women was often brushed off as a hormone-related issue and women themselves often lacked understanding of their own physical states. This was the finding of the in-depth research into women's health behaviours I conducted several years ago. The study looked at how women deal with their health and hormones throughout their lives. The conclusion, which actually ran to around ten slides of comprehensive text, could be fairly well summarised in just one short sentence: "Women are used to enduring hardship because it's part of being a woman." My recommendation at the time was to help women tackle that sad reality first and foremost.

The female body: a complex system
Our society has long viewed women's bodies as 'weaker' than men's. Women also tend to evaluate their health as poorer than men's. However, perhaps their bodies are just fundamentally different. After all, women menstruate, give birth and lactate. These and other changes to and inside the body can have a severe impact on a woman's life. Take the menopause, for example. Women going through the menopause may experience any of over 30 different symptoms, ranging from fatigue, mood changes and disrupted sleep to a decreased libido and hot flushes. The onset of menopause may also increase the risk of developing other health conditions, such as osteoporosis, heart disease and Alzheimer's disease. Although all of these

effects can dramatically affect a woman's quality of life, healthcare providers are often unable to answer their questions and concerns. In fact, research conducted by the start-up Gennev in 2019 reported that 94% of women don't get enough support to manage the symptoms and effects of menopause.

Earlier in this book, in the context of social transformations of Chapter 2.2, we touched on patient groups – **Solidarity** *(feel stronger united)* – that support people dealing with a certain disease or illness. Rather than relying on the opinion of just one medical professional, people are searching for communities where they can share experiences, pain management tips and solutions. Nowhere is this more evident than in women's health. There are groups for women dealing with certain conditions like endometriosis and PCOS (polycystic ovarian syndrome), for those going through certain periods of their lives like the menopause or simply for dealing with the menstrual cycle. Women are taking control of their own health and looking beyond the traditional, disease-focused healthcare system for answers.

The non-female-friendly environment

Although in recent years value-oriented care has increased the focus on the patient to a certain extent, healthcare has long been (and arguably still is) male-dominated. As such, it has contributed little to finding the right solutions for women. It's small wonder that 1 in 3 women don't trust the health industry, according to a 26-market study by Edelman.

A similar conclusion can be drawn regarding the investment in digital health solutions for women. Unbelievably, since 2011, only 3% of digital health deals in the USA have focused specifically on women's health. As late as 2019, FemTech received no more than 3.3% of total investments in digital health (RockHealth, 2020). Digital tools specific to women have been a niche category that has received only limited attention or interest. Nevertheless, things are slowly changing in ways that will impact the entire healthcare industry – and indeed, society itself – far beyond women's health.

Things are transforming now

New initiatives, often driven by female entrepreneurs, are now successfully being launched and scaled. They provide experiences that meet women's expectations better than ever before, by considering what's essential in women's lives to offer even more value. Furthermore, these solutions don't have a singular focus. They expand into related issues and 'treat' women as we would all love to be treated – as a whole person. In fact, it's true to say that women's health is turning into the epitome of healthcare, in a current that will ultimately lead to the end of healthcare as we know it.

TREATING THE WHOLE WOMAN

The **Maven Clinic**, based in New York, is a women's clinic that, on the surface, seems to offer traditional medical services for pregnant women and new mothers. However, they actually offer these services in a truly convenient way, allowing women to book video appointments and exchange private messages with a broad network of family and women's health practitioners. This telehealth solution may sound fairly obvious now, in the post-COVID era, but Maven have been doing this since 2014. They also offer services that don't form part of the traditional healthcare system at all, such as back-to-work and sleep coaching and appointments with relationship consultants and mental health therapists, in addition to specialists from 25 other sectors of medicine and wellness. To expand their services beyond the US, Maven Clinic picked up digital health start-up **Naytal** in 2023 to boost growth in the UK. Naytal also provides on-demand access to a network of healthcare providers, who are experts in more than 25 specialties in female health.

There are now many start-ups providing experiences that improve overall engagement with health, often in ways that were previously unheard of (especially in a medical setting). This means customers/patients will rightfully start expecting these kinds of experiences in every other healthcare setting too. FemTech is setting the tone, but it doesn't stop there.

Considering what's important in life

Outside the healthcare industry, it's becoming increasingly difficult for companies to differentiate themselves from their competitors with pleasant experiences. In order to create value for their customers today, those companies and brands consider what is vital to them in their lives: Their Life Aspirations. To do this, businesses need to create an experience that makes customers feel better, healthier and even happier. In a world focused on transformations, that is what people aspire to. FemTech, and companies focused on women's health in general, are showing us that this can be done in healthcare too.

Supporting your customers in achieving their aspirations requires looking beyond the mere touchpoints.

Supporting your customers' desires to achieve their aspirations requires looking beyond the mere touchpoints they have with your product, service or company. It demands understanding what is essential to your customers' lives. Helping someone develop themselves and become a better person can be a hard nut to crack for non-healthcare companies, but some manage it very well. For example, in 2021 Nike launched the (Cycle)Sync workout collection on their Training Club app – a collection designed to make women feel at their best in every phase of their menstrual cycle, and including workouts, nutritional advice and expert tips adapted to each phase. In Chapter 10.3 on the aspirational value of sports, we explore some more women-oriented transformations in sports.

Supporting aspirations

Supporting these Life Aspirations should be an easy fit for healthcare providers, but, again, this aspect is often overlooked. The overarching assumption is too often that people just want to 'have something bad removed'. However, aspirations are about the simple things in life you can desire or dream about – things that generally make you feel better or sometimes even healthier and happier. People want to live life to the fullest. That doesn't only mean going from sick to healthy, but about being as healthy as possible *whether you're sick or not*. This is the Healthusiasm I've extensively described in the first book. And FemTech has understood this very well.

SIMPLIFYING ACCESS TO ASPIRATIONAL SOLUTIONS

American women's health clinic **Tia** *digs deep into all things science, health and culture. They allow women to access assistance with their personal health, anytime and anywhere, through a monthly subscription. Moreover, Tia is building a new on-demand model of care for women that treats women as a whole, with an integrated Care Team including OB/GYNs, nurse practitioners, acupuncturists and various therapists. Their female-focused approach brings a new standard for women, making them feel* **Belonging (feeling accepted and included)**.

Kindbody *supports women in every step of their family-building journey by providing a transformational experience in tech-enabled clinics that are designed to feel like a soft coffee bar. Their approach brings science and compassion together to completely rewrite reproductive healthcare. Kindbody is focused on* **Kindness (being kind to myself and others)** *for women who are insecure about the future of their family.*

And it doesn't stop there. Just like Hello Fresh transformed the food industry by delivering healthy nutrition, **Nurx** *brings birth control and health tests, sexual and mental health solutions, skin and hair care products to your doorstep. They explicitly state that they're on a mission to transform healthcare as their team of experienced doctors, nurse practitioners, physician assistants, nurses and pharmacists meet the Life Aspirations of* **Calmness (avoiding stress and anxiety)** *and* **Consciousness (being aware and comprehending)**.

LOLA *has taken it a step further, turning home delivery into recurring deliveries. The company also works to normalise and destigmatise conversations about menstrual health, sex and sexual health, for example by providing young women experiencing their period for the first time with a starter kit that includes a digital guide and plenty of expert and accessible tips. They transform girls into young women by shaping positive rituals for the rest of their lives, trying to make them feel better, healthier and happier during this time of change. Their effort to shape positive 'rituals' from the first period shows* **Caring (being careful with myself and others)** *and helps with* **Autonomy (living independently and autonomously)**.

LOLA First Period Ritual Kit with free digital Guide

Aren't these aspirations to be as healthy as possible throughout life something every human being longs for? If you can include these aspirations into what you offer your clients, you're more certain to create engagement with your customer. That's precisely what these FemTech companies are achieving and there's no turning back now. Women will expect this level of transformation from every healthcare provider. And other areas will quickly learn that healthcare needn't just be something that answers a medical need only.

Providing a holistic approach

I'm not a big fan of the word 'holistic' because it's become such a buzzword. However, there's no better way to describe the key strategy that women's health is using to transform healthcare. These new providers recognise that women aren't fixated on just one single disease or condition. Instead, they seek support with managing their overall health.

"What does optimal health mean to you?"

"What does optimal health mean to you?" Women's health clinic Tia uses this question to unpack the unique goals that patients have for their care journey. It allows Tia to support women on their path, which will almost certainly go beyond one condition. They don't just want to treat a patient's disease, they want to set women up for better success. They're interested in the broader narrative. Their holistic view of health defines the personal experience, including Life Aspirations, and promotes overall health with a care plan that contains daily, weekly and monthly activities to optimise the patient's health. Like a personal trainer, the Tia care team also meets frequently with the patient to assess their progress and ongoing needs.

EVERY SITUATION HAS RELATABLE ASPIRATIONS

Menopause company **Gennev** *also offers a broad range of services specialising in gynaecology, primary care and lifestyle, while delivering natural wellness products and supplements that benefit the customer's overall health and lifestyle when dealing with menopause. It's about* **Strength (having power and resilience)** *as well as still living life full of* **Joy (having amazing experiences)**, *something that can be applied to different parts of the healthcare industry.*

And a trendy American telehealth company called **Hers** *has taken it a step further and offers convenient, more affordable access to prescription products and medical advice. They put the focus on healthcare that feels like self-care by combining medical care with health, well-being and lifestyle solutions, and aspire to make women feel healthy and confident in their own skin, with flaws and all, on their terms. This helps women with* **Self-Worth (feeling good about myself)**.

CASE IN POINT

For the past 170 years, our healthcare system has focused on solving and eradicating specific diseases, which is ultimately a highly fragmented approach. This leads to poor patient experiences, clinical errors and rising costs. This clinical, science-driven approach is the exact opposite of how we want to feel as human beings. We don't feel fragmented: we are a single, whole person. The holistic approach to 'treatment' offered to women by FemTech and women's health companies is a real game changer for the whole healthcare industry, and one that simply can't be ignored. They are leading the way. Others will follow suit.

Helping people live their best lives

The FemTech industry's approach should inspire you whether you are a healthcare provider treating patients, a project manager working on patient services for a pharma company or a marketer integrating health into consumer strategies. These examples show how a target group whose needs have been underserved for a very long time is now claiming its rightful place in healthcare settings and beyond. Female entrepreneurs have created businesses based on what it feels like to be a woman. They didn't approach the issue from a scientific, literary or disease-specific perspective only, but started with the human being and what optimal health looks like for that individual.

Start with the human being and what optimal health looks like for that individual.

Of course, that optimal health probably includes some medical needs to be treated, but businesses shouldn't limit themselves to focusing on that specific medical need. They must also consider the personal expectations and Life Aspirations of their customers. By being more holistic, they can support people in becoming engaged in their overall health and the lives they want to live, because the way we live our lives is the way we build our health. That's how FemTech companies are successfully serving women today – and how the healthcare system will inevitably change in the years to come.

It's not just FemTech changing the way in which people live and interact with their own health. In recent years there has also been a notable transformation in how we deal with different aspects of our health. One of the key areas to gain ground in recent years is fundamental to everything we do: our mental health.

7.2 Mental health is ele-mental to our health

The medical needs of women may often not be completely different from those of men. But being a woman is different. One may have different expectations, or one may have specific dreams and desires in certain situations. Women's health companies have been developed to meet this demand. They respond to what makes being a woman different. I expect that many other domains within healthcare will want to move in the same transformational direction by also taking into account what is essential in life for their target group.

But transformations can also arise from an urgent need for other solutions. A massive acceleration can suddenly occur when there are inadequate solutions for the (too) many problems. People then long for solutions that bring about change: transformations.

In this chapter, we will talk about the mental health crisis that is sweeping the world. For a health condition that perhaps more than other diseases revolves around feeling good, Life Aspirations are even more critical. This situation, therefore, requires transformational solutions. And that is also what is happening. In the following paragraphs, I will take you through the recent developments in this sector to introduce you to various transformations within mental care.

The history of mental health

Mental health is complex. It includes our emotional, psychological and social well-being. It ebbs and flows along a spectrum that ranges from thriving to coping, from struggling to treating mental illness. Over time, perceptions and approaches have changed a lot. Before the 18th century, mental disorders were attributed to demonic possession or divine punishment. Those affected were tortured or sent to insane asylums. Fortunately, things have evolved considerably since then.

Many people start prioritising well-being over welfare.

In recent years, there has been another very noticeable shift in public attitude as many people prioritise their overall well-being over welfare. Life has become less about amassing wealth than it is about maintaining health. People who step out of the rat race to pick up 'easier' and less well-paid jobs are no longer an exception. Millennials were the first generation to accept that they will earn less than their parents but it's spreading across other generations as well. That's a radical shift from what happened in the previous century. This is in part down to how much attention mental health is getting today. The combination of recent challenges like the COVID-19 pandemic, climate change, ongoing wars and economic recession have likely led to the worst mental health crises we are aware of. On top of that, it's clear that our current healthcare systems aren't fully equipped to handle this issue, with many seeing them as inadequate or even deeply flawed. The financial pressure of ageing populations on healthcare expenditure in society won't offer a lot of flexibility to solve this in the short run either. In a way, things are looking grim. But as with our own mental health, it serves to look at the positive transformations that are happening. Surely the future is brighter than we think.

The status of our detri-mental health

In 2022, the World Health Organization reported that the "global prevalence of anxiety and depression" increased by 25% in the first year of the COVID-19 pandemic. In fact, WHO expects depression to be the single largest healthcare burden by 2030, with a global cost of $6 trillion. (By comparison, this unimaginable amount equates to the total amount spent on healthcare worldwide in 2012.)

Over the course of the pandemic, the focus on mental health issues and the importance of caring for our mental health increased. Obviously, problems ranged much further than the loneliness and negative outlook that characterised that period. Technology has also played a massive part in our mental harm for many years.

CASE IN POINT

THE MULTI-CRISIS

Terms like glow faces, doomscrolling, smombies or pleasure trap apps describe the mental health impact of technology-related behaviours rather well. Meanwhile, filters and staged lifestyles create ideals that cause Snapchat dysmorphia, Adonis complex and wellness syndromes. The rise of online social behaviours like toxic positivity, echo chambers, gaslighting and love bombing should also take their part of the blame. We feel the polarisation as we are bombarded with fear-based campaigns, 'facts' about health research, the great resignation and predictions about a life-altering recession. Moreover, climate change, zombie viruses, plastic beaches and the prospect of soon-to-be-extinct animals create eco-anxiety.

One could say that we are on the verge of a full-blown existential multi-crisis while entire demographics are massively opting out of organised religion. Our minds are full, our bodies are burned out and we have stopped believing. It's omnipresent in (virtual and real) life and detrimental to our mental health.

A poll by the *American Psychiatric Association* showed that one-quarter of Americans made a New Year's resolution to improve their mental health in 2022. It's fair to expect similar numbers in Europe and Asia, because this is part of a wider social shift in which people are becoming more aspirational than ever. But this time around, being the best possible version of yourself comes with healthy moderation (see Chapter 4 and 5). It's no longer just about improving but also about preventing, accepting and enjoying. Nevertheless, this aspirational lifestyle may well be the main reason for this increased focus on mental health.

But while our aspirations may have become more moderate than ever, they can take a toll on our mental health. Because every aspiration – no matter how moderate it is – forces us to face a reality about ourselves. It might shine a light on the state of our own mental health. We aspire to be kind to ourselves because maybe we are too demanding; we aspire to look good perhaps to compensate for how we really feel; we aspire to feel safe because we are often insecure; we aspire to meaningful connections because we feel lonely. Every aspiration might come with or stem from a mental health issue. They are closely linked. As a result, we are looking for ways to deal with our mental health, similar to how we are looking to meet our (moderate) aspirations today. That's why I believe that the increased focus on mental health also finds its origins in being more aspirational.

People act like lab rats going from one great solution to another to experiment and discover what works best for them.

Therefore, we notice that people are ready to try different possible solutions from traditional medicine to technology companies, from wellness techniques to psychedelics. They are looking for solutions that affect different parts of their lives in different ways. People act like lab rats going from one great solution to another to experiment and discover what works best for them. This behaviour is often driven by the sad truth that professional help within the existing system is not easily or sufficiently available to them.

The dangers of experi-mental health

As more attention is given to this field, I expect to see new mental health treatment tools and strategies emerge. Global venture capital firm White Star Capital even dubbed this moment the "golden age of mental health tech", with funding for mental health start-ups topping 1.6 billion dollars in 2020. But the global 'mental health economy' encompasses more than these tech start-ups. It entails anything from alternative medicine to age-old therapies, from mood-altering real estate to mood-boosting foods. From a business perspective, mental health has enormous potential. For example, a survey by American Express (2021) reported that 68% of travellers worldwide will organise their next trip with a view to improve their mental health. Hence, it is no surprise that the Global Wellness Institute estimates the global mental wellness economy to be worth no less than $121 billion. Demand is higher than ever and the range of solutions continues to grow exponentially. Telehealth, consumer brands and workplace programmes are driving this evolution.

THE MENTAL HEALTH ECONOMY

CASE IN POINT

Late 2021 was marked by the remarkable merger of two mental health giants, **Headspace** *and* **Ginger**. *Headspace is a global leader in mindfulness and meditation, and Ginger is a leader in on-demand mental healthcare, including video-based therapy and psychiatric support. Together they now provide the world's largest, most accessible and comprehensive digital mental health and well-being platform. Meanwhile, other platforms are meeting this growing need for remote mental health support as well:* **7 Cups** *connects people in need to 320,000 trained listeners via anonymous text or voice chats;* **Coa** *wants to make mental health as common, accessible and fun as physical fitness. It offers remote therapist-led classes to make participants emotionally 'fitter'.*

Asics, *a Japanese sports brand known for its slogan 'Anima Sana In Corpore Sano' (healthy mind in a healthy body), launched a new project in 2021 to promote mental well-being. The initiative used Asics' face-scanning Mind Uplifter Tool to boost the workout efforts of small English communities. This focus on promoting the physical and mental benefits of exercise builds on Asics' existing campaign that encourages people not to exercise in an effort to look their best but to do it because it makes them happy. On World Mental Health Day 2022, Asics released an advertisement with almost identical images of models before and after their workouts. This departure from the typical 'before-and-after' photos used as celebratory images strengthens their vision: working out to achieve physical and mental* **Strength *(have power and resilience)***.

Consumer brand **KitKat** encourages people to not just 'Have a Break' but to take their break one step further. In a partnership with Australian suicide prevention charity R U OK, they want people to really check in with each other. KitKat has a worldwide focus on helping people with their mental health. In the Netherlands, they've introduced 'No Wi-Fi' zones that block all wireless signals within a radius of 5 metres so that people are encouraged to chat with each other while taking a break. In Colombia, the chocolate bar company instantly replied to Twitter posts that contained the word 'stressed'. The reply showed the location of the nearest KitKat billboard with tiny, vibrating motors that massage people while they're leaning against it (also encouraging them to meet other people). While many of these consumer examples are only brand activation campaigns, it shows how every brand – regardless of whether it is a 'healthy' brand or not – can help destigmatise mental health.

Finally, mental health became more visible in the workplace during the pandemic, as workers were forced to cope with endless days on Zoom and work from home. The result? Zoom fatigue and inbox infinity! This has caused many companies to adjust their policies to support mental health needs and prevent employee burnout and turnover. Numerous efforts have been made to support mental health, albeit rarely with any consistency or strategy. But it's a start. Some employers offer 'mental health days', Zoom-free days, counselling services or other resources designed to promote good mental health practices among employees. **Microsoft Teams** introduced 'virtual commutes' to create the boundaries and structure that physical commutes once provided. Scheduling a 'commute' for the beginning of a workday meant setting aside time to prepare for work, whether going for a walk or planning tasks with a cup of coffee. End-of-the-day commutes could be customised with prompts to reflect emotionally, celebrate accomplishments, add jobs to a to-do list for later and meditate with Headspace (yes, them again) to fully disconnect. Microsoft Teams also brought insights for managers and leaders into Teams. The aggregated view helped them identify whether teams and employees could be at risk of burnout from, for example, working long hours. Other initiatives, like the start-up **Misü**, can track your mood online. The workplace will (have to) be an essential driver for the future of mental health.

But there are dangers as a result of this surge in solutions. In an open letter to the *American Psychological Association* (APA), therapists expressed concern about unethical business practices, questionable marketing claims and low-quality services. Meanwhile, therapists on different tech platforms complained about aggressive patients and poorly paid compensation. On the other side of the spectrum, many patients also have negative experiences. They have reported receiving impersonal responses or being 'ghosted' by therapists altogether. More recently, I'm sure we've all read the case of an AI companion that seemed to suggest one person should take his life. These solutions designed to cater to our mental health are clearly not without their dangers.

Meanwhile, more people are choosing to share their stories about mental health on social media. This includes notable figures like Olympic athletes, celebrities and others who have started to open up about their struggles. They are using these platforms to talk openly about topics such as trauma, depression, anxiety, bipolar disorder, suicidal ideation and addiction. In many ways, this is a good thing. The more normalised it becomes to discuss mental health, the easier it will be for people to understand and identify mental health needs. This **Consciousness (being aware and comprehending)** can then help them seek the necessary **Healing (recover and restore)** when required.

But if everyone claims to have mental health issues too easily, finding the ones in (real) need becomes more challenging.

But while this evolution has helped break down the social stigma surrounding it, it does come with certain risks. First, many influencers and advocates speaking and advising on mental health have no (medical) background to inform others about more than just their own experience (which often happens nonetheless). Secondly, social media algorithms only prioritise 'popular' or more common mental health issues like anxiety or depression, causing many other problems to be ignored. Finally, there is also a risk that too many people will self-diagnose a mental illness because of this 'popularity'. However, there's a difference between a depressive period and depression, being anxious and having anxiety. Mental health conditions are hardly ever a binary state of being. But if *everyone* claims to have mental health issues *too easily*, finding the ones in (real) need becomes more challenging. This evolution, conversely, may even cause a new form of stigma around feeling okay or truly bad.

The funda-mental approach to mental health

The mental health crisis is worse than ever, the systems in place to address it are profoundly broken and the new solutions on offer are often still experimental. But as mental health is coming to the forefront of our lives, many are rightfully hopeful. A survey by Blackbox (2022) echoed this sentiment, with nearly 3 in 5 (58%) feeling optimistic about the growing discussions around mental health and well-being. And while solutions that tackle mental health issues are still growing out of their infancy, we must also acknowledge that they are already increasing accessibility and affordability. Additionally, these solutions help to develop ecosystems that can serve as health communities and contribute to a much-needed holistic approach to mental health.

The destigmatisation of mental health creates psychological **Safeness *(feel safe and protected)*** to bring up the topic in family conversations, neighbourhoods, schools, sports clubs and sometimes even at work. What better place to talk about mental health than where you feel best or find yourself most often? These communities or groups of people become safe environments where people dare to open up. Moreover, they are slowly starting to function as their own ecosystems, offering a growing set of solutions for people. They are laying the groundwork for the future of mental health. Customers/patients will rightfully start to expect these kinds of experiences in other healthcare settings as well.

MENTAL HEALTH COMMUNITIES

*In 2018, **Lidl** Ireland launched 'The Bakery' as a place where people could gather and discuss mental health topics while indulging in delicious baked goods. The space was created to provide events focused on increasing **Consciousness (being aware and comprehending)** around mental illness awareness. More recently, **Marks & Spencer** launched 'Frazzled Cafes' with a similar mission centred on mental health, community and supporting well-being. In 2022, **Gymshark** introduced a Pop-Up barbershop called **Deload** to allow men to comfortably open up to barbers with some education in mental health care. All barbers were trained in mental health, courtesy of **Calm**. The popular meditation app now also provides workshops to strengthen and normalise mental health conversations within communities.*

CASE IN POINT

In 2021, **Pinterest** *launched an initiative called 'Havens: Invest in Rest',* **a physical** *location in Chicago. The facility features pins of relaxing imagery, immersive art and community programming to help combat burnout and encourage viewers to come together, feel* **Belonging (feel accepted and included)** *and focus on* **Healing (recover and restore)***. Pinside Out – the platform's internal mental health community – curated the online collection of calming images, prompts for journalling and bedtime affirmations. In New York City, the* **Rubin Museum** *opened The Mandala Lab. It's a cultural healing space designed to encourage emotional wellness and inspire* **Relationships (have meaningful connections)** *within its own community.*

Another consequence of the current experimental evolution is the need for a more holistic approach. Mental health isn't just about your mind. Mental health is more than your relationships and the world around you. In fact, mental health is closely related to one's physical health as well. A holistic approach recognises how closely intertwined mental and physical health are. It will evolve into a better understanding of what primary mental care should be about (social, physical and mental). It will turn the focus away from linear diagnoses involving pills and procedures toward a greater emphasis on better overall health.

Mental health isn't just about your mind or your relationships and the world around you. Mental health is closely related to one's physical health as well.

This significant shift will profoundly impact how we care for our (mental) health. The person – not their diagnosis, symptoms or behaviours – will be at the centre of health management. And the way we manage our health will become a combination of Western medicine, advanced technologies and some of the world's greatest healing traditions (like meditation and acupuncture) to envelop our physical and social health. As such, previous experimental efforts will be combined and built upon to form a fundamental approach towards mental health that will include communities and physical health. But it won't stop here either. This new way of approaching mental health will be complemented by new scientific and technological instruments.

New instru-mental innovations

Innovations in the assessment and treatment of mental health problems are being shaped by progress in neuroscience, genetics, artificial intelligence and advanced technologies. The holistic approach will expand incrementally in the coming years. But three instrumental changes will surely transform the future of mental health in the coming years: biomarkers and genomics, nutritional psychiatry and the metaverse.

Blood tests for mental illnesses are one such advancement. They are still in the early stages of development but they have promise to become instrumental in diagnosing mental health conditions. Mental illnesses are complex and have biological, psychological and sociocultural etiologies. But this method could complement traditional diagnostic tools, which are often still trial and error today. Blood tests done after a diagnosis to find the root causes of mental illnesses like depression could in the future be done upfront. Because yes, research continues to show how the brain and the body are inextricably connected. These studies are often not 'large' enough to draw firm conclusions. However, the widespread availability of genetic data could help.

Genetic data will allow us to investigate the correlation between many small DNA sequence changes ('variants') and mental illness. These variants can then be *correlated* with blood biomarkers measured in routine blood tests, such as cholesterol, vitamins, enzymes and indicators of inflammation. (Correlation does not yet mean causality, but it's a start.) Genomics promises to be instrumental in mental health. It's been 20 years since the first human genome was sequenced but only 10 years since the birth of psychiatric genomics. This field of expertise aims to find genes that reveal the biology behind mental health disorders.

PSYCHIATRIC GENOMICS

Mental health genomic testing company **Genomind** *has already marketed a pharmacogenomic test called Genecept Assay. Since 2016, the test has aimed at guiding treatments for depression and Alzheimer's based on genetic profiling. The company even believes that science can now assess a person's predisposition to mental health.*

CASE IN POINT

> *The company launched its Mental Health Map ($599), which empowers people with* **Consciousness *(being aware and comprehending)*** *about how their genetic profile might influence behaviour, mood and stress response. This information lets people take action to optimise their mental well-being.*

Predicting a mental health disorder from a person's genome may not be fully scientifically proven yet, but the recent advances in Generative Artificial Intelligence will be instrumental in the near future. In fact, it's expected that the data from epigenetics and epigenomics will be unlocked far quicker with these smart algorithms and consequently mark a massive transformation in the diagnosis, treatment and management of (mental) health.

Artificial Intelligence will be crucial in another relatively new field called nutritional psychiatry as well. This discipline studies the role of nutrition in mental health care: what fuel does your brain need to take 24/7 care of your senses, your thoughts and movements, breathing and heartbeat? Researchers in this field of study explore the connections between gut bacteria and the brain. For example, studies have shown that patients with depression have lower levels of specific gut bacteria and that the abundance of several other gut bacteria may correlate with the severity of schizophrenia symptoms. There is still limited research in this area. Still, the SMILES trial (2017) examined the role of diet in treating moderate to severe depression and saw diets causing significant improvements in depression symptoms, including 32% achieving remission. Because of the relationship between the gut and brain, a person's food will affect their mood, cognition and mental health. Paying attention to how and when eating different foods has an impact will be instrumental in the future of mental health.

Finally, the metaverse will one day become instrumental in our lives, and mental health may be one of the best use cases in due course. The **mental-verse** has the potential to provide easy access to personalised experiences by removing barriers and creating impactful *virtu-real* **Relationships *(have meaningful connections)***. I will elaborate on mental-verse in Chapter 13.2.

Ele-mental to society and your business

In the next five years, we'll see the rise of innovations like biomarkers and genomics, nutritional psychiatry and the metaverse that will become instrumental in diagnosing, treating and managing mental health. Meanwhile current experiments will become more professional, health communities will further grow into safe havens and the physical side of mental health will be increasingly included. This will pave the way for one of the most transformational evolutions in mental health: it will become an elemental aspect of our overall health and of every business.

Mental health will become a more ele-mental part of our health management.

We live in a world that is arguably going through an existential crisis. Recession, endless wars, health scares, climate change and polarisation are detrimental to our mental health. Amid this harsh reality, we aspire to change things, starting with ourselves. We are looking for health solutions that help us face the challenges in different parts of our lives. Today, many of these solutions may still be in an experimental phase, looking for ways to mature as part of a broader context. But soon, we will see how these solutions can be combined as part of broader ecosystems based on a more holistic view of mental health and supported within health communities. This is the fundamental change in mental healthcare that we can expect in the short term. In the longer term, we will see how genomics, nutritional psychiatry and the metaverse will also become instrumental to our mental health. Meanwhile, I don't foresee less focus on mental health any time soon. Quite the opposite, in fact. There is an increasing and widely accepted belief that mental health is inextricably tied to broader health outcomes. As we start to build scientific proof on this, mental health will become an even more ele-mental part of our health management.

THE LINK BETWEEN MENTAL HEALTH AND OVERALL HEALTH

Poor psychological health can disrupt your ability to think clearly and make healthy decisions. But neglecting your mental health could also lead to serious health problems such as obesity, gastrointestinal issues and a weakened immune system. According to the US **Centers for Disease Control** *(CDC), depression and anxiety are associated with an increased risk of coronary heart disease and increased blood pressure. Depression is also considered to be one of the leading causes of disability, and people with severe mental health conditions die prematurely.*

Most studies on psychological health are observational and based on self-reporting from patients. This presents challenges to prove a cause-and-effect relationship. However, the large number of such studies makes it highly indicative and allows reasonable conclusions to be drawn about an association between negative psychological health and overall health risk. But the economic cost on society from, for example, obesity and cardiovascular diseases, is so high that these studies should be enough to prioritise the impact of mental health on our overall health. After all, cardiometabolic disease and obesity risk damaging our society severely in the future. Therefore, one of the most critical public health challenges is making 'mental health as elemental to our health'. In this way, mental health will soon claim an even more important place in everyone's health management.

Mental health touches every aspect of our lives, and not a single business can ignore this evolution, whether operating in a consumer or healthcare business.

Mental health touches every aspect of our lives, and not a single business can ignore this evolution, whether operating in a consumer or healthcare business. As a leader, it's your responsibility to reflect upon the role you can play in this changing world. You can be experimental, fundamental, instrumental or elemental in the mental health support of your customers and patients. The least you can do is to avoid being detrimental, of course. However, too many aspects of business today still negatively impact one's mental health. There's still a lot to be done there. Every business has a role to play in building transformations for a healthier and happier world. Look at how a study by American Express (Amex Trendex, Sept 2021) disclosed that 76% of respondents would choose better mental health over a new car. Better mental health is a more urgent need than new products. That's why it might be worthwhile for every business to reflect on your role in this. Because yes, in today's reality, it's elemental to make customers healthy and happy because that is what matters most to us.

LESS OBVIOUS MENTAL HEALTH SOLUTIONS

Smartphones have screentime-management and notification-less features to help people with **Nothingness (do, feel, see or hear nothing)**, *an aspiration that is also confirmed with the popularity of silent trains or slow travel in general. In that regard,* **KLM Airlines** *is suggesting a train route as a more sustainable alternative to the requested flight, feeding into the desire for* **Meaning (live life with a meaningful purpose)**. **Pinterest** *banned all weight loss product advertisements to prioritise mental health over ad revenue, supporting their users with* **Kindness (be kind to myself and others)** *and* **Self-worth (feel good about myself)**. **Herbalife market** *products focus on mood regulation, stress relief, and cognitive function to contribute to its customers* **Calmness (avoid stress and anxiety)** *and* **Strength (have power and resilience)**.

7.3 Aspirations turn metabolic health into meta care

Sometimes, we see changes happening without really realising it. This may also be the case with metabolic health. Many elements mentioned in this chapter will not seem utterly unknown to you. Only when you look at them together and from a little distance do you notice a change. In this case, it is also about a change to a more holistic approach that does not just look at the medical need but takes the entire person into account. It is not just about curing a disease but about making people healthier and happier through many solutions that help achieve universal Life Aspirations.

Metabolic health is about making sure that our metabolism is healthy. In technical terms, it can be described as having ideal levels (preferably without the help of medication) of blood sugar, triglycerides, high-density lipoprotein (HDL) cholesterol, blood pressure and waist circumference, to name just a few. In other words, excellent metabolic health means that a person is at low risk of developing metabolic conditions like weight gain, diabetes, hypertension, heart disease and stroke.

However, there is increasing evidence in scientific studies that the actual impact of our metabolic health is far more significant than previously thought. Metabolic health is about meta health. This is because metabolic dysfunction is increasingly linked to a chronic state of inflammation that might induce multiple inflammatory diseases, such as Alzheimer's disease and other cognitive loss, weakened immunity, cancer, pneumonia, kidney disease and hormonal diseases. One could thus easily argue that good metabolic health is actually the same as good overall health. That's also why I believe metabolic health has definitively shifted away from the notion of dieting. Today, it's seen as a means to manage your overall health. In my keynotes, I dub this trend 'Metabolic Mastery' and it is yet another example of how healthcare is becoming transformational.

Metabolic pandemic

Metabolic health has gained unprecedented attention recently, underscored by a surge in clinical studies, indicating that its impact extends well beyond cardiological conditions. This heightened awareness is driven not only by scientific discoveries but also by broader public interest, catalysed by two significant factors: the COVID-19 pandemic and a collective focus on immunity.

The world needs a global metabolic reset.

The term 'pandemic' became a household word in March 2020 due to the COVID-19 pandemic but also ignited debates about the importance of another pandemic: metabolic dysfunction. Studies cite that 88% of Americans are metabolically unhealthy. Though European figures are not as dire/bad, it is on a similar trajectory. This realisation has sparked discussions about whether the metabolic pandemic should be seen as a top priority; it arguably contributes to more deaths than the COVID-19 virus. The COVID pandemic also heightened the interest in metabolic health in public discourse, as people scrambled to bolster their immunity against COVID-19. After all, individuals with compromised metabolic health were at increased risk. Google trends reflect this surge in interest and scientific research has confirmed the intricate connection between metabolic health and immunity to the virus. This link is so profound that even the World Economic Forum has called for a global metabolic reset, noting that 3 out of the 4 leading risk factors for COVID-19 mortality were metabolic health-related. This sparked a wave of innovations that focused on metabolic health.

Continuous glucose monitoring

Metabolic dysfunction occurs due to abnormal blood sugar, lipids or inflammation. There are around 10 different biomarkers that could be tracked and optimised to deal with one's metabolic function but measuring blood sugar levels has recently become a vital indicator of metabolic health.

The launch of continuous glucose monitoring devices (CGM) in 2017 – like Abbott's Freestyle Libre and Libre Sense – opened a new realm of opportunity. These devices contain sensors that can track glucose levels non-invasively, thus changing the health experience for diabetic patients. But they were also attractive to athletes and top sports professionals who could improve their performance by mastering their metabolic health. Many start-ups – including Levels, Supersapiens, Veri, Vital, NutriSense, Signos and January AI – came to market targeting that segment in particular. Although none of these start-ups owned the CGM hardware themselves, they leveraged the devices that were made available by Dexcom and Abbott. With Apple, Amazon, Google and Fitbit expressing an interest in blood glucose monitoring as well, this market is bound to grow exponentially in the next few years.

Continuous Glucose Monitoring device

Initially designed as a medical device for patients, these devices have clearly become a tool for athletes to enhance their performance as well. However, these devices are undoubtedly going to hit big in the consumer market too. At the 2022 edition of the CES tech trade show – widely considered to be the most influential tech event in the world – Abbott's CEO, Robert Ford, revealed the launch of a more comprehensive monitoring device that will "offer consumers an unprecedented understanding of human metabolism". At the same time, Best Buy – a large American consumer electronics retailer – launched their 'Season of Me' programme to help consumers stick to their New Year's resolutions. Their 90-day membership includes a medical assessment, specialised app and a CGM device. We're on course for a world where data like metabolic health index or metabolic rate will be as widely used by consumers as step counts and heart rates.

Other metabolic health tests

There are many different ways to monitor your metabolic health that already exist or are in the process of being launched. Most analyse data and provide advice based on one vital factor of your metabolism – your metabolic flexibility. This is the human body's ability to switch back and forth between fuelling itself with fat and carbohydrates based on their availability.

MONITORING METABOLIC HEALTH

Lumen might be one of the most popular devices. This breath analyser claims to hack your metabolism by identifying the concentration of CO_2 in a single breath. This shows the user what type of fuel their body is using to produce energy. While this was previously only available to top athletes or hospital patients with metabolic disease, it is now being used by over 1 million people in 126 different countries. This growing audience, often inspired by influential biohackers, want to see how their metabolism is affected by sleep, physical activity and nutrition. With this **Consciousness (being aware and comprehending)**, *they can effect changes to their overall health.*

The market for at-home metabolic tests is expanding as well. This is definitely the case in the USA, where it is no longer necessary to go to a specialist's office or health clinic for a metabolism test. Today, home tests, like EverlyWell, myLAB and Allara, provide **Autonomy (live independently and autonomously)** *and allow individuals to collect their own blood and saliva samples to be analysed and discussed afterwards during a virtual appointment with a medical professional. Standard medical testing has been brought into our homes, but it won't stop there. Researchers are now working on an integrated 'smart toilet' system that will yield critical metabolic data.*

These solutions are bound to become more popular, in part because they reflect other essential trends like healthy homes (Chapter 10.1) and decentralised healthcare (Chapter 8.3). What's more, these solutions aim to answer widespread health issues like fatigue, anxiety, mood swings and weight gain. Who wouldn't want to get to the root of these issues from the comfort of their own home?

Navigating our food habits

Our metabolic health is primarily determined by what we eat. The old adage really is true: we are what we eat. Or, if we want to be technical about it, we should say "We are what we metabolise". In any case, it's no surprise that many metabolic health solutions focus on what we eat and drink. Keto diets and intermittent fasting are popular mainly because of their assumed impact on our blood sugar levels and general metabolism. They're a product of the Metabolic Mastery trend.

The negative impact of processed food is closely linked to the popularity of these diets. As you know, processed foods give us a quick jolt of salt or sugar that satisfies a craving, but they require less energy to digest due to the high content of refined ingredients. This means people expend less metabolic energy when consuming processed foods; recent studies have shown that this can slow our metabolism and harm our health in the long term. Processed food is out; local, fresh and organic food is in. The insights here are nothing new, but this trend is growing quickly now.

The metabolic health trend also has an impact on the market for nutritional supplements. Of course, supplements to boost your metabolism have been around for a long time, but the difference is that they are no longer simply linked to weight loss. The focus of these newer supplements, which often contain amino acids and polyphenols, is to benefit your overall health. This is also in line with the body positivity trend that helps people focus on being healthy rather than slim.

WEIGHT LOSS REFRAMED

Even when weight loss is necessary, it's better reframed as a metabolic reset. **Calibrate** *is a metabolic telehealth solution that coaches people remotely and holistically. Compared to other weight loss programmes, Calibrate believes more in biology than willpower. What they say is true: "Sustainable weight loss comes from good metabolic health". Even companies such as* **Novo Nordisk,** *which sells the miracle injectable weight-loss drugs Ozempic and Wegovy, are focused on nutrition and exercise to reignite the metabolism. Together with the University of Copenhagen, they are working on a Food-Navigator program that uses the analysis of continuous glucose measurements, images of meals, metabolomic data and gut microbiome samples to create a personal dietary profile with recommendations. Several supermarkets I've worked with stated that they have very similar projects in the works. Looking to the future, we can expect to see solutions that direct us towards the right foods meeting our aspiration to have* **Consciousness (being aware and comprehending)** *and pursue* **Self-development (grow and cultivate oneself).**

Finally, I wouldn't be surprised if ketones become the next big trend in biomarkers for metabolic health (please note that this is not a medical statement). Abbott's CEO Robert Ford has already hinted that the next Libre sensors will monitor biomarkers like lactate, alcohol and ketones. The Libre Keto will hit the market first, helping users understand when the body is in ketosis. This process happens when your body doesn't have enough carbohydrates to burn for energy, so it burns fat instead and makes ketones to use as fuel. If you've ever followed a strict keto diet, you'll probably be familiar with this method.

Ketones are also known as the fourth macronutrient. Fat, carbohydrates and protein are the more well-known first three. An increased level of ketones provides sustained energy, boosted endurance, enhanced mental clarity and better appetite control. It is tough to achieve this without fasting or following a strict keto diet. But a new drink will soon be launched to help with this.

DRINKABLE HEALTH FOR ATHLETES AND US

*Health Via Modern Nutrition (**HVMN**) is a metabolic health company and pioneer in drinkable ketone technology. The company aims to redefine the limits of human performance, metabolism and longevity. It's no wonder that cyclists in the **Tour de France** and the **Special Forces** are already using the product. Soon, we will all be able to experience the direct benefits of good metabolic health provided by this drink.*

CASE IN POINT

Circadian health

The final shift driving this Metabolic Mastery trend is related to sleep. Or at least, it is related to what happens in our bodies at night (when we are, or are supposed to be, sleeping). In 2017, a group of researchers won the Nobel Prize in medicine for the discovery of genes that build up protein at night and degrade protein during the day. This discovery highlighted the importance of our body's internal clock, known as our circadian rhythm. Remarkably, these circadian genes don't only regulate when we should sleep, but also control our heart rate, blood pressure, immune system, body temperature, hormones, mood and – of course – our metabolism.

The popularity of 'clock nutrition' might grow steadily in the coming years.

It's early days for circadian health. Plenty of research is still needed to understand what impact it truly has. However, lots of research has already been done on the effects of our internal clock, like how we metabolise calories better in the morning than in the evening. The idea behind intermittent fasting is also grounded in the science of our internal clocks. Whether or not this 'diet' remains as popular, I expect 'clock nutrition' – the awareness of when we eat – to grow steadily in the coming years. Circadian health will be an essential health and self-care focus that will foster innovation in lighting, food, exercise, sleep and the various environments we live, travel or work in. Ongoing studies about how sleep and meal timing affect our metabolic health will, without a doubt, also strengthen the popularity of Metabolic Mastery.

Feeding several of our most common Life Aspirations

There are several important Life Aspirations that make me believe that metabolic health has the potential to become a dominant health and self-care trend that could transform the approach to healthcare. Obviously it helps diabetic patients to feel **Safeness** *(feel safe and protected)* and protect them from severe hypoglycaemia. This is one of the biggest dangers of diabetes that we assume every patient wants to be protected from. But it also could protect people from developing obesity and related cardiovascular disease. Metabolic Mastery also feeds into the personal science trend (that we touched on in Chapter 2.1) that makes sports professionals more scientifically equipped to optimise their **Strength** *(have power and resilience)* and help them to further **Self-develop** *(grow and cultivate oneself)*. But most of all, having good metabolic health, or not having severe metabolic dysfunction, helps with **Energy** *(have vitality and stamina)*. In fact, a lack of energy or a feeling of fatigue is one of the most common struggles people discuss with their pharmacists.

Metabolic health is just one example. There are more.

The metabolic health trend shows that we are taking an active role in improving our own health, not just when we're 'in the healthcare system'. It confirms that there is more to it than simply meeting a medical need and that Life Aspirations are about living life to the fullest. We now see this evolution happening in other parts of the healthcare industry as well. The diagnosis and treatment of disorders of the gastrointestinal (GI) tract is evolving into a broader gut health approach, driven by people's Life Aspirations. It's about not feeling bloated, dealing with allergies and managing mental health through optimal gut health, regardless of whether people are sick or not. It's an interesting evolution sparked by the belief that our gut is our second brain, that will radically change healthcare in the coming decade. Another interesting evolution is happening in dermatology. This field is being transformed into skin health as it expands towards hydration and nutrition, turns cosmetics into health habits and focuses on sensitivities, allergies and ageing. In that regard, just like with FemTech, there is also a lot to learn from skincare. Businesses in this field make a very practical and clear distinction between all things medical, health, well-being and lifestyle. But more importantly, it's inspirational to see how they turn a clinical experience into a transformational one with appealing branding.

People seek a more holistic solution that meets several of their Life Aspirations. In the next chapter, we'll explore how such and other transformations could perhaps make individual diseases irrelevant, turn caregivers into care guiders and decentralise healthcare. These are possible future scenarios. Maybe they won't happen quite as I'll describe them here. Perhaps only a few partial evolutions will take place. Maybe I'm completely wrong. But either way, it will challenge you to think about how the Transformation Economy will impact the future of healthcare.

CHAPTER 8

FUTURES OF TRANSFORMATIONAL HEALTHCARE

I'm not trying to pretend that I have a crystal ball that allows me to predict the future. But I want you to reflect upon some futures with me. Even without a crystal ball, it could be interesting. I once saw the quote, "Out of three future predictions, seven will probably come true." It made me laugh but also think hard. This quote seems to make little sense. And yet, I mainly understand from this that there are multiple truths in one prediction. However, the future may be packaged entirely differently. Another quote about foresight and future forecasting stated that predicting the future is not difficult at all. In fact, the future already exists today. It is just not widespread yet. So you could pick up signals from the future quite easily today (that's how I spend my days, by the way) and you can build several scenarios if you place this in a broader context and analyse it from a distance. Some scenarios will be more plausible than others. Some may be possible, others rather preposterous. But they are all based on the same signals already here today.

Out of three future predictions, seven will probably come true.

If I look at signals of the futures within healthcare, I have to start with the Healthusiasm trend described in the first book. Healthusiasm is based on the assumption that we all want to be(come) healthy and happy. That has always been the case. But while humans had to rely on sacrifices and prayers a few millennia ago, we have more information and resources to improve our health and happiness today. This makes us more eager than ever to have an impact on our own health. In each keynote, I start with how this Healthusiasm trend accelerated in the 1980s. This has reached cruising speed recently, and I do not expect it to decrease in the next 50 years. Healthusiasm is a macro trend that has and will have many other smaller trends in its wake.

The three healthcare transformations discussed in the previous chapter exemplify such trends emerging from Healthusiasm. The common denominators within these transformations are essential when reflecting upon the transformational future of healthcare. We should estimate, interpret, and extrapolate them. These common elements are a more holistic approach, a shift from sick care to caring for your health, democratising advanced (medically approved) devices, and an even more popular health practice. It's not a coincidence that these elements were also described in the first book as the drivers of the Healthusiasm Trend, of course.

So, let us now look at some future scenarios in the following subchapters. I could have presented you with more scenarios than I can write down here. General and more specific health trends are part of my portfolio of keynotes. But I specifically chose these scenarios because they appear to be particularly relevant in the Transformation Economy, which is, of course, what this book is about.

A first scenario builds on the transformations discussed in the previous chapter. Indeed, in women's, mental and metabolic health, we have seen a shift away from merely treating diseases to addressing health as part of life. In a certain sense, the diseases themselves are fading into the background. In the first subchapter, I want to discuss this further with you and look at a scenario where diseases could become irrelevant.

A second future builds further on this. Here, we think about the consequences of healthcare transformations for healthcare providers. The tsunami of digital solutions plays a significant role here, but how patients will increasingly take their health (and not just their illness) into their own hands also contributes to this.

Finally, we tackle a future known as the decentralisation of healthcare. But again, we expand beyond sick care because we can no longer see health management separately from ill care. These are often seen as two separate things today, but in the future, they could become very close to each other. Especially from the patient's point of view, little distinction will be made (or will be wanted to be made). In this last subchapter, we will, therefore, give a broader interpretation of the decentralisation of healthcare.

Now, let's dive into those futures together.

8.1 Diseases become irrelevant

Transformations can be driven by an underserved population (women's health), an urgency (mental health) or advances in technology and science (metabolic health). But the common denominator of our increased interest in women's, mental, metabolic, skin and gut health is that there is less interest in treating only one condition. People realise they need to look at the whole package to be happy and healthy as a person. Individual diseases are thus losing their relevance, as we will see in this chapter. This might be one of the biggest transformations in healthcare.

This Healthusiasm trend means two things: The healthcare system will focus more on prevention, and/or people will focus more on self-care.

You've surely heard healthcare professionals talking about moving away from sick care and towards *health*care. I'm sure we can agree that until now the healthcare system has been mainly focused on sick care; that is to say, only taking care of people's health when they are sick. It indirectly implies that people only 'care' about their health when they are sick, but even if that were once the case, it's certainly no longer true. People are paying more attention to their health than ever before.

This Healthusiasm trend means two things. The healthcare system will focus more on prevention, and/or people will focus more on self-care. Whatever way you look at it, it all boils down to the same thing: Diseases will become less relevant. Let's look at why.

Prevention is more prevalent than sick care

The healthcare system is starting to focus a bit more on preventative health to postpone or prevent the onset of diseases. At the same time, people are taking care of themselves, turning increasingly to self-care to optimise their health and happiness. This Healthusiasm is everywhere and is taking a crucial stand against diseases. That being said, I'm not so naïve as to think that all diseases will disappear as a result, but I do think that they will become less relevant. Just do the numbers. Look at the number of people playing an active part in their own health (even when they're not sick) compared to the number of sick people. It's a pretty straightforward calculation: There are always more people focused on prevention and self-care. This has the potential to radically outweigh the focus on sick care. Disease, as such, will therefore become less relevant because there will be many more opportunities to talk about preventative health and self-care.

Prevention is more generic than sick care

And there's another factor that will make disease less relevant. Sick care is very disease-specific. At any given hospital, you have departments for every sub-domain of health: cardiology, oncology, gynaecology and the list goes on. Meanwhile, prevention and healthy lifestyles are more generic. They are relevant beyond and across conditions. As a result, healthy living has more potential to scale and is doable regardless of whether or not you are sick.

Prevention and healthy lifestyles are more generic. They are relevant beyond and across conditions.

More companies and brands are already using this Healthusiasm to speak to a wider audience. It empowers them to bring to market better products, services and experiences, which, in turn, will radically increase the uptake of health and wellness initiatives in the coming years. As a result, there will be more preventative solutions than 'medical' solutions. This will radically shift the focus of the health discourse, in which diseases will become less relevant.

Health start-ups are covering larger areas of health

If you work with start-ups, or if you've been monitoring the start-up market in the past couple of years, you may have noticed the same change: there's less focus on diseases, while the attention paid to entire health areas is growing. And even if start-ups kick off with a single focus, after a few years, they aim broader. For instance, rather than claiming to solve depression or anxiety, companies approach mental health from a more holistic angle. Rather than honing in on diabetes or weight management, they'll talk about metabolic health. This fits perfectly with how people are looking to manage their own health. There is plenty of interest and motivation to work on more than just curing a single disease. People make health-related decisions ranging from lifestyle choices to well-being, from preventative to curative medical decisions. More people want support when it comes to those decisions. As we've seen in previous chapters, the women's health market is a perfect example of that. It's seldom only about menopause, PMS or fertility. It's about the broader picture, about how women can optimise their own health regardless of specific disease struggles.

Health is everywhere. Diseases are not.

Pharma companies are partnering with wellness applications. Wellness retreats are providing programmes for recovery from long COVID, cancer treatment or surgery (see Chapter 9). Gyms are offering medical expertise and treatment (see Chapter 10.3). Sports brands are supporting women during their menstrual cycle. This random sample of initiatives shows how health has become an integral part of our daily lives, which will be extensively covered in Part Four. Health is everywhere. It's a Healthusiasm world. The same cannot be said for diseases. In fact, the most frequent feedback from patient research is that they don't like to be addressed as patients because they don't feel or consider themselves to be sick most of the time. As we discussed in Chapter 6, we're only a patient in specific situations. We may have particular needs in that situation, but we remain the same person with the same expectations and Life Aspirations. We are still human beings who care about our own health and happiness.

"We are only a patient sometimes."

Good health is about more than not being sick

In many ways, the COVID-19 pandemic was a very enriching experience. We were confronted with the (additional) risks of not being in good health, which increased the focus on self-care and prevention. We learned that fear-based, paternalistic communication has a limited impact over time. We saw people actively looking for health-related information and solutions beyond the medical field. But we also saw that many people preferred to run the risk of infection rather than stay indoors. When it comes to your health, it's not just about avoiding disease but also (and increasingly so) about your overall health. Sometimes, your mental health takes precedence over hiding from a virus. To be clear, I'm not trying to undermine the health restrictions that governments put in place during the pandemic. I'm just trying to show that even when a potential disease is lurking, people still look beyond the disease itself. Good general health is more important than trying to avoid illness at all costs. In other words, for many people, a disease is less relevant than good overall health.

Technology changes the healthcare game

In addition to changes in society, human behaviour and clever business strategies, there are still two more important aspects that can be mentioned in the same breath: progress in science and technology. For instance, the development of different vaccines is expected to grow massively. Several life-science companies were already designing vaccines but during the pandemic, biotech companies were able to test new technologies and scientific breakthroughs in an environment that had more urgency and very little business risk. Take the use of mRNA for vaccines for example. While this particular research was already promising for several decades, research got fast-tracked by the urgency of the pandemic. Governments limited the risk of further research by buying the products upfront at a pre-defined price. COVID vaccines were identified, developed and brought to market faster than ever before. But it also sparked the development of a wave of new vaccines for influenza, Zika, HIV, cancer and many others. It's fair to expect a huge wave of new vaccines in the next decade that will prevent various diseases. Diseases may thus become less relevant because they will also be less prevalent. We can hope so, anyway.

At the same time, plenty of start-ups have already invested heavily in tools to diagnose possible diseases early enough before the actual onset of a disease so that the risk of developing the disease could be postponed or avoided. There's also plenty of research on identifying predispositions to disease using DNA or microbiome analysis, again allowing us to postpone or delay the onset. These solutions won't make diseases go away just yet. However, they are changing the conversation from curing to prevention and are, in turn, making disease less relevant.

TRANSFORMING DIAGNOSIS

Californian biotechnology company **GRAIL***'s Galleri test can detect 50 different types of cancer with a single drop of blood before symptoms develop. Currently, cancer is often diagnosed at an advanced stage, which can be fatal. Early detection is challenging, as there are no widespread tests for the majority of cancers that lead to death, and available tests usually focus on only one type of cancer. If integrated into annual screenings, this could cut late-stage cancer diagnoses by half and reduce cancer mortality by 39% among those detected early. Pharma giants like Bristol-Myers Squibb, Celgene, Merck, Johnson & Johnson Innovations, and tech heavyweight Amazon are among GRAIL's early investors. Valued at over 1 billion euros, GRAIL is gearing up for an IPO. Initially, GRAIL's test was only available in the US as part of the PATHFINDER study. The PATHFINDER study was a pilot non-randomised study to evaluate how patients and clinicians would respond to a blood test to screen for multiple cancer types. The screening test identified a cancer signal in 1.4% of participants, 0.5% of whom were confirmed to have cancer. In the vast majority of cases, the test accurately predicted the type of cancer. It has now been released for prescription use as Galleri and is being tested in the UK on 140,000 people who do not have cancer. GRAIL faces competition from start-ups like Thrive, which is developing multi-cancer tests, and Freenome, which focuses on colorectal cancer and is backed by Google's parent company, Alphabet. Meanwhile this evolution is visible in other therapeutic areas as well. French start-up Ziwig has developed a salivary test for endometriosis – a disease that currently takes on average 7–10 years to diagnose.*

The end is in sight

The end of the disease era and the predominant focus on sick care could very well be in sight. Being sick is no longer the dominant driver of our health-related decisions. We aren't inside or outside the healthcare system, but are constantly involved in our own health. Rather than worrying about a particular disease, we are generally more concerned with our overall health. And start-ups are cleverly playing into this trend by bringing health-related rather than disease-specific solutions to market. Companies from other industries with little to no prior affinity with health are providing health-related services in all parts of our lives (see

Chapter 10). This all shows that the focus is no longer on disease management, but on health optimisation. Health management can also be more focused on the positive side of things: people's enthusiasm to be healthy and happy. Or what I call Healthusiasm.

We aren't inside or outside the healthcare system, but are constantly involved in our own health.

This shift is already taking place. This means that I would love to rethink how we approach caring for sick people and instead care for the whole person, in sickness *and* in health. But what will this transformational shift mean for healthcare providers? Will this change the way in which they work and provide healthcare? We'll explore the role of healthcare providers in the next chapter.

8.2 Caregivers become careguides

People are taking more control of their own health than ever before. They're not waiting for an illness that sends them to the doctor to then take medicine. They want to do more for their own health before they reach that point. I don't want to bang on about the COVID-19 pandemic, but it was an accelerator of this evolution.

The pandemic was characterised by specific situations that sparked the desire to be more in control of our health. Health systems were inaccessible to regular, non-COVID patients for significant periods, making people suddenly more reliant on themselves. A shortage of health workers put pressure (and still does) on the viability of specific healthcare segments, making many not want to end up there (ever). The empathy for government COVID-measures quickly wore out, as people preferred to live according to their personal health priorities. The limitations of 'sick care' became apparent, making people focused on preserving health. Boosting immunity became an obsession for many, making it one of the most popular health ambitions ever seen.

Of course, the need for a sound healthcare system was emphasised by this urgency. It was an argument to highlight how important it is, bring attention to it and the investments it has lost over time. But in the meantime, another vital evolution happened on the other side of the spectrum. The world was accustomed to being empowered in common industries like banking, travel and retail. In light of the pandemic, people also looked to take their health into their own hands. By intensifying self-care, we aspired to avoid the parts of healthcare that seemed broken or provided a horrible experience. It wasn't surprising when Ipsos (2023) found that 83% of people wanted more control over their health decisions. It also disclosed that 65% of Europeans are likely to make everyday decisions based on their health. People are more than ever focused on what matters most to them: their health and happiness.

Health happens outside of healthcare

While healthcare was shaken up, self-care took an even more solid stance in areas that could impact our physical and mental health. But self-care, and the closely related wellness business, is more than fitness, spas and nutrition. It has started to claim its place alongside healthcare. After all, 99% of caring about our health happens outside of healthcare. To put it in the words of the World Health Organization, an average person spends less than an hour a year with a healthcare worker versus over 8.700 hours a year in self-care (8,700 hours = all day, every day). In this statement by WHO, self-care stands for all the actions we undertake every moment of every day to be healthy and happy, regardless of whether we are sick or not. Therefore, self-care is not just the prevention of diseases but part of the entire continuum of health management. It can be considered the soft side of medicine and is gaining importance within and outside of the healthcare system.

99% of caring about our health happens outside of healthcare.

The Yin and Yang of health management

Health management as a combination of health and self-care is ubiquitous in to-day's world. Consumer industries are becoming active facilitators in the management of one's health as we will see in Part Four. Meanwhile, wellness initiatives integrate more medical practices into their approach and healthcare organisations have started combining modern medicine with more wholesome, holistic methods. In the next 2–5 years, self-care will solidify its position alongside healthcare. These two (often) opposing, (currently) non-communicating forces will turn out to be the yin and yang of health management. The different 'cares' will be *tuned* to one another. Initiatives will rise from both sides to unlock access, empower people, make smarter decisions, design a better experience and achieve better outcomes. Early initiatives already showcase how this will facilitate more collaboration and tuning between health and self-care.

Health- and self-care will need to be tuned to one another.

TREATING THE WHOLE HUMAN

CASE IN POINT

Merging medicine and wellness

There is perhaps no better visual representation of this convergence of health and self-care than the **Sangha Retreat** *in Suzhou, China. This establishment is built around a central corridor that links a wellness area with a clinic for conventional medicine. During their stay, visitors can freely tune the care they are given to their needs.*

Spanish clinic **SHA Wellness**, *in Valencia, offers a 360° integrative approach to health that combines holistic and medical practices. In the wake of the pandemic, they launched a programme to address the long-term effects of COVID-19 using wellness therapies and clinical treatments.*

Healthcare providers transform into health guides

Self-care will continue to grow in our lives, complementing healthcare with more accessible, understandable and convenient solutions. From prevention to diagnosis, people will increasingly be supported by tools and solutions they can use themselves. The participation of the patient will also radically increase their involvement in treatment and disease management, while earlier discharges from hospitals will give the patient new and more elaborate responsibility. Because of these evolutions, health and self-care must be tuned for better experiences and outcomes. But that is precisely the challenge for a healthcare industry that has always been closed off and protected from external interference. Tuning health and self-care will now demand dedication and openness by the healthcare system to be successful.

It wouldn't surprise me if this evolution were one of the major transformations in healthcare. In fact, I expect that the role of frontline healthcare workers will shift radically in the future because of this. They will have to *guide* patients and health consumers much more than they do today. That doesn't mean that they will just be guiding them through the maze of the healthcare system. Instead, patients will need to be guided through a much broader health and wellness ecosystem that goes beyond their current, primary knowledge and expertise. It will be broader and much more complex. These new *careguides* will help people navigate through a maze of health and self-care solutions, regardless of whether they are looking for information, prevention, diagnosis, recommendations or alternative treatments and (perhaps even) whether or not the solution is part of the recognised healthcare ecosystem.

These careguides will help people navigate through a maze of health and self-care solutions.

This might seem like a somewhat exaggerated portrayal of where we are going, and of course it's clear that this isn't going to happen overnight – but this transformation has already started. The battle for the frontline is picking up speed; that much is apparent in the digital efforts being made by health insurance companies, pharmacists and doctor's associations. They all seem to be claiming the same space on the frontline with similar initiatives that go beyond healthcare. It's also already clearly visible in how patients and health consumers approach their health.

CASE IN POINT

LIFESTYLE MEDICINE

Lifestyle Medicine is another practice of tuning health and self-care and of how healthcare providers will help in tuning health and self-care. Its popularity is driven by the conviction that lifestyle changes can treat (and possibly reverse) specific chronic conditions. In the coming years, a growing wave of healthcare professionals will be certified to apply evidence-based, whole-person, prescriptive lifestyle changes. Lifestyle medicine tunes healthcare with self-care-related actions such as healthy eating, physical activity, restorative sleep, stress management, avoiding risky substances and maintaining positive social connections.

The global movement toward Lifestyle Medicine is supported by a growing number of organisations advocating for health transformation through lifestyle changes. The Lifestyle **Medicine Global Alliance** *unites healthcare professionals worldwide to combat non-communicable diseases by promoting Lifestyle Medicine. The* **American College of Lifestyle Medicine** *leads the charge in the U.S., training clinicians in six key lifestyle pillars to prevent and reverse chronic conditions. In Europe, the* **European Lifestyle Medicine Organization** *is dedicated to improving life expectancy and quality of life through evidence-based lifestyle medicine, and the* **British Society of Lifestyle Medicine** *focuses on behaviour change to improve overall well-being. The* **International Board of Lifestyle Medicine** *sets standards for professionals in the field, indicating a structured approach to credentialing. These initiatives collectively underscore a powerful shift towards integrating lifestyle medicine into healthcare, emphasising prevention, and empowering individuals to manage their health beyond sick care.*

In Chapter 14, I'll elaborate on how this shift from healthcare providers to care-guides will be reinforced and accelerated by transformational technologies. But let's first have a look at another future transformation in health care.

8.3 Decentralised Health and Care

Decentralisation is transforming various industries. It happens by distributing power from central entities to a more widespread network. It's been a more common topic of discussion since innovations like crowdfunding, Open Source platforms, Blockchain technology, Non-Fungible Tokens (NFTs), and Decentralized Autonomous Organisations (DAOs) took the stage. But it's a trend that has been going on for much longer. And there is a good reason for it. Decentralised systems offer several benefits. They are more flexible and quick to respond to (local) needs because they function in smaller groups with fewer bureaucratic procedures. It makes them more efficient and agile in providing better solutions for specific situations. It improves innovations, which plays a vital role in the necessary adaptability and competitiveness of businesses in modern reality.

DECENTRALISED INDUSTRIES

Home renewable energy, energy storage solutions and localised grids that can operate away from the main power grid are decentralising the energy industry. Ride-sharing apps (and soon autonomous vehicles) offer personalised transport options without centralised scheduling. In finance, digital currencies and ledger technologies, like cryptocurrency and blockchain, function independently of central banks. At the same time, other financial services are being distributed to a more widespread network of Peer-to-Peer (P2P) lending and crowdfunding solutions. Online courses are part of the decentralisation of education. Streaming services, podcasts, and content platforms like **YouTube**, **Twitch**, *and* **TikTok** *created a distributed entertainment ecosystem.*

Decentralisation in healthcare most often refers to the application of telehealth and telemonitoring solutions, which the pandemic has accelerated as certain barriers were removed. It transformed telehealth from an opportunity to a necessity. Hospitals became trauma and ICU centres, while other care services were delivered in a community, home-based or virtual setting. This achievement was heralded as significant, but I couldn't share this joy with perhaps the rest of the healthcare system. The technology had been around for decades and was already well established in other parts of our lives. The fact that it took a global health scare to remove barriers and fix processes was more disappointing than it justifies celebrating. Did it indicate a lack of willingness to decentralise healthcare? I'm not entitled to claim that, but what seems inevitable is that decentralisation will continue and even broaden.

Healthcare providers are no longer at the centre of the health universe, but patients are. Circling these patients are various solutions that sometimes aren't part of the healthcare system.

What the current and future transformations in healthcare seem to indicate is what I explained in Chapter 6 as the Corpernican Health Revolution. Healthcare providers are no longer at the centre of the health universe, but patients are. Circling these patients are various solutions that sometimes aren't part of the healthcare system, look at disease and treatment differently, and already gather far more data than is currently available in the healthcare system. I hear the arguments that most of these solutions aren't centrally approved and that the data is not validated or labelled. That might still be true in many cases (for now). But would the healthcare system quickly welcome data and insights from 'a more decentralised network'? I'm looking forward to it happening because it would accelerate innovation.

The Copernican Health Revolution also means a broad range of health-related solutions that are not centrally endorsed will 'interfere' with how people go about their health. This has always been the case. But the difference is that these solutions will be more impactful tomorrow than praying was 500 years ago. In Chapter 7.2 we explored how mental health has seen valuable new solutions because the central healthcare system can't cope with the influx of patients. What part of the healthcare system is already occupied with circadian health to optimise metabolic health? Which hospitals will soon be organised in clusters of diseases like the longevity or geroscience is doing? And how, if at all, can the personal science trend, mentioned in Chapter 2.1, be extended in healthcare? These look, to me, like good reasons for more decentralisation, but most importantly, it guarantees more patient-centricity.

DO-IT-YOURSELF ARTIFICIAL PANCREAS

The #WeAreNotWaiting movement is a community of patients with diabetes taking disease management into their own hands. They organise themselves and develop applications, platforms, and other solutions to help each other manage their disease. The movement, initiated by Dana Lewis, emerged from the frustration with medtech companies' slow progress in diabetes care. In 2016, Dana and her husband created their DIY artificial pancreas at home and shared the blueprints on Twitter.

CASE IN POINT

This DIY artificial pancreas automatically gives patients the proper insulin doses based on their real-time blood glucose level. The software was created entirely by the patient community with no contribution from medical professionals. It is to be said that this software is the most personalised code on GitHub, a platform and cloud-based service for software development and version control that allows developers to store and manage their code. After all, almost all patients tweak the code to suit their personal biological response. In other words, the app is designed from the ground up to be fully configurable to suit individual needs. Despite lacking regulatory approval from central bodies, the open-source, decentralised artificial pancreas system gained traction among patients.

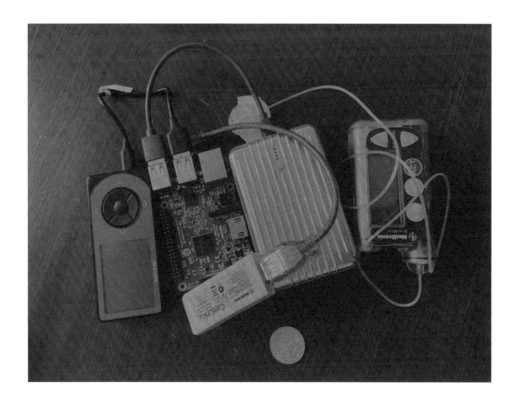

Wilson's first Open Artificial Pancreas System created in October 2016. Credit: Orla Wilson

Decentralisation has challenged multiple industries. It even created burning platforms for sectors like entertainment or journalism. A 'burning platform' is a critical and urgent situation that demands immediate action to avoid a potential failure, but which healthcare has never faced. Healthcare has never had to deal with a burning platform because it is primarily protected by the central organisation (or monopoly) in science and its related procedures. That was until now.

Decentralised science, commonly called 'DeSci', represents a new approach in the scientific community that leverages emerging technologies like blockchain and Web3. DeSci aims to address critical issues within the traditional, centralised scientific system. The current standard model for funding science is, for example, assumed to be vulnerable to biases or even politics. It's also difficult to publish research via traditional channels because it relies on free labour from scientists, requires a high publishing fee and doesn't always reward researchers transparently.

PATIENT-CENTRIC DECENTRALISED SCIENTIFIC INITIATIVES

Vibe Bio, LOVE DAO, and PsyDAO represent a new wave in healthcare, emphasising a human-centred approach through Decentralised Autonomous Organizations (DAOs). **Vibe Bio** *empowers patients with rare and neglected diseases to search for and fund potential cures. Unfortunately, this is necessary because the best science and medicines often never receive funding. This is not because the science is not promising but because traditional centralised systems optimise for different metrics like prestige in academia, the lowest financial risk in biotech, and influence in government. Vibe Bio aims to fund promising treatments often overlooked due to these traditional systems prioritising different metrics.*

In the following decade, science will become widely available to many (or at least more). One example is the popularity of synthetic biology. This field of science looks at biology as if it were Lego, calling it the most advanced building technology on the planet. And indeed, biology has been built since life on Earth began. Synthetic biology is, therefore, often called the revolution that has been 3,5 billion years in the making. Synthetic biology has the potential to program cells to make everything, from extinct flowers to growing coral reefs to designing bacteria as a medicine against cancer. Despite common overestimations of short-term progress, synthetic biology's potential in a decade is often underestimated. But to achieve its potential, it needs to democratise access to technology with inexpensive, user-friendly tools and methods available for public use, including DIY instructions for building DNA manipulation devices. This might seem ludicrous, but it's already happening.

BIOLOGY BY DESIGN

ODIN *is making advanced biological research and experimentation more accessible to the general public. It provides DIY genetic engineering courses and kits online. ODIN's courses cover various topics, including CRISPR gene editing, and are designed for different levels of expertise, from beginners to more advanced enthusiasts. The kits come with all the equipment, reagents, and materials required to conduct experiments. A $ 600.- course includes all the materials you need to learn to program DNA.*

CASE IN POINT

These resources provide a hands-on learning experience and promote a deeper under-standing of genetic engineering principles and techniques. By making these tools and knowledge more widely available, ODIN contributes to a growing community of citizen scientists and enthusiasts exploring the potential of genetic modification and bioengi-neering outside traditional academic and industrial laboratories. This approach aligns with the broader movement of DIY biology and biohacking, which seeks to make science more open, accessible, and decentralised.

A fantastic concept in this field is **community biolabs**. *It is based on the idea of 'Sce-nius', a concept that emphasises a community's collective intelligence and creativity. In the context of 'synthetic biology', Scenius could be seen as the driving force behind these collaborative spaces where individuals from diverse backgrounds converge to explore and innovate in the field of biology. These community biolabs are typically open-access labs that provide the public with the tools and resources to conduct biological experiments and projects, including hobbyists, citizen scientists, and researchers. This model fosters a cul-ture of open science, democratises access to biotechnology, and encourages a decentralised approach to scientific exploration and learning.*

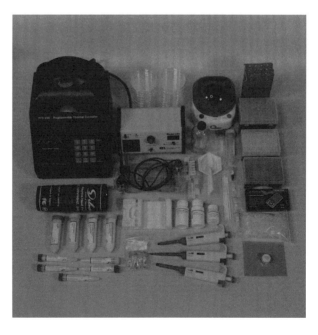

Genetic Engineering Home Lab Kit via the-odin.com

Decentralisation is one of the most impactful transformations in healthcare. As we have seen in this chapter, this decentralisation goes beyond telehealth solutions or home monitoring. It drives up an entirely new dynamic on the outskirts of the healthcare systems that might radically change the system. It has been impossible to decentralise healthcare until now. But I expect some advancements in the coming years, not least because one sector can no longer claim health(care). Many other industries are also moving into that space because health and happiness are also essential for their customers. It was the core message of the first Healthusiasm book, but you will see in Part Four that The Transformation Economy also drives this trend.

Conclusion

But perhaps it is appropriate first to look back at how healthcare transformations are necessary and already emerging today. This is what Part Three was mainly about. Patients are, of course, the primary motivators here. They demand that health solutions not only address medical needs. Their expectations are at least as important to be met. But of course, in the spirit of the times, patients have also become more aspirational. Their dreams and desires remain at least as important even when they are patients. However, it sometimes feels as if these simple things, which make someone feel good about life, receive little attention in healthcare.

However, these are the Life Aspirations that can lead to better care. People will be even more motivated and committed. We see this happening today mainly in women's health, which has specifically started to take 'being a woman' into account. We also know the importance of Life Aspirations in mental health, not least because feeling good in this domain is perhaps even more essential. Both domains, therefore, go further than simply curing a condition. There is a shift towards a more general health approach that we are gradually seeing becoming dominant in other domains as well. We talked extensively about metabolic health and mentioned gut and skin health as exciting examples of a more holistic, transformational approach.

Healthcare thus becomes more than just medical care. It will have a self-care component that will play an increasingly important role in health management. In fact, self-care could quickly become so ubiquitous that diseases could become irrelevant in the future. Numerous rich insights and intelligent solutions then motivate people to be involved in their own health. More and more solutions will fuel this motivation, which may require healthcare providers to take on more of a role as care guides. Patients want to be assisted by these care guides in the oversupply of health solutions that provide them with diagnoses, recommendations and perhaps treatments. But at the same time, this will also lead to further decentralisation of healthcare. New solutions to optimise your health are increasingly not centrally managed (or approved). Just look at how people today already have access to innovations that have not (yet) been confirmed by the national (or central) health system. Therefore, this future decentralisation of care could go much further than teleconsultations or monitoring.

In Part Four, we're going to take this decentralisation of health even further. It focuses on the impact of the Transformation Economy on the average business, but you will soon notice that many Customer Transformations are self-care-oriented. This is not surprising because they respond to people's Life Aspirations, those dreams and desires that make them feel better, healthier and happier.

PART 4

TRANSFORMATIONAL BUSINESS

CHAPTER 9

CUSTOMERS SEEK TRANSFORMATIONS FROM COMPANIES AND BRANDS

The Transformation Economy significantly impacts the healthcare industry, as we have seen in Part Three. It does not come as a surprise, as the entire industry is focused on making their customers healthy & happy. Transformations must be an essential part of that industry. But not only the healthcare industry is moving towards the Transformation Economy. In the following chapters, I want to take you on a tour to other sectors that are even (far) ahead of the healthcare industry in that regard. Our dreams, desires and values are present in our lives at every moment and place. It is a constant in our lives. The different parts of our lives certainly contribute to these Life Aspirations, to feeling better, healthier or happier. And the more time we spend in or near certain places, with particular objects or performing certain activities, the more impact they can have on us, and the greater their value in the Transformation Economy.

Many parts of our lives can obviously be instrumental in making us feel better, healthier or happier.

We spend plenty of time at home, in our car and at work. Most of us exercise, have sex or listen to music. We are occupied with our finances, our food and sleep. We wear glasses, watches, jewellery and clothing near our bodies. In each of these moments, businesses could help their customers pursue some of their Life Aspirations. The different chapters in this part will showcase how some places, activities or objects are valuable to you in the Transformation Economy. It exemplifies how the Life Aspirations in these moments bring value to your business once you start thinking beyond fulfilling immediate needs. To illustrate how to create such value, let's look at one of the first transformational sectors: the travel industry.

The travel industry

The travel industry may not be the first sector that comes to mind when you think of innovation, perhaps because we often associate the word 'innovation' with new technological solutions. Nevertheless, the travel industry has always been an early adopter of innovating the value it provides for its customers.

Travel is something that we, as humans, attach great importance to. We save our hard-earned money to travel for pleasure once or twice a year in an attempt to leave behind the stress of our everyday lives. Given that investment, we don't want anything to go awry. We want the journey to go as smoothly as possible, the accommodation to meet our needs and the overall experience to leave us feeling transformed. In short, we want to receive great value. This is why the travel industry has always placed such importance on creating value for its customers.

Back in the 1950s and before, travel was just about getting out of the house and enjoying a change of scenery. So people would rent a house, a caravan or some other place where they could spend some time away from their own home. In the 1960s, however, the travel industry realised that people wanted more. This was the start of all-inclusive packages created by travel companies like Club Med. Rather than simply renting a place to stay, the focus switched to receiving endless services during your holiday so that all of your needs were taken care of. Another shift occurred in the 1990s, when people started to seek new experiences. Instead of just lounging by the pool with a cocktail in hand, people wanted to go on whisky-tasting tours in rural Scotland, horse riding in Ardèche or hiking in Iceland.

This is how the travel industry came to create more customer value: by shifting from product to service to customer experience, quite literally. In recent years, the travel industry once more raised the bar by focusing on customer transformations. So more and more people are setting off on 'holiday' to climb Kilimanjaro, meet and stay with indigenous people, clean beaches or simply just return to nature. The purpose of travel today is to feel transformed by the time you come home. This is what people strive for because it makes them feel like the best version of themselves. It makes them feel better, happier or perhaps even healthier.

The purpose of travel today is to feel transformed by the time you come home.

The transformational travel trend can be grouped into three main categories: sustainable travel that leaves the tourist feeling guilt-free; trips that aim to develop a better understanding of diversity in our society; and retreats focused on health and self-care. The latter, in particular, is a booming sector that's proof of the Healthusiasm trend I wrote about in my previous book. But it is also a great example of how customer transformation creates additional value. This may not come as a surprise to you. After all, travel has long been a key part of our health as a means to rest, relax and recharge. Travel, health and happiness are all top priorities for us. It makes perfect sense to add some health and wellness to your holiday or even to travel exclusively for that purpose. So let's take a look at some examples.

Wellness travel

Travelling to improve your health and well-being is far from a new phenomenon. Over 5000 years ago, people travelled to specific places in India to practise yoga and Ayurvedic medicine. In ancient Rome, people visited particular destinations to relax or heal, like the hot springs in Mesopotamia and the iron-rich mineral springs in Switzerland.

Conversely, the rise of the all-inclusive holiday package represented excess, leading travellers to drink and eat more than they usually would. Instead of continuing their healthy habits, holidaymakers would laze around the pool or party endlessly. However, that approach is no longer the gold standard. Now, people want to use their time away to improve their health rather than see it deteriorate. And not only do they want to continue their healthy lifestyles and routines while away from home, they want to build on them and take new ones home.

THE POPULARITY OF WELLNESS TRAVEL

Wellness travel currently makes up almost 20% of all travel spending, but the market is expected to double between 2022 and 2027 to attain a value of 1.4 trillion euros (Global Wellness Institute, 2012). This kind of travel appeals to everyone, regardless of age, gender or social class. Research published by American Express in September 2021 showed that 68% of travellers intend to plan trips to improve their mental well-being. Meanwhile, research by Expedia in the same year shows that more than half of US travellers believe that travel should be a healing experience.

The first thing that springs to mind when you think about wellness travel is people travelling to destinations or for experiences focused on wellness, including dedicated retreats or activities centred on health. However, the Global Wellness Institute has calculated that this segment represents only 14% of wellness travel today. Nevertheless, this sector has some exciting new trends, from dedicated retreats to wellness labs and sabbaticals.

There are retreats to suit all tastes, with yoga retreats probably the most familiar. However, did you know there are retreats where all the activities, food and sleep are based on your DNA and/or gut health? You can also combine the calming relaxation of yoga with the vibrancy of dancing in Ibiza's renowned nightclubs. Whether you're looking for silence, digital detox or tantra, to reconnect with spirituality or religion, to recover from divorce, burn-out or addiction, or to boost your immunity or fertility, there's a place and a retreat for you.

Every Destination has something Unique to offer

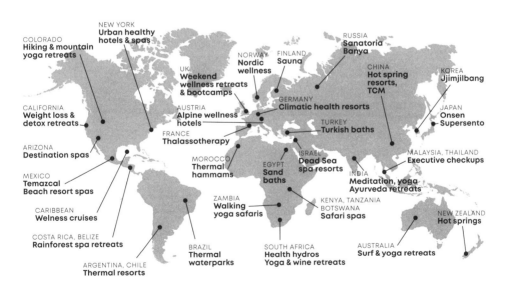

Source: Global Wellness Institute, Globel Wellness Tourism Economy, November 2018

HOLIDAY IN A HEALTH HAVEN

Kokululu *in Hawaii is a retreat where you can recover after a serious diagnosis such as chronic illness, chronic pain or cancer.* **Zulal** *in Qatar is designed to improve* **Strength (have power and resilience)** *quality through better nutrition, physical activity and spa treatments. Meanwhile,* **Foxhill Manor** *in Worcestershire accompanies women through the difficulties of menopause.*

Every visitor to **Playa Viva** *in Mexico is supported by a holistic health coach who designs their personalised well-being programme. Meanwhile, the* **Peninsula hotels** *in New York have a digital wellness portal as part of their Life Lived Best initiative. This portal serves as a health concierge that accompanies the visitor through every step of their wellness journey.*

A more recent trend in the travel industry is the wellness sabbatical (otherwise known as a working holiday), which lasts around one month and aims to strike a balance between the pursuit of wellness and the need to work. This trend responds to the recent surge in burn-out and allows people to benefit from the freedom of being able to work from home (or elsewhere).

COMBINING WORK WITH WELLNESS TRAVEL

TUI Group, *a German travel and tourism company was one of the first big companies focusing on these wellness sabbaticals, supporting visitors with work-related support while staying at their holiday destinations. But there are of course many initiatives focused on* **Clarity (be mindful and focused)** *and* **Joy (have amazing experiences)**. *Here are some noteworthy examples:* **Amble** *offers one-month destination sabbaticals in national parks across the United States.* **Gather** *is a one-month programme for those who want to work remotely in Israel and experience the communal Kibbutz lifestyle.* **Kamalaya**, *in Thailand, schedules treatments,* **Healing (recover and restore)** *and* **Self-development (grow and cultivate oneself)** *therapies to fit around the visitor's work schedule.*

*Employers are also adapting the trend to their needs. Also here, **TUI Group** seemed to be a first mover in launching TUI WORKWIDE. This policy provides employees, who are not permanently tied to one location, the possibility to work from abroad for up to 30 days a year – in a holiday destination, their favourite city or simply a place they particularly like. The tech giant **Salesforce** leased a work-and-wellness centre in California and provided it to employees as a Corporate Retreat called 1440 Multiversity (before the price plummeting stocks made them pull the plug on this centre).*

Beyond the travel experiences based primarily on health and wellness, wellness activities are also becoming more routinely integrated into normal business or leisure trips. This is because every traveller wants to find ways of better taking care of themselves when they travel. It represents 86% of wellness travel spending and goes much further than salads and neck rubs. From airlines to hotels, sectors throughout the travel industry are starting to include specific health-focused solutions in their standard offering.

Wellness travel

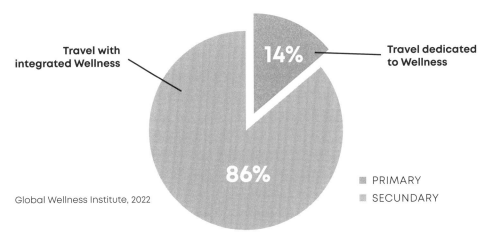

Travel with integrated Wellness

14%

Travel dedicated to Wellness

86%

Global Wellness Institute, 2022

■ PRIMARY
■ SECUNDARY

TRAVELLING IN WELLNESS

Airlines are offering health solutions before and during flights to provide **Calmness (avoid stress and anxiety)**. **Fuji Airways** *provides passengers with healthy dinners before flying so they don't have to choose between sleeping and eating on the plane.* **Etihad Airways** *calls their cabin crew 'wellness ambassadors', who are devoted to providing comfort and relief. The meditation app,* **Headspace**, *collaborates with 10 airlines to offer passengers in-flight exercises to help them relax, sleep or learn a new skill. Meanwhile* **Qantas** *is building well-being zones on their aircraft, complete with on-screen fitness content, healthy snacks and a hydration station.*

Some hotels and resorts are starting to integrate wellness into their activities, buildings and holiday plans as standard. The **Hilton** *in Beverly Hills has a biohacking human upgrade facility next to their pool, presented as a health haven with over 15 customised high-tech experiences designed to power you up with* **Energy (have vitality and stamina)**, *rejuvenate your appearance to be* **Looking good (be attractive)** *and amplify your brain power with* **Creativity (Imagine and invent)**.

Hotels are also getting involved. **Marriott** *hotels in New York trialled ASMR (Autonomous Sensory Meridian Response) videos in their rooms as part of their bedtime stories programme to help guests sleep better. They also provide an app, TakeCare Level30, to encourage people to come together and compete in exercises aimed at improving* **Strength (have power and resilience)**. *At* **The Standard** *in London, guests exchange their mobile phone for a polaroid camera during their stay in an effort for more* **Nothingness (do, feel, see or hear nothing)**. *They can also order an ice bath on their balcony or ask for IV drips and* **Peleton** *bikes to be provided in their room.*

Medical tourism

Travel combined with health and well-being isn't restricted to adding health and self-care to your holidays or business trips. You can also travel for your medical treatment. Medical tourism has long been defined as 'travelling to access affordable healthcare in another country'. However, the main reasons for medical travel today are seeking out the most advanced technology (40%) or better-quality care for necessary procedures (32%) – according to a study conducted by McKinsey and Company more than 15 years ago! Lower cost of care was only mentioned in 15% of cases. It's clear that the aforementioned definition is outdated and that a revision is long overdue.

Medical tourism	Wellness Tourism
Travel to receive treatment for a diagnosed disease, ailment, or condition, or to seek enhancement.	Travel to maintain, manage, or improve health and wellbeing
Motivated by desire for lower cost or care, higher quality care, better access to care, and/or care not availalable at home.	Motivated by desire for healthy living, disease prevention, stress reduction, management of poor lifestyle habits, and/or authentic experiences.
Activities are reactive to illnesses, medically necessary, invasive, and/or overseen by a doctor.	Activities are proactive, voluntary, non-invasive, and non medical in nature.

Source: Global Wellness Institute, Globel Wellness Tourism Economy, November 2018

In recent years, medical tourism has been professionalised and is increasingly recognised as a valuable healthcare option. Some countries and cities, like Canada and Düsseldorf, are boosting their image and economy by focusing on medical tourism. Meanwhile, prestigious medical centres – including Harvard, Boston University, the Cleveland Clinic and Johns Hopkins – are looking to establish hospitals or partnerships with hospitals in other countries. Currently, there are over 930 hospitals and medical departments that are globally accredited by the Joint Commission International (JCI) to guarantee identical (or better) hygiene, safety and reputation.

The main reasons for medical travel today are seeking out the most advanced technology or better-quality care.

A growing number of professional organisations are supporting this growth in medical tourism. For instance, the Medical Tourism Index provides an unbiased assessment of a place's attractiveness for medical travel. It supplies an extensive description of how and why a country or city is an excellent destination for medical tourism. Meanwhile, the *International Medical Travel Journal* celebrates outstanding achievements with its Medical Travel Awards. Hospitals can receive recognition as the 'destination of the year', 'cancer centre of the year' or even for 'best customer experience'.

CASE IN POINT

FACILITATING MEDICAL TOURISM

Travel agencies, whether independent or government-run, are also playing a role in medical tourism. **Singapore** *recently established International Patient Service Centres (IPSCs) that act as medical travel agencies and mediate between international patients and Singapore-based healthcare providers.* **Meditourz** *is a start-up that brings patients from a particular country to foreign hospitals, working with exclusive agreements with certain hospitals.* **Healthtrip** *earns a commission for every patient they bring to their partner hospitals, while* **Qunomedical** *allows patients to find and compare quotes online for various medical procedures in accredited clinics around the world.*

Medical tourism is growing quickly but it's difficult to estimate its current market value. Estimated numbers vary from 11 billion (Fortune Business) to 439 billion (NewtonX). Nevertheless, it's clear that this trend is on the rise and isn't likely to slow in the near future. People are searching for an overall better experience, for both their procedure and their recovery time. Who wouldn't want to do some **Healing (*recover and restore*)** from surgery while having some **Joy (*have amazing experiences*)** in an idyllic setting on an Adriatic island? Isn't that what transformations are all about?

Transformational travel and other business

Travel responds to people's needs, but it really becomes valuable when it meets their Life Aspirations. We can see now how travel brings **Meaning (*live life with a*** *meaningful purpose)* by adding volunteering work to the programme, while working from a holiday destination will bring a feeling of more **Autonomy (live independently and autonomously)** as you're not obliged to *go to* work. But in general, such destinations help to achieve more **Calmness (avoid stress and anxiety)** as well. This is also the case for medical tourism where people – on top of medical care – aspire to more **Joy (have amazing experiences)** and a better **Healing (recover and restore)** than would be the case in a regular healthcare institution. The latter is also the case for many wellness retreats.

Travel is no longer about escaping the day-to-day, but about coming back transformed. Transformations have thus become essential for any kind of travel – from holidays to business trips and medical procedures. It sets the tone for other industries that will also have to focus on how they too can enable those customer transformations. Your business may not be involved in the travel industry, but perhaps you can still find ways of providing that 'just back from holiday' transformational feeling?

If Customer Transformations are about making customers feel better, healthier and happier, there are many parts of our lives that can be instrumental.

This part of the book serves as an inspiration for every company or brand to think beyond customer needs and see opportunities beyond one's own industry. Even if you are not working in construction or real estate, perhaps there is some value you could bring into the homes of people. Although you are not a financial institution, your transformations might help your customers with their financial wellness. Or the sexual transformation could be something you can contribute or take away from.

If Customer Transformations are about making customers feel better, healthier and happier, there are many parts of our lives that can be instrumental. The next chapter will shine a light on transformations already happening in essential parts of our lives, like in our homes, at work or when exercising. The last chapter of this part will highlight where to expect other transformations in about 5 years from now.

CHAPTER 10

FIVE MAJOR TRANSFORMATIONS IN OUR EVERYDAY LIVES

When we are at home or work, don't we always aspire to feel good in that moment? Aren't these the places where we always want to work on ourselves a little? Perhaps we want to come into contact with ourselves, avoid stress, or feel safe in that environment. It is part of our daily lives. We spend the most time in those places. Home and work are often referred to as the first and second places in our lives. It goes without saying that if we want to live life to the fullest, these places greatly influence it; we will be involved in our Life Aspirations because the moments we spend in these places affect our mood, happiness and often even our health.

It goes without saying that if we want to live life to the fullest, the places we spend most time greatly influence it.

In the first subchapter, I detail what is important to us in our home. What are the typical Life Aspirations that mainly concern us at home, and how could companies respond to them? Our home can be quite a transformational space. You may think this may be less important for your business because it is not active in real estate, interior design or house construction, but that is not true. Many products or services will be used at home. But you may even find other connections: How can you help people relax or heal? What role do you play in the relationships that people maintain or receive at home? Our home is the epicentre of our Life Aspirations.

Another epicentre could, of course, be work. After all, we often take home how we feel at work. So, of course, I also want to talk about what's important to us there and how leaders can help with the Life Aspirations of their employees. Maybe you are already satisfied with the corporate well-being plan you have set up. But you will probably discover new ideas if you surf the relevant Life Aspirations I want to explain here. In this section, I also launch an alternative idea to make these Employee Transformations more impactful.

In addition to the places, some activities significantly influence how we feel. In this chapter, I would like to discuss three activities that most people know or 'practice'. I'm talking about exercise, food and sex here. All three have undergone quite a few transformations in recent years. It is no longer about meeting a need, but expectations and Life Aspirations are involved.

In the part on sports, we will see similar trends in women's health. It is about a holistic approach that goes beyond physical aspects. In addition, the medical aspect of sports has also become more attractive. We find the same elements in how we eat today. There are several Life Aspirations that we look for in how we deal with nutrition. And how we view sex has correspondingly changed. Here, too, it goes further than merely meeting a need. Sex and sexuality can be considered a good mirror for today's social and transformational changes. By better understanding the changes these activities have undergone, companies can also get closer to their customers.

This chapter looks at the society in which we all live and do business. In the Transformation Economy, it is important to feel these changes carefully to discover for yourself what your role can be. How can you set up Customer Transformations that make people feel better, healthy or happy?

10.1 Homes are the epicentre of our Life Aspirations

Travel can be transformational, and it is therefore a great case to show how customer transformations generate more value. The places we go to or find ourselves are essential in our transformational journey, for our health & happiness. Business and healthcare organisations must take note of this. IDEO, the world's most famous design firm, said it best: "Every business has a part to play in building better health." And it does not go unnoticed as many physical places are turning into transformational spaces. This chapter helps you the find what you(r business) could mean in these spaces.

CREATING TRANSFORMATIONAL SPACES

Lululemon's *flagship store in Chicago allows customers to do yoga exercises, meditate or drink a healthy juice at the bar. No longer is that store focused on just buying trendy yoga gear, it is about finding your* **Energy (have vitality and stamina)**. *Sex products brand* **Maude**, *then again, had a temporary sex shop that radiated a feeling of* **Safeness (feel safe and protected)** *and* **Kindness (be kind to myself and others)**. *They wanted their customers to cherish sexual wellness when discovering their products in that space. With their serene but (more) colourful interiors, funeral service company* **Exit Here** *wants to transform heavy farewells into moments of* **Calmness (avoid stress and anxiety)** *and* **Gratitude (have appreciation and be thankful).** *The waiting room in the plastic surgery clinic* **Raveh** *in Tel Aviv is elegantly designed for patients not to face each other, creating a space with more* **Safeness (feel safe and protected)** *than your average waiting room, while on the other hand, elderly care homes in Blancafort (Spain) and Drøbak (Norway) are more thoughtfully organised to stimulate* **Relationships (have meaningful connections)** *between its residents.*

Equally, in parts of cities, like **Circus Street** *in Brighton, residential buildings are designed to instigate more* **Relationships (have meaningful connections)** *in the neighbourhood as well. To meet that same Life Aspiration, former train tracks (high lines) in cities of New York, Bangkok and Paris are turned into walking parks. These green spaces serve to find some* **Nothingness (do, feel, see or hear nothing)** *in busy, crowded cities too. Meanwhile* **Singapore** *has publicly announced its plan to transform into a city in nature (don't read this the other way around), as a transformation away from cities taking over nature.*

Saudi Arabia is taking it yet one step further. As part of their **NEOM** *project near the Red Sea, Saudi Arabia commenced the building of* **'the Line'** *in 2023. This mirrored linear city that runs through the reddish, sandy Nafud desert has an unusual shape: it is 170 kilometres long, 200 metres wide, and 500 metres high. It is designed from scratch to provide its 9 million future residents with 100% renewable energy, abundance of nature and the ultimate healthcare experience. In Spain in 2023, global architecture firm* **Gensler** *received the permits to build a new city from the ground up as well. This city, called Elysium, is expected to be the most transformational space in the world.*

The Line, The City of the Future in Saudi Arabia (via neom.com)

But it's fair to say that there is no place more important than home. It's where we spend most of our lives. Our homes see the highs and the lows, they carry us through our everyday lives. Other than having four walls and a roof, heating and hot water, a bed and sanitation, with which they're meeting our basic needs, how can our homes help us fulfil our Life Aspirations? That is a vital question I'll try to answer for you in this chapter.

Our homes are the most important investment in our health.

For most of us, our homes are the most significant financial investment we ever make. But we're now starting to realise they are also one of the most crucial investments in our health. The vast majority (83%) of construction companies in the United States believe that consumers are willing to pay more for a healthy home (US National Association of Home Builders, 2020). Moreover, our health is one of the two crucial factors driving us to invest further in our homes (Shelton Group, 2020), especially as many of us want to continue working from home.

Needless to say, the Transformation Economy is entering our homes. We want the spaces where we spend time to be healthy and transformational. The Life at Home Report (IKEA, 2021) stated it as follows: "We want our homes to be clean, healthy places with well-being built into the design." This sounds rather vague but in fact it can easily be translated into some very specific areas in which many businesses can make a difference and help customers achieve the transformations they're looking for. Whether you're in construction, furniture, household appliances, lighting or gardening, there is sure to be a business opportunity for you. But other consumer companies or healthcare providers might discover as many opportunities. Maybe it suffices to ask ourselves what people aspire to at home. Let's have a look at some important ways in which people are aspirational inside their homes.

Safe spaces

In 2016, research by the UK Green Building Council had already showed that the most important feature of an ideal home is "feeling safe and secure". And then the pandemic hit. It forced us to retreat to the safety of our own homes to protect us from the outside world. Our homes really needed to be our safe havens, the only place we don't have to worry about getting infected or catching a virus. This importance of **Safeness** *(feel safe and protected)* became awkwardly obvious when the inquiries to join Vivos, the largest bunker survival community in the world, grew by 2000% in the first months of the lockdown. But even now that the COVID-19 pandemic has subsided, we are still set on making our homes clean and safe environments.

Vivos, the largest bunker survival community in the world (via Vivos)

Safeness can entail anything from securing locks to child-friendly staircases, from avoiding sharp edges to slow burning materials, and much more. But the indoor air quality is (still) one subject of particular interest to many. Even before indoor air quality was all over the news during the pandemic, 66% of millennials were already worried about it (EcoPulse, 2019). After all, research by Nielsen (2018) confirmed that we spend 90 per cent of our time indoors, while the US Environment Protection Agency (2018) stated that there is 5 times higher levels of Volatile Organic Compounds inside our homes compared to outside. If we want to feel safe indoors, air quality is clearly something to pay attention to.

CLEANING THE AIR

Fifteen years ago, **Renson***, a Belgian company active in ventilation, had already decided to differentiate itself from competition by putting forward customer transformations. Instead of competing on price or performance, it went to market as a solution that makes homes healthier. Their ventilation systems are called a Healthbox and their products are turned into experiences with automatically increased ventilation flows when odours, humidity and high levels of CO_2 are detected. I'm pretty confident this company will remain at the forefront of making indoor quality even better, perhaps by injecting natural micro-organisms into our homes to mimic the air quality of nature as much as possible.*

Many other companies are now trying to obtain that same transformation, albeit through different approaches. **IKEA** *launched air cleaning textiles that are, for example, used in their curtains. Cleaning brand,* **Frosch***, provides products with less chemicals than other brands, avoiding your indoor air to be contaminated. At one point, you could even have Frosch test the indoor quality of your home (to convince you about the necessity to use their products).*

Mindful Hybrid Spaces

We are easily distracted by everything happening around us, not least by the constant push notifications on our digital devices. In fact, we pick up our phones more than 300 times per day. Our attention easily slips away in today's always-on culture. But there is a counter movement of digital detox with smartphones putting out more ways to manage notifications, the relaunch of non-smart phones like the Nokia 3310 or the popularity of noise-cancelling headphones and earplugs. There is an increased desire for not being distracted, to maintain focus and have **Clarity** *(be mindful and focused).*

However, the range of activities taking place in our homes – work, sport, life, enjoyment, hosting, school, recovering, cooking and so on – have increased in recent years. More than ever, we need to find new ways to be in the moment and not get distracted when we do one of these things. How our homes are organised will play an essential role in this. The Life at Home Report (IKEA 2021) indicated that "having control over the space and place where you live" is important for 84% of the respondents. Some may have the means to foresee different rooms per type of activity. According to the National Association of Home Builders (2022), adding a home gym is one of the most popular requests. But less affluent people (i.e. most of us) will have to organise their rooms as hybrid spaces that can serve these different activities. Homeowners are now designing these rooms with multiple purposes in mind and finding furniture and décor pieces that serve multiple functions. After having focused on one particular task (e.g. work), we want to be able to shut it out or hide it away: Foldable desks, compact fitness gear, hidden kitchen. Nobody wants to be constantly reminded or confronted with a mess of all the things you've done or should be doing. It is important that our homes remain a place that provides **Clarity** *(be mindful and focused)* when we are occupied with one activity or when we want to relax – as we will see in the next piece.

A space to relax

We have already elaborated on the mental health crisis and some of the many ways people are trying to cope with it. Meditation apps are one such example. The Global Meditation Apps Market is predicted to grow at an annual rate of 34.90% between now and 2031 (Insight Ace Analytic, 2023). Another great example is the 'mental health playlists' that grew 200% in recent years (Spotify, 2021). I personally loved the White Noise album by Lego, which sounded weird and comforting at the same time.

FINDING WAYS TO RELAX: LEGO

Lego *has created a playlist named 'White Noise' to help people relax. This playlist includes various audio tracks that only use sounds from 10.000 Lego bricks, which many people know and love. People shuffling through the blocks, or the clicking sound when two blocks are put onto one another. These sounds work like white noise, helping you to feel calm and peaceful, because our brain links it with a relaxing activity many of us enjoy(ed). It's great to listen to when you want to sleep or relax, much like you would be when listening to the sounds of nature.*

Lego White Noise on Spotify

The fact that Lego launched a playlist on Spotify to relax people did not entirely come as a surprise. Playing with Lego is known to make people feel better. In fact, research by Lego found that 91 per cent of adults felt noticeably better after playing with the building blocks, while 86 per cent said that it made them feel more relaxed. No wonder, Lego also launched building kits for adults, like Lego flowers or design objects one could display in house.

Relaxing is essential in our lives. But it is our home that – for many – will be the best space to unwind, recharge and become ourselves. It's a place where we crave to 'chillax', have some me-time, or find some **Calmness (avoid stress and anxiety).** Even more than before, our homes have turned into health sanctuaries where we 'actively' find peace and rest. In fact, according to IKEA's Life at Home Report again, 55 per cent claim that relaxing is the most important activity at home. It is essential to achieve a sense of well-being in life. Therefore, your home space should support your head space.

Your home space should support your head space.

There are many ways in which people try to increase the **Calmness (avoid stress and anxiety)** at home. They include colours that instil a sense of reassurance, comfort and internal peace, or interior styles, like Japandi, that create serene, safe environments. We also see nature being integrated into our houses again, with more focus on plants and in-house trees, organic materials and scents, or large windows and nature views. Even with the increased activities happening in our homes, it remains our sanctuary to relax. And it's something people do consciously, for example making sure our home is not a big, disorganised mess of clutter.

Tidying Expert and best-selling author Marie Kondo actually turned tidying up and decluttering your home into an act of self-care. "Life truly begins only after you have put your house in order" is one of her favourite quotes. And it does makes sense of course. Research published in *Personality and Social Psychology Bulletin* (2010), found that cortisol levels rise when rooms feel cluttered and that organised homes reduce feelings of depression. Isn't that what we all long for, a place to find **Clarity (be mindful and focused)**?

And many more Life Aspirations

Our homes provide Safeness, Calmness and Mindfulness, but they also could play a pivotal role in fulfilling many other Life Aspirations as well. Being at home can enhance our daily **Energy (have vitality and stamina)**. Recent in-house innovations are, for example, focused on aligning with our circadian rhythms. Think of natural lighting to invigorate us by day and softer, warmer tones to cue relaxation at night. Smart home technologies further personalise environments, adjusting conditions to energise or calm us as needed. Our houses also function as hubs for nurturing **Relationships *(have meaningful connections)***. We design our living spaces to be comfortable and accommodating, fostering meaningful connections with family and friends. And for those seeking care, the home is increasingly the preferred sanctuary for ageing and **Healing *(recover and restore)***. Designs are adapted to support recovery post-hospitalisation, and for home or elderly care.

HEALING FROM HOME – AGEING AT HOME

CASE IN POINT

Remote care is transforming healthcare by providing accessible and convenient medical services at home, for those in remote locations, with mobility issues, in need of regular care or after being discharged from hospitals. For many years, there has been a trend of decreasing bed capacity in hospitals, discharging patients earlier and managing their health remotely. Our bedrooms are then (temporarily) turned into hospital rooms, rarely to the dismay of patients who prefer to heal – and often heal better – at home. The same can be said for elderly care, as more people long to spend their older years in the cosiness of their own homes, tiny houses, or cohousing places in city centres. Technology is, of course, a big driver of this transformation. Innovations in telehealth and -monitoring allow professional medical care to be effectively delivered at home, adding to the comfort and convenience. Meanwhile our houses, our gardens, cities centres and the delivery of different services at home are being transformed to facilitate this evolution. Research by **Seniorennet** *(2017), a Belgian website dedicated to the elderly, learned that 50 per cent of respondents want to renovate soon to make everyday life easier and to be able to live independently for longer. Senior cohabitations like* **De Living** *in Belgium,* **Arqbag** *in Spain or all projects by Danish* **RealDania***, are steadily growing like mushrooms and the rest of the planet is following suit. Meanwhile older people are put at the centre of urban transformations as the majority are still – and would love to continue – living in the heart of urban communities (and not in rest homes at the outskirts of cities). Plenty of businesses are adapting to this changing reality as well, from supermarket* **Jumbo** *having slow cashiers where the elderly feel at ease and don't have to rush to digital solutions like* **Helpper** *who let the neighbourhood take care of elderly living at home by helping them with errands or even personal care.*

Our homes are the epicentre of many Life Aspirations

Our homes have evolved into multifaceted environments where personal care routines are enjoyed and plenty of Life Aspirations sought after, reflecting the broadening role of our personal spaces. They have become the foundations for not only our daily routines but also our long-term health and well-being. In short, most of our possessions are used (or stored) at home and most activities are (also) done at home. It's very likely that your business also has a facet related to the homes of customers. This means that – technically speaking – almost every business can find opportunities for transformations in homes. It's only a matter of finding how you can help them with the Life Aspirations mentioned in this chapter.

Another place where every business can find opportunities for transformations is at the workplace. It's the place we spend about eight hours per day. Time to tackle that in the next chapter.

10.2 Distinct Life Aspirations for well-being at work

We spend a lot of time at work. It defines a big part of who we are, who we want to become and how we feel day in and day out. I'm sure I'm not the only one to believe it is important for companies or organisations to keep that in mind. Several studies have shown a direct correlation between employee well-being and company performance. How involved a company is in its employees' well-being is a key consideration for workers as well. In fact, according to a survey conducted by Deloitte in 2023, "60 per cent of employees and 75 per cent of the C-suite are seriously considering quitting for a job that would better support their well-being". People want to become the best versions of themselves; they want to be healthy & happy, and they want to fulfil their Life Aspirations, also at work.

Customer Transformations can be called Employee Transformations in this context. Therefore, let me start this chapter by translating Chapter 3 into what it means for Human Resource departments or team leaders all together. Then I'll deep dive into the difference between creating a healthy working environment and making employees healthy and happy. The difference will be made clear by referring to the different relevant Life Aspirations. I'll finish this chapter by reflecting upon some better ways of organising this approach to make employees healthy & happy.

Employee Transformations

In recent years, marketing departments were often surprised by the sudden, new expectations of customers. Or at least, they seemed to be new expectations. Often these were only new in their sector. The same expectations had existed for some time in other sectors and customers had become familiar with them. Needs may differ per sector, but expectations are less sector-specific. These often remain similar across sectors. People like a certain experience, get used to it and start to expect it 'somewhere else'. As a customer, you also want the speed and ease of use of amazon.com's services with your telecom operator, your doctor or the children's school. Companies often do not notice it at first because they monitor their customers too closely in the context of their own sector, which is called their own customer journeys. However, customer expectations often remain the same wherever you are purchasing products or services. This insight formed the basis for writing the first *Healthusiasm* book: Which expectations are so essential that they should not be missed by another sector, such as the healthcare sector, for example.

Work and private life are so intertwined that expectations are no longer distinguished.

This insight is also valuable for HR departments or managers. After all, employees are the same people with the same expectations, just in a different situation. Their needs as employees differ from when they are in a situation as a customer, visitor or, say, patient. However, general expectations will remain quite similar throughout these situations. They do not simply want a product or service that merely meets their needs but want an experience that is equally personal, easy, accessible and relevant to themselves. Failure to meet these expectations creates an experience less likely to engage customers or patients. Customer Experience has, therefore, been the main focus of marketing for almost 10 years. But the same is actually true for Employee Experience.

As a company, you must also be able to guarantee an experience that corresponds with the expectations that the employee has appreciated outside the company or even outside the working environment. In the past, the two worlds were completely separate. This is no longer the case. Work and private life are so intertwined that expectations are no longer distinguished. People are no longer a different person at work than in their private lives. We are the same person, in a different situation. There is, therefore, no reason why we should accept that the experience at work is different from outside it. As an employer, you will know well which needs need to be met. However, it is the expectations associated with meeting these needs that will largely determine the commitment of your employees. For example, expectations regarding the IT Helpdesk can impact overall satisfaction, or a corporate well-being programme can completely miss the mark if it does not meet people's expectations.

These recurring expectations (across sectors or situations) were the important insight and unique approach in my first Healthusiasm book. But in this book, I emphasise another radical change that has occurred in recent years: People want more than ever to become the best version of themselves. This can be explained based on Maslow's Hierarchy of Needs. In our Western society, functional and emotional needs are increasingly being met. This means that people have a greater need to develop themselves or to get the best out of themselves. This is also visible in purchasing behaviour today. The preference for sustainable brands, healthier products, or companies with a social commitment has noticeably increased in recent years. This choice makes the customer feel committed to a good (or at least less bad) goal. People want to do good. These choices can make you feel like a better person, so to speak. This superlative of a good customer experience is the experience that makes people personally feel better. You can literally call it a transformation. These customer transformations ensure the greatest commitment among customers. Because in this way companies help their customers pursue personal values and priorities. What is more engaging than something that makes you personally better, healthier or happier? If you, as a company, want to engage your employees or make them feel better, you can better help them to become the best version of themselves. That's where employee transformations come into play. That's where a company needs to focus on Life Aspirations. But first, let's have a look at the current ambiguity in corporate well-being.

Healthy working environment vs. healthy employees

The professional world is dealing with unprecedented rates of workplace stress and burn-out and corporate well-being has quickly become essential to any company's coping mechanisms, as well as becoming part of their branding in the war for talent. However, I feel corporate well-being is still an orphan trying to find out where it belongs within a company. Even sincere and valuable initiatives tend to lack a longer-term vision and strategy.

Corporate well-being is still an orphan trying to find out where it belongs within a company.

I believe that the main struggle lies in knowing exactly what the aim of corporate well-being should be. Do companies need to create a healthy working environment, or should they focus on improving their employees' overall health? Due to this ambiguity, most health and well-being solutions don't fulfil either objective very well and thus don't achieve their intended goal. In the worst-case scenario, health and well-being initiatives may even come across as indulgent bribes to make up for demanding workplace expectations. In the meantime, hardly anything truly changes within the company.

This is why there is a general consensus that these two objectives need to be separated and approached in a different way. We need to realise that 'creating a healthy working environment' is far more than ergonomic chairs and well-adjusted screens. On the other hand, we also need to understand that supporting employee health and well-being is much more than just team-building activities. They are different aspects that influence different things. But today I still see too many solutions that don't make a clear distinction between the two. Team-building activities are wrongfully expected to create a healthy working environment while ergonomic chairs are expected to make employees happy and healthy. That happens when the means becomes the objective. Similar to a digital strategy (see Chapter 6), it is important to know 'what' you want to achieve before focusing on the means to achieve it. That's where Life Aspirations come in handy again.

Creating healthy working environment

Making employees healthy & happy

Individual well-being initiatives

Corporate well-being initiatives

EMPLOYER
AMBITION IN
WELL-BEING

THIS WILL DEPEND HEAVILY ON **WHO** TAKES THE HEALTH & WELL-BEING DECISIONS

Life Aspirations to the rescue

Life aspirations are the values and priorities that are important in one's life. Deep down we all have such aspirations in life. And we all want to be guided, supported or motivated to achieve these. As we spend a big chunk of our time at work, the workplace contributes to this a lot (or not). I believe that every employee well-being programme should take into consideration the universal Life Aspirations of their employees. Moreover, it should make a clear distinction between the Life Aspirations that contribute to a healthy work environment and the ones that help in feeling healthy & happy.

Safeness is undoubtedly one of the predominant conditions for a healthy working environment. In the next paragraph, I'll elaborate firstly on that Life Aspiration. But others bring value as well. Autonomy, Caring, Kindness, Belonging, Solidarity, Realness and Self-Development are essential pillars for creating a healthy working environment for every employee. On the other hand, Calmness, Clarity, Nothingness, Joy, Strength, Healing and Energy would make every single employee healthier and happier while at work. I'll briefly touch upon these Life Aspirations in the subsequent paragraphs, but I'll pay some additional attention to the meaning we all seek in our jobs as well.

Distinct Life Aspirations

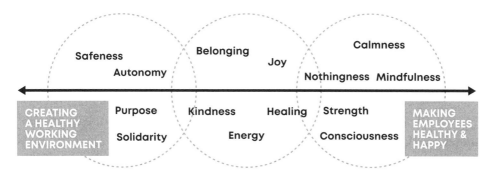

Creating a healthy working environment

First, let's address the elephant in the room: *Individual* employee well-being initiatives won't help create a healthier working environment. Instead, the working environment relies on corporate culture to make people feel psychologically safe. Only an environment that breathes trust and empathy can create this much-needed psychological **Safeness *(feel safe and protected)***. Only then will people dare (!) to talk about and deal with unhealthy work-related situations that are causing stress and burn-out. Whether this is related to their responsibilities, purpose or the social support available within a team, only psychological safety will allow them to talk about it. This is the foundation of any healthy working environment.

> *Psychological safety is the foundation of any healthy working environment.*

Like Safeness, *Corporate* well-being initiatives designed to create a healthy working environment should be directly related to the work itself. Can we provide enough **Autonomy *(live independently and autonomously)*** by, for example, allowing flexible remote work and avoiding micromanagement? Are we displaying **Kindness *(be kind to myself and others)*** and **Realness *(be genuine and true to myself and others)*** in the way we communicate with employees? Are we paying enough attention to inclusivity, diversity and equity so that different groups of people feel **Belong-**

ing *(feel accepted and included)* at work? Do we show **Caring *(be careful with myself and others)*** to our employees by taking into account their personal attributes? Are we facilitating the working environment with, for example, adequate furniture and food options to maintain or optimise their **Energy *(have vitality and stamina)***?

Working with a purpose

Such good working conditions are thus set up as corporate well-being initiatives. These initiatives look *internally*. But as a marketing expert, I would also recommend engaging employees by looking *externally*. The employees' desire for a healthy working environment makes them also wonder about the **Meaning *(live life with a meaningful purpose)*** of their work. What is their contribution to society? What greater purpose is being served? What does this really mean for your customer? Everyone can confirm that meaningful work will engage staff. Fortunately, today there are actually more opportunities than ever to give work meaning. After all, customers want to be helped in their quest to get the best out of themselves (hence the importance of customer transformations). This aspiration to do good can be the perfect marriage between a customer strategy and personnel policy. A marriage that will find an organic raison d'être in the company's purpose.

After all, the purpose of a company is the very reason why a company or brand exists. This is translated into the vision, mission and values of the company. Sometimes these (often generic) values find their way into the objectives of the staff. But it is challenging to make these values come to life in a company. A recent study from MIT Sloan School of Management (2020) showed a gap between official values and the cultural reality on the ground in most organisations. When companies grow, they slowly slip in a process-based and hierarchical system and the company's purpose will disappear into the background. Tasks become smaller and based on efficiency and effectiveness. It distances staff from the original reason for a company's existence. They keep the course and the engine running but often no longer remember why they are doing it.

If you look at the reasons for the existence of almost every company or brand, it usually has its origins in 'doing better'. It is usually described as 'this is what we do for someone else'. Kellogg Company, recently mired in controversy as CEO suggested that the poor eat cereal for dinner, wants to 'Nourish families so they can flourish and prosper'. ING will 'Empower people to stay ahead in their personal and business lives'. Facebook wants to 'bring people closer together'. The raison d'être is somewhat lost today. It has often been replaced by a sales strategy that guarantees continued existence.

CSR programmes should not even be necessary anymore.

Today, the real purpose of a company is often found only in Corporate Social Responsibility programmes. However, these socially committed projects are totally separate from the company's operation. They are sometimes seen by critics as polishing the (sales) image. But in a world where people want to become a better version of themselves, this does not have to be the case. In fact, CSR programmes should not even be necessary anymore. Because customers look for companies that are committed to a clear purpose, and employees want to feel committed to the purpose of their job. It is precisely this commitment to the raison d'être of a company that will ensure the greatest commitment among its employees. It is also a contributor to a healthy working environment as it helps with the employee's Life Aspirations.

Making employees happy & healthy

Corporate well-being solutions that facilitate a healthy working environment typically serve the company's culture. Meanwhile, *individual* health and well-being solutions are designed to help the person *for* the person, not for the culture. Of course, companies can benefit indirectly from healthier employees, simply because a healthy employee is likely to be more productive than an unhealthy one. These *individual* solutions typically focus more on the non-work related Life Aspirations, but contribute to a healthier & happier employee in the end.

MAKING EMPLOYEES HEALTHY AND HAPPY

Workplace Options *is a US-based corporate well-being solutions company with a global presence. They provide corporations with everything from emotional, physical and practical support to solutions for individual and organisational effectiveness. Their focus tends to lean more towards reactive care (eg. Rapid Response Hotline) and creating a healthy working environment, although some wellness or life coaching is also part of their offering. That is somewhat in contrast with companies like* **NOOS** *that represent a corporate well-being ecosystem that focuses on employees' well-being. With wellness vouchers, employees can freely select one of the 3500 available preventative and personalised sessions.*

Providing solutions like psychotherapy consultations, personal coaching or vouchers for wellness centres will bring a return on investment. In fact, studies have proven that every euro invested in well-being can provide a return on investment of at least 271 per cent (Harvard Business Review, 2010). And yet, I still see too many companies trying to redo that same calculation for themselves. Well-being initiatives are thus launched as an itemised checklist of activities that at least x per cent of employees must complete. These checklists are made for the company, not for the employee. As a result, they become simply yet another thing that people are expected to do at work.

These individual well-being initiatives are supposed to be for the employee, serving those who want to be(come) healthier and happier.

It can be tempting to itemise and track health and well-being initiatives as you would a budget, but that's not how humans work. That's not how you go about making people healthier and happier. These *individual* well-being initiatives are supposed to be for the employee, serving those who want to be(come) healthier and happier. However, this corporate focus on itemising and tracking health and well-being initiatives is a massive pitfall for digital health solution providers that choose to work with corporate customers. It means these health solutions need to invest time and money in appealing to the corporate market, and, in the process, they lose sight (to a certain extent) of the actual user. This is the problem with this current corporate well-being market. It might provide a company dashboard that offers insights into the employees, the active participants and the return on investment for the initiative. But all the time and money invested in these tracking efforts would have been much better spent on solutions that actually engage the company's employees more.

It is similar to what was explained in Chapter 6. The traditional healthcare system may prescribe a particular treatment plan, but whether or not patients adhere to these solutions depends more on the solutions themselves than the patients. That is likewise the case in a corporate environment. If the employees don't use corporate well-being initiatives, it simply means the solutions aren't engaging enough for them. And unfortunately, there's a greater risk that solutions in a corporate environment won't be sufficiently engaging because they are (also) made for the company rather than (primarily) for the end user.

An individual approach to health & well-being at work

It's also important to remember that not everyone will become healthier and happier in the same way with these health & well-being initiatives. And yes, it is probable that those who are already healthy might benefit more. Human Resources departments must think about such *individual* health & well-being initiatives in terms of individuality. Everybody has their own interests, personality and pace of going about something. It's important to bear that in mind. I believe companies should treat these health and well-being initiatives more like training and educational initiatives. When a company organises training for its employees, there's no expectation that everyone will benefit from it in the same way, simply an intention to provide them with professional development to boost their skills. The change happens at their own pace, with their own capabilities and driven by their own interest. The return on investment is rarely calculated for training and educational initiatives. And it should be the same when it comes to health and happiness.

We need to make health and well-being solutions more focused on the employee than the company, which is why I could perhaps see value in a somewhat different marketplace – one that will avoid this pitfall as well. This new marketplace could be compared to a company car leasing service. Like other perks of the job, cars are welcomed by most employees because they help them live their lives. Nor does leasing a car come under the umbrella of 'just another task you need to complete at work'. Even in the war for talent, digital health solutions, similar to car-leasing benefits, could provide a welcome corporate advantage for those who just want to be healthy and happy, even when they're not at work.

Company cars aren't made for companies, but for employees. Corporate well-being solutions should be no different.

I'm fairly positive that (digital) health solutions could be managed in a similar way as a car policy: a benefit that clearly helps the end user but one that isn't an obligation. To achieve this, these solutions need to be built for the end user first and foremost. After all, company cars aren't made for companies, but for employees. In this new marketplace for health solutions, employees would select a health or well-being benefit from a catalogue based on their personal interests and desired experience. This type of catalogue of solutions would be administered by the equivalent of a fleet manager, who wouldn't be part of the human resources department or be responsible for building a healthy working environment. Instead, their role would be to negotiate a catalogue and discuss the options and prices with a company providing leasing of digital health solutions. This person would understand the impact or experience of specific digital health solutions for individuals but would never influence the actual solution. They would be a digital health specialist, a careguider (see Chapter 8), helping employees make the most of the benefits offered *by* the company, not directly *for* the company.

No such marketplace currently exists (at least, to my knowledge), but I could imagine a leasing-like market becoming a reality. Existing marketplaces of corporate well-being solutions currently act as aggregators, conveniently bundling various solutions and adding their own service offerings. However, they are currently too heavily focused on creating a positive impact for companies. That's not necessary and is even counterproductive when it comes to the health and well-being of individuals. That's where there's room for change. Because it allows more focus on the Life Aspirations of employees.

It is far from certain whether this marketplace will actually come into existence. What is certain is that business leaders today have the opportunity to be meaningful for their employees by thinking about the Life Aspirations they want/can fulfil. Plenty of opportunities exist to set up a healthy working environment or to make people healthy and happy. Whatever you choose, you can't make a wrong choice. The most important thing is clearly distinguishing between the two objectives and setting the right expectations when selecting. A healthy working environment does not make employees healthy or happy. And vice versa. Setting the right expectations for yourself and communicating them to your employees is essential. The Life Aspirations model can be helpful here.

10.3 The aspirational value of sports

Sports is one of the four pillars of the 'Wellness Bingo' I mentioned in Chapter 5. It's not surprising that sports are part of an aspirational lifestyle. Many Life Aspirations can be achieved through exercise, working out or sports. And this is how it works best: trying to achieve a goal (Life Aspiration) by choosing a means (sport). Not the other way around. No wonder that sports can be a transformational activity for many.

What's more, the fitness industry serves as a textbook example to clarify how Customer Transformations create more value for a business. It is consistently featured in every one of my keynotes because people can easily relate to it. Let me lay out for you how, in recent years, value has been created in the fitness industry.

Value creation in the gym industry

If you want to work out, you can buy a bunch of dumbbells for about 20 euros. With those *products*, you can then exercise your entire life. Working out your whole life with those dumbbells costs 20 euros. However, you could also go to the gym, which already has plenty of exercise equipment. They did it for you. How valuable is that? Well, it's a *service* you are willing to pay 20 euros for per month. In the past decade, however, we saw the rise of spinning and CrossFit classes. They provide an enjoyable *experience* with others that is way more engaging than going to the gym alone. Again, that is why you are willing to pay more – 20 euros per session in this case. It's (again) more expensive than a gym membership, but that is what this experience is worth to you. How much would you be willing to spend if someone personally trains you, informs you and helps you achieve your personal Life Aspirations? Whether you are focused on **Looking good** *(be attractive)*, building **Strength** *(have power and resilience)*, working on your **Self-development** *(grow and cultivate oneself)*, or wanting to have more **Consciousness** *(being aware and comprehending)* about living more healthily… this trainer will help you achieve those specific aspirations. That *transformation* is most valuable to you. That is why you are ready to invest up to 60 euros per session with a personal trainer.

Feeling transformed is what we value most.

We are ready to pay more if it is more valuable to us. And what this example very concretely shows is that we are willing to pay more for services than products and more for experiences than services. But feeling transformed is what we value most. Transformations are what we are ready to invest most in. In you didn't know it already, this is called the Transformation Economy.

Value creation in the gym industry

CUSTOMER VALUE

CUSTOMER DIFFERENTIATION

Sport is all about aspirations

Does this mean that only personal trainers can provide customer transformations? Definitely not. Personal trainers can help their clients with specific Life Aspirations, while gyms or other sports clubs might be better equipped to meet different Life Aspirations. Queer Gyms can help their customers with **Belonging *(feel accepted and included)*.** Women-only centres provide them with **Safeness *(feel safe and protected)*.** At the same time the training programmes are adapted to their menstrual cycle to bring **Healing *(recover and restore)*** or **Energy *(have vitality and stamina)*.** In the first Healthusiasm book, I mentioned that the elderly are the fastest-growing gym population and that weightlifting is a highly popular discipline in that age group. Their gym programmes need to be built differently, focusing on **Strength *(have power and resilience)*** and a lot of **Caring *(be careful with myself and others)*** for their bodies.

WOMEN'S FITNESS

ONE LDN *is a gym in London that offers more than workouts. It›s a community with top-notch facilities and a professional training team. A couple of years ago, they introduced a new body Transformation programme called The Curve, tailored for women to align with their menstrual cycles. The Curve also aims to move away from hyped diets and instead focuses on understanding each woman's body rhythm. This programme empowers women to use natural cycles to achieve their best physical shape and health. It's an innovative and healthy approach to helping women achieve their fitness goals. Another lovely example comes from* **Psycle***, which recognises that over 40 per cent of women feel their menstrual cycle adversely affects their workout routine. They've introduced the 'Psycle with your Cycle' programme to address this. Developed with input from NHS doctor and personal trainer Dr Frankie Jackson-Spence, this programme aims to help women sync their exercise with their menstrual cycle. It utilises hormonal fluctuations to enhance training efficiency, boost results, and lessen PMS symptoms. The programme suggests intensive workouts during the follicular phase when oestrogen levels peak, enhancing muscle building and recovery, and shifts to lighter, bodyweight exercises like barre and yoga during the luteal phase to prevent injury and improve bone density.*

> **The Hogarth Club** *is also a great example of Customer Transformation for women. They even have specific classes for older women. The Hogarth champions the benefits of exercise for women in their later years. Recognising that the ageing process naturally brings a slowdown and the possibility of falls, The Hogarth encourages strength training to enhance muscle function and bone density. The club underscores the significant gains awaiting women who remain active as they age, offering a supportive environment for their journey to better health.*

I love how even entire sports leagues are playing into universal Life Aspirations. The FIFA anti-racism campaigns in which the most famous football players appear is all about **Solidarity *(feel stronger united)*** and creating an atmosphere of **Belonging *(feel accepted and included)***. Wimbledon allowed women to wear colours other than white shorts as it made them feel vulnerable and insecure during their menstruation – a much-needed act to make these women play with **Spontaneity *(act spontaneously)***. The Soccer for Life (SLF) League in Japan, a league for people over 80 years of age, is, then again, a great example of maintaining **Self-worth *(feel good about myself)*** while also working on your **Strength *(have power and resilience)*.** The same can be said of the Senior Women's Basketball Association (SWBA), the National Senior Games or any other of the growing senior sports leagues.

There are too many examples of Life Aspirations already mentioned to be pleasant to read, but there are still more. Bear with me here and let me refer to one more essential sports trend I don't want to keep from you: Going back to nature. I alluded to it in Chapter 2 on planetary transformations. Since we enjoyed nature during the pandemic and with the extra focus on the ecological crisis we face, people want to return to having some **Joy *(have amazing experiences)*** in nature again. There is only one planet, and we are an integral part of that planet. We need to take care of it; we need to enjoy it; and we need to have some **Gratitude *(have appreciation and be thankful)*** for it. After all, we are part of nature. We are nature.

NATURE IS POPULAR

*So many people are climbing **Mount Everest** that they have to queue to reach the top. The litter found at base camps is also evidence of the many groups that pass. While only 12 people ever reached the top in 1963, that number has now been multiplied to 600 climbers annually. For **Kilimanjaro**, that number rises to 30.000 per year. People return to nature to exercise and be challenged. For that reason, we saw the popularity of trail or ultra running grow by more than 2.000 per cent in the past two decades. Also swimming in nature is very attractive today. The **UK outdoor** swimming website has 1 million unique visitors per year (vs. 67 million inhabitants), and cities like London, Paris, Brooklyn and Manhattan are cleaning up their rivers for that reason.*

Part of 'nature's popularity' comes from IceMan Wim Hof, a Dutch motivational speaker focused on cold therapy and breathing techniques. This Wim Hof Method – which has more views on TikTok than the popular Barbie movie – advocates a return to nature to reawaken the inherent vitality within humans. Historically, humans thrived against the challenges posed by nature, with harsh climates and predators ensuring that their physical and mental faculties remained robust and alert. In contrast, modern comforts and technology have led to a sedentary lifestyle, diminishing these natural defences, and making people more prone to illness, stress, and a lack of focus. This method suggests that by embracing the elements in nature from which humanity has retreated, we can restore our body and mind to primaeval **Strength *(have power and resilience)*** and **Clarity *(be mindful and focused)***.

Sport is more than sport

Sport is all about aspirations. So, no wonder many Life Aspirations fit in very well with various disciplines. The previous paragraph had an overabundance of such examples. But what it finally shows is that sport is more than sport, exercise or workouts. Sport is more than performance or competing. It has become an integral part of a more holistic approach to health and happiness. The many different Life Aspirations that can be pursued when doing sport, workouts, or exercises, therefore, provide new opportunities for gyms, sports leagues, clubs and disciplines. It also has brought a breath of fresh air into the sport industry. Many sports apparel brands also see opportunities to move beyond products or services and concentrate on customer transformations.

WORKOUT TRANSFORMATIONS

*It's no coincidence that **Nike** is the highest-valued sports brand in the world. Nike has been very innovative in creating added value for their customers. Sure, they have great running shoes, for example. But Nike also provides services on top of these products. The Nike Run app and the Nike Training Club are freely offered to help you with your workouts or sports. The Nike app, then again, generates a hybrid shopping and community experience. The experience with the SNKRS app is one for sneakerheads who love to hunt exceptional launches. But the Nike experience is even felt when you participate in sport. First, with the Nike+ iPod sensor that had to be put in a running shoe, then with the iconic Nike Fuel band and today with the Nike version of the Apple Watch, the company has put incredible effort into changing the sports experience. But they did not stop there. The more you work out, the more exclusive experiences you can access that could help you feel transformed, from conversations with personal trainers to discounts for online classes, and from testing products to buying exclusive sports gear.*

VALUE CREATION

Products	Services	Experiences	Transformations

The Nike examples shown above are remarkable in themselves. But an announcement made by Nike on June 13th, 2023, was one of the most notable moves in the sports apparel industry. It went largely unnoticed unless you followed them on social media and saw the @niketraining handles switching to @nikewellcollective. This came accompanied by the statement, "Nike wants to connect with what matters most for everybody: a life well lived." Besides echoing 100 per cent what I've been speaking and writing about for the past five years, this statement also indicated a radical shift from being a pure sports brand to a company focused on holistic health. Nike Well Collective *aspires* to help customers across five pillars: movement, mindfulness, nutrition, rest and connection. They will create holistic fitness content, programming and experiences across Nike's entire ecosystem. Nike also engages with a diverse roster of world-class and award-winning academics, researchers, scientists, medical professionals, and academic authors across its holistic fitness pillars, such as Deepak Chopra. As a result, Nike will now turn their retail shops into transformational experiences, focusing more on holistic health instead of shopper experiences.

"Nike wants to connect with what matters most for everybody: a life well lived."

HOLISTIC SPORTS

Although no other sports brand has made such a radical shift towards holistic health as Nike, many other brands were already aiming for less-obvious Life Aspirations in sports. Mostly known for its recovery device Theragun, **Therabody** *makes a case as a mind-body wellness company by adding skincare, eye masks, muscle stimulators and many other products. Their app is focused on breathwork, sleep and relaxation, while their well-being programmes for corporations are about instilling a culture of wellness, mindfulness, and body awareness. Meanwhile, you can enjoy a full wellness experience (read: customer transformation) in their retail concept called 'Reset'. Therabody's mission is to empower everybody to live better, longer and healthier lives.*

CASE IN POINT

*Lululemon is, then again, a clothing brand for yoga and running that calls itself a mindful movement. They help their customers redefine their active lives through textural sensations in clothing, online mindfulness sessions and stores that function as community hubs for classes and workshops. You also might know the Japanese sportswear brand Asics. The name is an acronym for the Latin phrase anima sana in corpore sano, which translates to 'a healthy mind in a healthy body'. With this statement, they want to make people understand that you don't just exercise to look good but to feel good. On World Mental Health Day in 2023, an Asics advertisement showed people 'before' and 'after' workouts. However, there was no physical difference between both pictures. Accompanied by the slogan 'Not all transformations are visible', the advertisement strengthened their sentiment that working out is good for mental health. Asics also wants to avoid bias in sports images created by Artificial intelligence programs, which typically generate people with 'six packs'. Not every sportsperson looks like that. By uploading your workout pictures with #AItraining, they'll make sure that AI tools learn what exercise really looks like. Finally, in another effort to promote the mental benefits of exercise, they launched their Mind Uplifter tool in Retford and during Milan's city run. This face-scanning tool measures people's mood before and after, to capture how exercise affects 10 emotional and intellectual metrics, including calmness, confidence and positivity. Or in Life Aspiration terms: **Calmness (avoid stress and anxiety), Self-worth (feel good about myself)** and **Joy (have amazing experiences)**.*

Medical gyms

Medical gyms are another trend in sports centred on overall health and offering a holistic approach. It is closely linked to some Life Aspirations that are worth mentioning here. This trend finds itself at the intersection of **consciousness (being aware and comprehending)** and **Healing (recover and restore)**. People don't 'just' exercise anymore but want to be aware of and comprehend the impact of their efforts. People also don't 'just' exercise anymore but consider recuperation an integral part of sports. The latter is visible in how sports wearables from Garmin, Whoop or Oura Ring have specific parameters to measure it. The former relates very well to the Personal Science trend explained in Chapter 2.1.

With medical gyms I am not referring to rehabilitation or physical therapy centres in hospitals. These centres provide *services* to help patients recover, for example, after angioplasty or bypass operations. But a medical gym is a *transformation*, an engaging experience that mixes fitness and healthcare like never before. It's not only about fitness and it's not only about healthcare either. Medical gyms actually show how the future of healthcare and fitness is interwoven and centred on helping people lead happier and healthier lives. These motivational gym-like programmes are combined with medical insights and are emerging in both healthcare institutions and fitness clubs.

In the first Healthusiasm book, I described how wellness should be the front door of hospitals to become more relevant and pull people into their ecosystem. This is already happening in the United States. US hospitals consider their role in their community, and medical gyms are essential here. According to the Medical Fitness Association, the number of medical gyms that are part of, or tied to, healthcare institutions has grown to 1.400 worldwide in recent years. Hospitals get involved in these programmes because it has been proven that membership lowers the risk of hospitalisation by 13 per cent and the risk of mortality by 60 per cent.

MORE THAN MEDICAL CLINICS

CASE IN POINT

Hancock Health, *a member of the Mayo Clinic Network, was one of the early innovators. In 2009, they set up the first Hancock Wellness Center to deliver care and improve health outcomes. Hancock Health now has three state-of-the-art medical fitness centres that are helping to transform the region's health.*

In Europe and the Middle East, some clinics are also starting to use their fitness facilities as a place to welcome people other than those accessing medical care. **Clínica Planas**, *a cosmetic surgery clinic in Barcelona, has a medical gym that leads customers through personalised training programmes designed by physical trainers. To address the diabetes epidemic in Kuwait,* **the Dasman Diabetes Institute** *offers scientifically designed fitness programmes for diabetics. But they also welcome people without diabetes to improve their fitness and lifestyle in their medical gym.*

Similar to hospitals, we see health and well-being centres adding a gym-like layer to become medical gyms in themselves. These health centres are beautifully designed, wellness-like environments focused on preventative medicine and holistic health. They are a rather recent phenomenon but continuously evolve and grow with their popularity. Their integrated approach primarily consists of diagnostic procedures, medical consultations, and holistic wellness methods. Today, we see them adding gym-like programmes to this foundation.

CASE IN POINT

ADDING A FITNESS LAYER

Lanserhof at the Arts Club *in London is a fantastic combination of a cutting-edge medical health and wellness facility with an elegant private gym. The interdisciplinary team of medical experts and specialists advise on examinations and will design the ultimate tailor-made plan. They combine the best in research, innovative technology and medical expertise from qualified doctors to empower people to live longer, healthier, and happier lives. Their advanced diagnostic procedures even include an MRI scan that brings an unprecedented, sophisticated health screening level in gyms. Personal trainers closely monitor your progress on your journey to optimal health.*

* **Leadlife** *in Belgium is another health centre that functions as a medical gym. They help their customers to take control of their life by first measuring, scanning and analysing DNA, blood, exercise, body composition, and mobility. This is followed up with a tailor-made improvement plan guided by health specialists. It wouldn't be surprising at all if hospitals soon work together with leadlife to follow up with patients in need of lifestyle medicine or preventative approaches.*

Fitness clubs are also increasingly pivoting towards becoming medical gyms as well. They might have no affiliation with hospitals, but their medically trained staff oversees customers as they work towards their goals. Sometimes, the staff works closely with local primary care physicians, physiotherapists, sleep centres and retail clinics, as they often don't have the time (and expertise) to offer people the support and guidance they need. Medical gyms are the perfect setting to offer these medically sound fitness recommendations.

ADDING A MEDICAL LAYER

Barbell Medicine *is a medical gym in San Diego that integrates modern medicine into strength and conditioning exercises. This fitness centre was founded by Jordan Feigenbaum, an experienced strength coach with a medical degree who wanted to provide high-quality content and products along with medically oriented coaching. Their team is made up of rehabilitation therapists, dieticians and other healthcare professionals who support local power lifters and fitness aficionados.*

CrossFit *turned fitness into an experience and then turned it into a transformation. Near the end of 2021, CrossFit announced the launch of Precision Care, a new boutique gym model that partners CrossFit-trained doctors with CrossFitters. Their focus was on specialised testing and data that you probably wouldn't get from your general practitioner. Doctors and health coaches at CrossFit Precision Care would use detailed genomic profiles, advanced labs for blood testing and biomarkers from wearables to help each person build a personalised care plan to protect and improve their health. However, the advantages of Precision Care were not only felt by CrossFitters themselves. Physicians, who often feel alienated or stressed in their practice, were also able to build a closer relationship with their patients as part of the CrossFit community. Precision Care was later sold to* **Wild Health** *that currently offers it as virtual service via telemedicine.*

In short, sports have become more than sport. More Life Aspirations are pursued when working out or playing sports today. Therefore, sport has become an integral part of holistic health. Business has taken note and many brands are moving towards a more holistic strategy as well. The same happened in hospitals that added a layer of fitness, while fitness and wellness centres moved towards a more holistic approach by adding a medical layer. That is the aspirational value of sports. After all, it is one of the four pillars of health management. Now let's shift to another pillar of health and how it increasingly contributes to our Life Aspirations in ways like never before: Eating.

10.4 Eating good food is a good 'act'

Like the other activities mentioned in this chapter, eating is a common activity. We need food to survive. It's an essential human need. But there is much more to food than nourishing oneself. People want to do good to feel good about themselves? Well, that is even more true for the food choices we make every day. That's why Life Aspirations have become very critical in what, how and when we eat. This provides new opportunities for different companies and brands to bring value through Customer Transformations.

Taking action to do good with food

We can find a lot of **Meaning** *(live life with a meaningful purpose)* in how or what we eat. One-quarter of the world's greenhouse gas emissions are caused by food production, and about half of the world's habitable land is used for agriculture. Agriculture requires 70% of global water withdrawals. In the wake of climate strikes and the often-mentioned positive impact of lockdowns on our planet, it is only natural that people are looking for ways to reduce their ecological food footprint through their food choices as it brings them **Meaning** *(live life with a meaningful purpose)*. New innovative businesses using science and technology to tackle this need are arising. Consider the quick uptake of meat replacement companies like Impossible Foods or the dairy alternatives by, for example, the Not Company. These companies offer the experience of traditional foods and the feeling of non-guilt and pride of doing something 'good' for the planet.

Consumers are, in their activism, being supported by different such (digital) solutions as MyLabel that can indicate per food whether pesticides were used, farmers were rightfully remunerated, or whether the product adds to biodiversity. It quickly offers consumers answers to their environment-friendly questions and makes them feel better about their choices. Being able to 'easily' avoid palm oil feels like a transformation if you want to become that better person.

Consumers increasingly want to have the experience of knowing food comes from 'nearby' as is the case with organic, local food or even vertical farming. Why? It presumably comes from healthier soil, is relevant to the community, and generates less waste. An estimated 1,3 billion tonnes of food, or roughly 30 per cent of global production, is lost or wasted annually, according to the UN Food and Agricultural Organization (FAO, 2014). About 8 per cent of the gas emissions originate from food waste. More people will focus on actual food waste in their quest to be better. Biodiversity is also crucial for ensuring everything from human health to ecological stability. But today, five animal and 12 plant sources comprise three quarters of our food consumption.

ACTIVELY CHOOSING 'GOOD' FOOD

Too Good to Go *is a global community of about 60 million waste warriors and almost 154.000 stores and restaurants, saving more than 139 million meals. Everybody could experience the good feeling of being part of this large community of Waste Warriors. Its success has meanwhile inspired companies like Gander in Ireland or SpareEat in Israel to specifically combat food waste in supermarkets.*

These food waste solutions are making food relevant for consumers. That is a recurring expectation for consumers. Similarly, **Electrolux** *Karma Fridge is transforming its consumers. In Stockholm's central underground station, consumers can buy products via the Karma food waste app and pick up food on their way home. Beyond being a convenient solution, consumers also experience a 'relevant' good deed.*

Launched in mid-2019, furniture retailer **Ikea** *is helping consumers with their 'Future Food Today' cookbook that overhauls all non-sustainable foods in today's fridges and pantries. Ikea seeks to offer answers to consumers on how to make more biodiverse food choices by helping them to discover new delicious flavours or sustainable and healthy ingredients. Also in 2019, Unilever's* **Knorr** *and WWF launched a similar initiative called the 'Future 50 Foods' as a report that promotes a more sustainable global food system. And don't be surprised if newer ingredients become massively popular, like, for example, watermelon seeds, algae or passionflower.*

Activating oneself with 'good' food

The Healthusiasm trend I wrote about in my first book influences more than half of the population. The healthiness of food has, therefore, become one of the biggest reasons to prefer one or the other food or beverage. The function or the benefit a product can bring is one of the most crucial buying decisions today. This is partially driven by the fact that 24 per cent of adults feel they don't get enough diverse nutrients (FMI 2017). But it is also emphasised by increasingly being used to personalise offerings. People are now looking for more functional nutrition beyond their diet preferences. It addresses their personal needs (or at least that of their personae) and *activates* their **Strength *(have power and resilience)*** and **Energy *(have vitality & stamina)***.

Professional sportspeople have been using functional food and beverages for over two decades. As we saw in Chapter 2.1, people have turned to personal science, and these functional foods have moved towards the recreational sportsperson and even the fit consumer to make the market grow by over 25 per cent in recent years. But unsurprisingly, the most significant growth in functional food is expected in the field of 'anti-ageing', growing at a pace of 50 per cent per year (Tastewise, 2019). The 60+ generation today is radically different than before. They start businesses, have the highest divorce rate, and travel widely. But they are also the biggest and the fastest growing customer group for the fitness industry and more likely than any other generation to choose nutritious protein-rich foods. Perennial, for example, *activates* older people's potential, not only because they need it but mostly because they want it.

Chapter 7.2 elaborated on how elemental our mental health has become. With about 13 per cent of the world population suffering from some common mental health illness like anxiety or depression, and with loneliness being recognised as an epidemic, there is an increased focus on mental health from brands across all industries. Mood-elevating foods will become hugely popular in the coming months and years. Also, sleep-inducing, stress-reducing, and beauty-boosting are becoming increasingly popular as activated food functions. As these self-care markets are being set, medical activation is also expected to occur as food becomes increasingly crucial for optimising patients' disease management.

85% of the money spent on healthcare is because of diseases caused by poor diets.

Food as medicine will not sound new to you. About 85 per cent of the money spent on healthcare is because of diseases caused by poor diets. Most people also believe eating healthily can help prevent and treat health problems. More and more people are paying more attention to how their food choices affect their overall health, including their immune system and mental well-being. They choose what to eat to avoid health issues like being overweight, having diabetes, or high cholesterol. This popularity might increase as more people get older and chronic diseases become more common. How we eat can prevent diseases and improve our quality of life and how long we live. The trend of using food as medicine, including meals made for specific medical conditions, personalised nutrition plans, and using food to help mental health, is becoming more popular. This approach to nutrition is becoming more personal, similar to how Spotify recommends music. This idea is not new; the ancient Greek doctor Hippocrates once said, "Let food be thy medicine, and let medicine be thy food" as it will help you with **Healing *(recover and restore).***

RETAIL HEALTH

US-based retail grocer **Kroger** *is doing many great things to grow the 'Food as Medicine' idea. They held the Nourishing Change Summit to talk about how food can help improve health and are working with* **Performance Kitchen** *to make special meals for people with diabetes or heart disease. But these meals are, of course, also meant to be nutritious and improve the overall health of all customers. To accelerate this ambition even more, Kroger is raising $250 million to research how food can be used as medicine and is also starting to be involved in clinical trials. The first study they're focusing on is about gut and immune health, especially looking at signs in the body that might be linked to colorectal cancer. Closer to everyday shopping, they have a feature in their* **Kroger** *app, OptUP, that rates food based on its health qualities, approved by their dietitians, making it easier for people to choose good food when shopping. This system is part of the Kroger app and gives each food item a score from 1 to 100. With a new loyalty card, then again, Kroger motivates people to buy these fresh, healthy foods. But this advice not only happens inside their stores or apps. Customers can also get advice about food and nutrition from home via online telehealth services. These efforts show Kroger's commitment to combining health care with their services, focusing on the vital role of food in keeping us healthy.*

Meanwhile, healthcare institutions and start-ups won't be left behind. At **Geisinger** Hospital's **Fresh Food Pharmacy**, patients with heart disease and diabetes get help from dietitians, attend health workshops, and receive fresh food (within the hospital's retail store) to prevent serious complications. Doctors have seen significant improvements in their patient's health, like better blood sugar levels and blood pressure and healthier lifestyles, including more exercise and home cooking. **Season Health** offers a 'digital food pharmacy' with personalised meal kits for chronic conditions, working with health systems, grocery stores, and food delivery companies. **Uber Health** started a service for delivering physician-prescribed groceries to people who just left the hospital. Meanwhile, **Instacart**'s health division delivers medically tailored meals for health conditions in partnership with **Boston Children's Hospital**. It is also conducting studies with institutions like **Mount Sinai Hospital** and the **Stanford Cancer Institute** to see how these food-as-medicine programmes help different patients, especially those in low-income and food-scarce areas.

Actively fulfilling your specific dietary needs

Food plays a vital role in how we feel each day. Just like with sports, food impacts our overall health. But while activity trackers have taken the market by storm, there aren't many valuable solutions that allow people to track their food consumption easily. MyFitnessPal has almost 50 million registered users. That may seem a lot, but it has lost three quarters of its users in recent years since it requires manual input of the food consumed. People don't *expect* such a cumbersome experience anymore.

Meanwhile, Pinto and Calorie Mama are starting to use deep learning on images to track nutrition successfully. It may sound like an impossible gimmick for now, but it's learning. Imagine the convenience of almost accurately tracking your food intake and nutritional value by simply taking a picture of your meal. But looking into the future, food logging will one day become even more 'ambient': a personalised sensor mounted on a tooth, developed by researchers at the Tufts University School of Engineering, will one day link your diet and health directly.
Why is this so important? It's about **Consciousness** *(being aware and comprehending)*. People want to know about the food they consume and be *actively* guided in

what (not) to eat. It confirms the previously mentioned Personal Science trend and explains the recent popularity of subscriptions for blood tests, genomics and microbiome testing. People desire to know how allergies and (diet-related) diseases impact their food choices. Similar 'real-time' solutions like Nima will soon be taking away the fear of eating, for example, for people with a gluten allergy. Tellspec, a hand-held scanner that offers real-time food-safety testing in the distribution chain, will soon help consumers know even more about how the nutritional value of food matches their needs.

We are *what* we eat. Researchers at Cornell University calculated that we take 226,3 micro-decisions per day related to food alone. Most of these decisions are likely subconscious. But what if they were made consciously? What if people actively measured the impact of everything they eat? Richard Sprague did just that in 2019. Using Abbott's Freestyle Libre, a patch that monitors blood glucose, he learned how his body reacts to food and how he can personalise his daily life. These real-time insights allow us to adjust and have an active impact. They are not expensive and insightful for non-diabetic people as well.

KNOWING WHAT TO EAT

Levels *is a program designed to help you improve your metabolic health, which can lead to a longer and healthier life. It benefits anyone with fitness goals, whether fine-tuning their diet, enhancing their exercise routine, or just aiming to stay healthy. The program focuses on monitoring your glucose levels to personalise your diet and optimise your metabolic health. Levels recognises that everyone's metabolism is unique, and even foods considered 'healthy' might not suit everyone, as they can cause blood sugar spikes and energy crashes. The Levels program includes a continuous glucose monitor (CGM), a small device you can easily attach to your arm to measure your blood glucose in real time. Over 30 days, this data is analysed by the Levels app, which acts like a personal metabolic coach. The app gives insights into how your food and exercise choices affect your metabolism and provides suggestions for improvement.*

CASE IN POINT

Additionally, Levels provides comprehensive monthly reports with real-time data and actionable steps for improving your health, showing your progress, identifying the best and worst foods for you, and offering recommendations for the next steps. This structured approach is aimed at helping you eat the right foods at the right times to enhance your fitness performance, recovery, and mental clarity. While continuous glucose monitoring devices are medical devices, they are now sold by electronic retailers like **Best Buy** *and synced with the* **WeightWatchers** *app to show users how foods impact their personal glucose levels.*

But, we are *when* we eat, as well. Circadian health has been booming these past years by bringing circadian rhythm-supported lighting into homes, restaurants, planes and hospitals. However, we've learned that circadian health is about sleep and how the circadian clock controls our entire brain and body systems as well. It means that the timing of eating will become something we need to measure and manage as well because *when we eat* has profound consequences, as was briefly mentioned in Chapter 7.3. More than just focusing on what to eat, circadian eating stresses the importance of when to eat, promoting regular and consistent meal times in harmony with our body's natural and personal processes. This consistency is believed to benefit mental health, help reduce the risk of obesity, improve heart health and enhance sleep quality.

Even if 'actively' might become one day ambient or embedded in our environment (or tooth), the need to 'actively' track and adapt food choices will only grow. We want to know and act upon <u>what</u> to eat <u>when</u> because people aspire to **Consciousness *(being aware and comprehending)*** to feel better, healthier or happier.

Being in the actual moment when eating

Calm is helping people to be in the moment, for example, when going to bed or before a sports game. Headspace helps you in the same way before going on a date. Screen-time information by Apple and Google motivates people to use their phones less. Meditation and yoga are two of the most significant health trends. Decluttering and other Marie Kondo cleaning approaches are considered acts of self-care. Restaurants like the Lucky Cat in London and Montreal's new Four Seasons restaurant have interiors that are less Instagrammable and more tactile, which allows people to live in the moment. Customers at the Abu Ghosh restaurant in Jerusalem receive a 50 personalise discount when their phone is turned off. Why? Because people have been overwhelmed with notifications and other distractions. They are submerged in information (but hardly ever build knowledge anymore) and never have peace of mind. That's why people need help to be in the moment and enjoy it.

Related to food and eating, people don't only want an experience that facilitates convenience, transparency and personalisation to create peace of mind when choosing food (e.g. meal plans). Neither do they only desire to be supported with Mood Elevating Foods that help their mental health. But they want to have **Clarity (be mindful and focused)** while eating. More and more people realise the importance of food beyond its nutritional value: The social aspect of it, as well as the conscious tickle of all senses. How can we make 'being in the *actual* moment' part of a plan or routine integral to the eating experience?

But also cooking is becoming part of the actual moment of eating. Home-cooking chefs, team building around cooking and family cooking have already created a new form of togetherness in what used to be a lonely, obligatory task. But now co-cooking kitchens, where people can cook together, are turning cooking into an enjoyable, social moment.

Just as restaurants and bars increasingly create transformational spaces that allow people to be in the *actual* moment, a similar initiative is also entering the retail spaces we mentioned before. Driven by our fast-paced society, where people have hardly any time to relax, unwind and be in the moment, many retail spaces offer precisely that: a transformational space to unwind even when not having a ton of time. Coffee bars, gas stations, and airport lounges have served as fast-serving spaces for quite a while. Now, retailers focus even more on zooming out. Until recently, supermarkets were primarily focused on operational convenience. Today, they increasingly turn into health centres delivering health & care. Convenience was once the primary *service*. Today, it's about *transformations*. It will create more personal experiences that make people feel more because they feel more **Calmness (avoid stress and anxiety)**, **Clarity (be mindful and focused)** and sometimes even enjoy some **Nothingness (do, feel, see or hear nothing)**. We feel better in that *actual* moment.

The act of eating good food

Customers want to become better, so they make several conscious decisions every day. In making these (conscious decisions), people strive to impact their health, society or the planet. Also, when it comes to 'the act of eating good food', people make these types of decisions. As reported with the four most crucial active food trends, it is clear that these are indeed all about **acting** to be(come) a better version of oneself. Playing into these trends allows brands and companies in the food and dining sector to help their customers with their Life Aspirations. It helps them to be valuable in this world focused on transformations.

People estimate making an average of 15 food- and beverage-related decisions daily. But the truth is that they make more than 200 such decisions. The opportunity with people making so many more food decisions than we are aware of is that these small decisions are moments where a person can be influenced for their own good. And that is precisely what you can do. As a company or a brand, you can satisfy a customer by making them a better version of themselves; you can help them become aware of making 'good food' decisions. But what about good decisions related to sex or sexuality? That's the subject of the next chapter. And also here, it's valuable to understand the recent trends to take an aspirational position in society, because sex could perhaps be considered the mirror of society.

10.5 Sexual wellness as a mirror of society

We've talked in previous subchapters about the places we spend the most time and some of the activities we do most often, like sports or eating. These are important to understand because the aspirational needs in our lives can be fulfilled in these moments. And as a company, it can be interesting to comprehend these trends to create deeper connections with customers. And that is certainly also the case for the subject discussed here: Sex.

A NOT SO OBVIOUS SEX SHOP

*The importance of this trend really hit me when seeing the pop-up store by **Maude**, a modern sexual wellness brand created to simplify sex with body-safe essentials like vibrators, butt plugs, condoms, lubricants and other personal care goods. Whether or not you've ever been to a store that sells such products, I bet you can picture what it typically looks like. But not in this case. There were no coloured neon lights, no red carpet, no shiny objects or rickety racks. It was a serene place, with lots of plants, wooden furniture and… a large cosy bed with white sheets. The sex toys and care products were designed in earthy tones and were displayed as if they were art objects in a luxurious living room. While I've never been lucky enough to visit the place in New York, it sure seemed to radiate a calm, open atmosphere. And that's when it hit me: "This is how it is supposed to be."*

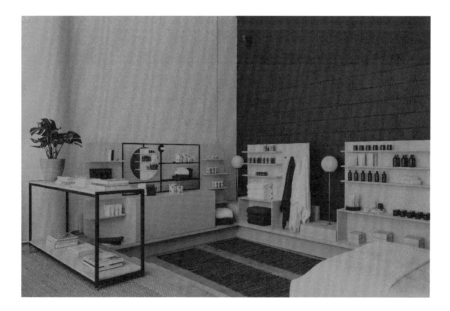

Maude 'Staycation Pop-up' by Collector Design Studio (photo by Nicole Franzen)

Sexuality and sexual satisfaction speaks to all of us, I presume. But the fact of the matter is that it has always been a rather male-focused topic that left at least 50 per cent of the population largely unattended in this conversation. Biology and reproduction taught us this: Sexual pleasure is something that men experience and women offer. Our society has long been entrenched in these patriarchal norms that influence our professional, social, personal and even sexual interactions. Luckily, we are now seeing conversations on sexual experience shifting.

Sex has historically been kept behind closed doors but is now positioned as a fundamental element of a 360° holistic health approach and valued as an equal part of the wellness bingo that contains sleep, exercise, nutrition, mental health (and also financial wellness as we will see later). Pleasure has become an essential pillar of our health, and sex care has turned into a new form of self-care. It's about tuning in to your body, connecting with your mind and learning what you want and what you don't want.

MINDFUL SEXUAL HEALTH

Launched in June 2019, **Ferly** *is an audio guide for mindful sex that merges meditation and masturbation. The app offers podcast-style thought pieces on everything from anatomy to setting sexual boundaries; guided self-pleasure meditation practices; and sensual stories. The* **Pornhub Sexual Wellness Center**, *the (in)famous website's free resource for information about sexuality, health and relationships, raises awareness of the social and cultural taboos associated with sexuality and promotes positive sexual health.*

CASE IN POINT

Only in recent years have we made some significant strides to dismantle these age-old, stereotypical norms of anatomy, reproduction and pleasure. But it's been years in the making and several moments could be considered accelerators that paved the way for true Sexual Wellness.

One of the first stones were laid in 1969 with the introduction of birth control. Contraception made women feel (more) empowered to have control of their own (reproductive) health. It was a remarkable society-wide liberation that laid the foundation for (often) healthier, more positive sexual experiences. It's no wonder that the consecutive decades were characterised by (even more) sexual exploration and liberation. We navigated through the hippy '70s to explore "make love, not war" and to recognise same-sex pleasure more openly. The extravagant '80s continued down this same path as popular culture doubled down on 'sex sells' while sexually transmittable diseases were part of the global conversation. This really was the era in which Sexual Wellness kicked off.

In 2017, the #MeToo movement served as another powerful catalyst. It challenged and often broke down the oppressive social dynamics that forced (primarily) women into accepting harmful and often criminal sexual experiences. This movement provided a voice to trauma caused by unwanted sexual encounters. A voice that was amplified by social media and heard by the entire Western world. The importance of positive sexual experiences took front stage.

As described in Chapter 2.2 on social transformations, social media (and a wide variety of dating apps) accelerated an even broader discourse, also on positive sexual experiences. Individual sexual desires and pleasures were no longer on the 'do-not-discuss' list. Just like 'money' or 'death', sex was brought to the forefront of public discussions. A more receptive culture around sexuality, known as sex positivity, has emerged. It fostered more fluid perceptions of gender, sexuality and even forms of love; it broke down traditional taboos and stigmas surrounding sex; it accepted different sexual orientations and preferences more than ever; it gave more focus to awareness of and empowerment for safer sex; and it simply recognised pleasure as an essential part of health. After all, every individual, regardless of their preference, should be able to explore, express and enjoy their sexuality without any fear of judgment or shame. And that's what this Sexual Wellness trend is all about.

It is apparent that women, and even feminism, have played a pivotal role in this Sexual Wellness trend. And they still do. Just as the contraceptive pill empowered women 60 years ago, FemTech is now empowering women again (ironically enough by revoking the use of hormone-based contraception). In earlier chapters I wrote about how FemTech is changing healthcare for good by focusing on the Life Aspirations of women. But this focus on women's health is also changing sexual experiences for good, bringing new attention and solutions to age-old struggles.

The sex industry is on a swing from a male-centric vice industry to a femme-led wellness industry, and that's a pretty big change. Sex is also becoming a more public part of everyday conversation, which helps shed light on high-quality products within the industry. Our sex lives were permanently stuck at the bottom of our massive, constantly regenerating to-do lists. Now, people are more committed to getting the satisfaction they deserve and it does much more than just improve one's sex life. It can be an avenue for overcoming the many blocks that keep us from putting our well-being first. Sex care is the new self-care.

SEXUAL WELLNESS HAS HEALTH BENEFITS

In a titillating awareness campaign that shows the wriggling feet of a person masturbating, **Helan** *wants to make it clear that Valentine's Day should not just be about love for someone else. "On the contrary, the most important relationship you have in your life is with yourself," says Rik Selleslaghs, CEO of Helan Independent Health Insurance Fund. "We want to make self-love a topic of discussion, in all its facets. An ad that portrays masturbation in a loving way is part of that. We want to show that it is completely okay to like yourself. Mentally. And physically. And without guilt. You deserve as much loving attention as the people around you." And guess what: We spent almost as much on sex toys as on personal hair care.* **PWC** *calculated the size of the global sex toy market at $19bn in 2021 (up from $11bn in 2016) making it roughly as big as the market for hair-styling products.*

As part of a content and commerce initiative extolling the skin health benefits of mas-turbation, **Consonant Skin+Care** *recently launched its Come & Glow Set. Accord-ing to the brand, the pack is "designed to help satisfy your curiosity about all the ways masturbation can become part of your skincare practice". Erika Schwass, MSc, science and wellness manager at Consonant states that masturbation can soothe stressed skin and mind by releasing happy hormones like serotonin and oxytocin, decreasing stress hormones and decreasing your risk of psychocutaneous skin conditions.*

Male sexual wellness and pleasure will also be redefined by a new mindset that is already being welcomed by the younger generations. It is emerging as an in-creasingly popular topic, gaining attention and shedding old taboos. Education on this subject is expanding, but societal pressures around sexual ideals remain. The deep connection between mental health and sexual well-being are now starting to be recognised and the link between anxiety, depression and sexual concerns is more openly discussed. The importance of testosterone levels and male fertility is becoming more acknowledged as well. As we (slowly) move away from the ste-reotypical male norms, in the next 10 years tapping into emotions and practising self-care will be seen as a marker of masculine strength.

DISMANTLING TOXIC MASCULINITY FOR BETTER WELLNESS

@boysinpolish and **The Good Men Project** *are part of a wider movement that rejects toxic notions of masculinity and teaches how to be different. Sexual wellness will be presented as fun and cool with current start-ups such as* **Roman** *offering products for erectile dysfunction, premature ejaculation, hair loss, herpes and more.* **Hims** *is another men's wellness brand addressing hair loss, skincare and sexual wellness in a very approachable, trendy and consumer-appealing way.*

Angel investor Laura Behrens Wu says that investing in SexTech is like investing in any other healthcare market. And guess what? In 2020 sex toys were eligible for inclusion at Customer Electronic Show (CES) for the first time, as they were showcased as part of the show's health and wellness section. Similarly helping the growth of sexual wellness are the hordes of celebrities suddenly moving into the sexual wellness industry – and I'm not just talking about Gwyneth Paltrow's Goop. Lily Allen launched her own sex toy, Cara Delevigne is now the co-owner of a sex tech business, as is Dakota Johnson of the aforementioned Maude. These public, sometimes high-profile, conversations about sex toys play a huge role in helping to reduce some of the stigma still tied to all aspects of the sex industry. "These celebrities are giving a new group of people permission to explore self-pleasure." Also in the media and on streaming platforms, Sexual Wellness becomes mainstream. From *Sex, Love and Goop* on Netflix to Davina McCall's *Sex, Myths and the Menopause* on Channel 4, mainstream channels have extended the invitation for exploration around Sexual Wellness. The Sexual Wellness trend has been evolving from novelty toys to a more holistic approach to sexual health and is turning into a part of our general health and wellness experience. But what does this all mean for your business?

Contributing or taking away

Every company could ask themselves to what extent they are contributing to or taking away from sexual health, sexual pleasure, sexual justice or sexual well-being. I don't expect many companies to see immediate opportunities there, but it might be worthwhile to hold a brief brainstorm. You might be surprised how your company is still stuck in this age-old typical patriarchal dominance. Or you might see ways to amplify the diversity in pleasure or support the possibility of reproduction. In any case, Sexual Wellness and pleasure is important for most (if not all) of your customers. Sexuality represents one of the most profound pleasures in human existence.

SEXUAL WELLNESS FOR HEALTH'S SAKE

During COVID, single Dutch people were allowed to meet with a 'sex buddy' when contact between households was restricted. Irish health authorities gave their citizens recommendations on masturbation. Colombia's health ministry dispensed guidance on the use of sex toys and consensual cybersex. **Sex with Cancer** *is an integrated sex shop, art platform and public campaign devoted to opening up conversation and confidence around its namesake. The initiative aims to provide people with cancer or in recovery, as well as their sexual partners and loved ones, with practical and creative resources centring on pleasure and ownership of their sexual well-being. Disability awareness consultant Andrew Gurza and his sister Heather Morrison are the co-founders of* **Bump'n**, *a start-up creating sex toys for disabled people. With* **Pulso Solo Essential**, *you can even enjoy masturbation without an erection, perfect for those with erectile dysfunction or older people who might just like some extra help.*

Sex (or the lack of it) plays a vital role in people's lives indeed. Next to reproduction, sex also establishes an intimate experience that strengthens relationships, deepens sleep,... and even improves our health and happiness in general. So, when society is focusing on (sexual) wellness, it means that people will typically try to aspire to achieve a range of things that are important in their life.

The Sexual Wellness trend is an intriguing example of the Transformation Economy. In the quest to be(come) healthier and happier, people also have Life Aspirations that can be (or even should be) met during sexual experiences: people want to feel **Safeness (feel safe and protected)** and **Belonging (feel accepted and included)**. Sexual experiences should embrace **Spontaneity (act spontaneously)** and **Realness (be genuine and true to myself and others)**. We might be looking for **Meaning (live life with a meaningful purpose)** in (intimate) connections and we want to feel **Loving (love or be loved)**. It could provide us with **Joy (have amazing experiences)** and **Energy (have vitality and stamina)**. Perhaps sex might make us feel **Looking good (be attractive)** or even boost our **Self-worth (feel good about myself)**. All these 'Life Aspirations' are tightly linked to such a personal and intimate experience that also is a considerably important aspect of our lives. No wonder it is an integral part of feeling better, healthier and happier. But what this part may have made strikingly clear is that this sexual wellness trend is intrinsically linked to bigger societal events. One could even state that it is a mirror of society.

Sexual wellness is a mirror of society. Therefore, it's important to understand what it means for your customers.

Therefore, it is interesting to somehow understand what Sexual Wellness means for your customers. Sexual Wellness can about safer sex, improved sexual pleasure and acceptance of diverse forms of sexuality. This helps in maintaining good sexual health, from the prevention and management of sexually transmittable diseases to fertility management and reproductive choices. Sexual Wellness drives a culture that welcomes inclusivity and diversity (=sexual pleasure) while guaranteeing privacy, safety and legal support when necessary (= sexual justice). Thanks to diverse Sexual Wellness initiatives people should feel comfortable with their own sexuality, sexual experiences, and sexual relationships (=sexual well-being). In short, Sexual Wellness provides us with the ability to have a satisfying, fulfilling (sex) life in a healthy (sexual) relationship with ourselves and others.

Conclusion

As seen in this section, businesses from every sector are already stepping up in different places or activities in life. From our homes to work, from sports to eating and sex, numerous business initiatives help people fulfil their life aspirations and lead a happy and healthy future. Will the future continue down that same path? Let's explore that in the next section, in which I'll dig into future transformations in the automotive sector, the finance world and the music industry.

CHAPTER 11

FUTURES FOR TRANSFORMATIONAL BUSINESS

Today, people want to transform themselves, society and the planet. This stems from the urge or desire that people today have to be the best version of themselves. Do you know this feeling: Looking for ways to do just that little bit better, to learn something, to have an impact somewhere? Today, we are all a little more aspirational than ever. And many also pursue those aspirations. But of course, it is not easy, and it does not stop at things that we can do ourselves. Often, we look to others to help us. They have to do it, and then we feel good about choosing them. That's pretty much what we do when we look to companies and brands to help us with our Life Aspirations. People want to feel better by choosing the companies that help them with those transformations. We call this the Transformation Economy.

In the previous chapter, we explored some sectors that already operate in the Transformation Economy. The food industry might have been the least surprising example. After all, what and how we eat significantly impacts individuals, society and even (the fate of) our world. It's easy to find relevant Life Aspirations that contribute to those transformations. The impact that we can have on our lives at home or at work perhaps also did not come as a surprise. These spaces are fertile ground for transformations because of the time we spend there. The recent evolution in how people view sports might be slightly newer for some. How sexual wellness mirrors societal shifts might be the most surprising, as it is more recent.

Trends in different industries hint towards the Transformation Economy.

However, it won't stop there, of course. All signals in different industries hint towards the Transformation Economy. In these next subchapters, I'll dig deep into some of these signals. How is the automotive industry becoming transformational? Why should finance become the 5th pillar of health? Can music be more than entertainment? You'll discover that even less obvious industries are commencing to invest in Customer Transformations. Even if you are not active in the automotive, finance or music industry, you'll learn that the boundaries of each of these industries are slowly blurring in the Transformation Economy. If you are present in one sector, you might be able to ignite transformations in another. It's a matter of discovering that your customers' Life Aspirations match your company's DNA.

But I'm sure you'll be inspired anyway because the trends in other industries might similarly hit yours.

11.1 From driving to health experience in the car

"We look after our car better than ourselves." This statement has been a mainstay of my keynotes for the past 10 years. I'm not just talking about people who don't smoke in their cars to not damage the interior, despite what the habit is doing to their lungs. I'm talking about how well we maintain our cars. The thing is that we know our cars better than we know our own bodies, simply because there are more sensors both inside and outside the car. We're notified of the slightest (even suspected) defect so that it can be taken care of. This service is, of course, not yet available for our personal health. But soon our cars might be taking care of our health.

On average, we spend more than eight hours a week in our cars. That's 18 days a year and more than 4 years over our lifetime. Besides our workplace and our home, it's the place where we spend the third most time. Much of that time is wasted in traffic jams or looking for a parking space, things that are hardly conducive to feeling happy and healthy. It's thus the perfect environment for Customer Transformations. We all know how exhausted we can feel after a three-hour car journey, so what if we could instead feel healthier when we step out of the car than when we got in?

Car manufacturers focus more on creating health experiences than optimising the driving experience.

Today, we see car manufacturers starting to focus more on creating health experiences, rather than just optimising the driving experience. They are shifting gears from customer experience to customer transformations. And it's shifting the entire automotive industry. So, let's look at how some of these initiatives today are fulfilling particular Life Aspirations. While I consider this one of the vital transformations for the future, I'm not looking to the future with these examples. They already exist today. But I just expect these to accelerate in the coming years.

Steering towards Safeness

Our homes are our safe havens and psychological safety is the most critical aspect of a healthy working environment. It's no different in a place like the car. Passenger **Safeness *(feel safe and protected)*** is non-negotiable requirement in the car industry. Traditionally, cars have been built to protect passengers by being sturdy and robust in case they would crash. Today, cars are using new technologies to avoid these crashes. They correct their trajectory if they deviate across lanes or brake automatically if they detect a pedestrian or object in their path. More recent cars also look 'inside' to avoid crashes. Cars now include technology to identify unsafe driver behaviour and can determine if drivers are intoxicated, overly tired or distracted and take action.

CARS AS FIRST AID STATIONS

Volvo's XC90 has cameras that analyse the driver's reaction speed and eye movement to identify if they are intoxicated or distracted. If they ignore alerts, the car can react by itself. Volvo aim to ensure that nobody is killed or seriously injured in a new Volvo. Some Volvos in the Netherlands are also equipped with an automatic external defibrillator to ensure life-saving first aid can be administered more quickly. This is called the Volvo Lifesaver project. The recruitment of Volvo drivers who want to participate in the pilot has started. Volvo is working together with HartslagNu, the national call system for resuscitation.

CASE IN POINT

Volvo Lifesaver, external defibrillator, picture via Volvo.

MyTaxi *have a similar initiative. Although it was the first app of its kind on the market, MyTaxi quickly lost out to its competitor Uber due to their speed of launch. In response, MyTaxi decided to install defibrillators in their cars and train their drivers in how to administer first aid in case of an accident. They then used a slogan to show that their taxis arrived on the scene faster than ambulances. Interestingly, MyTaxi was acquired in 2014 by the* **Daimler Group***, which also owns* **Mercedes-Benz** *(we'll see what they're doing a bit later in this chapter).*

As mentioned related to the Safeness we want in our homes, we want the air quality to be healthy enough in our cars as well. According to research carried out in China in 2021 by Ipsos, consumers consider a healthy configuration to be even more important than safety when purchasing a car. In fact, 69% of respondents asserted that they would focus mainly on the health experience. In terms of what this means for product features, more than half of respondents expected air conditioning to be equipped with germ filters or for the interior to have antibacterial properties.

THE CAR AS POLLUTION FILTER

This shift plays into the hands of Chinese car brand **Geely**. *Through their healthy car programme, they make vehicles with advanced health technologies. For instance, the pressure inside the vehicle can be automatically adjusted to prevent contaminated or unhealthy substances from entering. If any pollutants do make it in, they are sterilised and deodorised by the intelligent air purification system. As a result, mould, bacteria and viruses don't stand a chance in Geely's cars.*

Mindful driving

Some manufacturers aim to create a feeling of **Calmness *(avoid stress and anxiety)*** and **Clarity *(be mindful and focused)*** in their cars to contribute to their customers' well-being. One of the easiest ways, of course, is by filtering out unwanted or stressful sounds. Buyers often pay extra to have a Bose sound system installed in their cars, because they know the sound quality is unparalleled. However, many don't know that Bose have also been working since 2010 to filter out unwanted engine noise.

THE CAR AS A MINDFUL SANCTUARY

Lincoln, *Ford's luxury car brand, now offer a free subscription to meditation and mindfulness app Calm with the purchase of a Lincoln car. It's a tiny financial gesture – a subscription to* **Calm** *costs $69 per year – for a purchase of around $70,000, but it highlights how important Calmness and Mindfulness is to the drivers of their cars. And that's why Life Aspirations are the new needs to focus on.*

> *Delivering sanctuary is at the core of the Lincoln DNA. Through warm and personally crafted approach to design, they aim to make your experiences effortless and your journey rejuvenating. Offering Calm is simply a continuation of their ongoing commitment to well-being. In fact, Lincoln says its commitment to wellness has never been stronger, because travel can be stressful. Studies have shown that mindfulness has positive benefits before you get behind the wheel: It has been associated with positive behaviours such as improving Mindfulness and Calmness, along with decreased engagement in problematic driving behaviours (phone usage, aggression, stress).*

Some innovations go a step further to optimise health rather than keeping out stressful noise or offering subscriptions to meditation apps. Faurecia, a world leader in automotive technology, launched the wellness seat in 2017. This is a smart seat that uses various sensors to collect and process data on heart rate, respiratory rate and body movement. It also takes into account critical information about the environment, including the time of day, driving conditions and the driver's preferences. This data then allows the seat to identify the position in which the driver would be most comfortable and adapt accordingly. It is the first seat in the industry to detect the mental and physical condition of driver and passengers and to help reduce stress.

While Faurecia mainly use the seat as a sensor, KIA have achieved a similar goal using cameras. In 2019, the manufacturer launched the SEED Car with Real-time Emotion Adaptive Driving technology. These cameras make it really easy to use certain vehicle functions, allowing effortless control with a virtual touch gesture. But even more importantly, the cameras can also detect and decipher a driver's emotional state by examining their facial expression, heart rate and other factors. The system can thus personalise the driver's environment, adjusting lighting, sound, temperature, vibrations and smell. KIA optimised the driving experience but – more importantly – improves the driver's emotional state.

Physical fitness, strength and energy

People are more concerned than ever with their physical fitness, which doesn't align with sitting in a car for long periods of time. Our sedentary lifestyles are often equated with smoking in terms of the harm it causes to our health. So car brands are right to look for ways to mitigate this risk and help drivers in building up **Strength *(have power and resilience)***. Jaguar is such a brand. They have developed a 'morphable' seat that uses a series of components in the seat to constantly create micro-adjustments tricking the brain into thinking the person is walking. Jaguar and Land Rover's Chief Medical Officer (yep, you read that right) Dr Steve Iley states that "the well-being of our customers is at the heart of all our technological research projects". Another car brand that uses R&D to empower people around the world to live better lives is Renault-backed electric vehicle brand BeyonCa. To drive a historic transformation in the automotive industry, BeyonCa, short for BEYONd the Car, employs visionaries from the health industry. Together they want to renew the way we interact with cars and bring unparalleled health technology inside the car.

A few years earlier, in 2017, Mercedes-Benz launched the Fit and Healthy car – the Mercedes-Maybach S-class – as a holistic ecosystem that offers something for all the senses. The car monitors the driver's vital signs and the environment to then run specially designed programmes. These include stimulating exercises, revitalising or relaxing massages, different vibrations and climate control, all tailored to the driver's mood and traffic situation. The car is thus able to reactivate the body and mind, to bring some **Energy *(have vitality & stamina)***.

The Mercedes-Maybach S-Class Fit & Healthy

They've even taken the experience beyond the car with the Mercedes Me app that helps drivers to maintain a healthy and active lifestyle 24 hours a day. Based on the data collected, the app can make personalised recommendations such as specific health training. This initiative falls within Mercedes-Benz's broader health strategy. For years, their website has contained a plethora of health information, often more than the website of the average healthcare provider. The brand is thus clearly on its way to focusing on health experiences beyond the driving experience.

At the same Customer Electronic Show (CES) in 2017, Hyundai presented their own version of this Fit and Healthy car as well. Six years later, Mobis, the automotive parts of the Hyundai group, converted this technology into a cockpit, called the Smart Cabin, that could be integrated in any car. This Smart Cabin contains a 3D camera that captures a driver's posture, an ECG sensor mounted on the steering wheel to measure stress, an ear-set sensor to measure the brainwaves flowing around the ears, and an HVAC sensor to measure the temperature or humidity and carbon dioxide level of the cabin. It then analyses the recorded vital signs, including posture, heart rate, and brainwaves. Hyundai aims to turn vehicles into "moving health check-up centres". In the future, it is also expected that the Smart Cabin will be able to guide a car to an emergency room in case of emergencies, such as cardiac arrest.

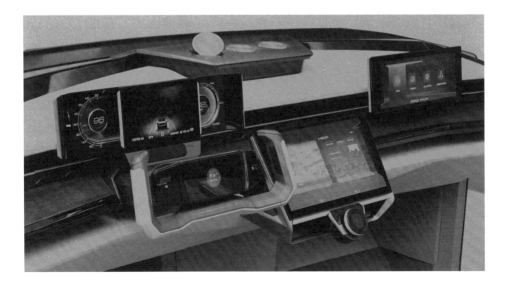

The Smart Cabin by Hyundai Mobis

In 2018, Transparency Market Research predicted that such in-car health tracking will reach a market value of $10 billion by 2030. Seat belts, the steering wheel and anything else the driver touches could easily be turned into a biometric sensor to obtain information about the driver's health, while cameras are indeed able to read our vitals. Within all this tracking, heart-rate monitoring is expected to become an essential feature in cars. Research has shown that around 70% of over-65s are at risk of cardiovascular disease. In the case of a cardiac event, this could result in loss of control of the vehicle and consequently a very dangerous situation. The difficulty in the car, however, lies in collecting reliable data while moving with various noises, vibrations and other disturbances. Nevertheless, we will have **Consciousness *(being aware and comprehending)*** of our health while driving our car. At least, if we are still driving our cars ourselves...

CARS AS HEART MONITORS

*Ford have established an automotive wearables experience lab in Michigan, while **Ferrari** have appointed a new CEO in 2022 with extensive expertise in the sensor industry. **Toyota** are currently testing existing technology used to detect atrial fibrillations and **Mercedes** Trucks are experimenting with integrated ECG (electrocardiography) sensors linked to an online algorithm.*

CASE IN POINT

The Transformational Car Business

All the previously mentioned aspirational innovations point to the growing importance of Transformation Economy in the automotive industry. And so, health experience will become more valuable than driving experience. This also fits perfectly into the future of self-driving cars which will in any case make the 'driving experience' secondary. Cars will become those transformational spaces we mentioned earlier.

A comfortable car to drive does not create enough value today.

SELF-DRIVING ELDERLY TRANSPORT

Self-driving cars will also contribute to increased health and happiness by definition. For instance, they will allow older people to continue living independently in their own homes for longer. Voyage Auto, now renamed **Cruise**, *was one of the first start-ups in the self-driving sector to make this happen. Funded by* **Honda**, *they offered self-driving cars for door-to-door travel within retiree communities in California, thus making the elderly less dependent on carers.*

But other macro trends such as sustainability and urbanisation are playing a huge role in the Transformational Car Business as well. The automotive industry has long realised that creating added value for customers is not just about launching new products or services. A car that is comfortable to drive no longer creates enough value either. People want to travel in an ecological and healthy way that's also quick and efficient. How they do that is less important. It's about mobility. The automative industry is transforming into a more sustainable mobility industry. They are creating Customer Transformations that meet the Life Aspirations of their customers.

Today, cars are still one of the biggest polluters on the planet. And it's well known that the polluted air we breathe negatively affects our health. The transition to electric cars could change this, but there are still significant limitations preventing them from being implemented quickly and on a large scale. Meanwhile, we're seeing more and more ecosystems designed to reinvent mobility. This new mobility-as-a-service model offers customers solutions in their urban environment, whether or not they own a car. We no longer believe we need to have a car. Instead, we want a solution that offers a seamless transport experience through an ecosystem of car-sharing and rental companies, parking assistance, charging stations and location-based mobile lifestyle apps. Such joint ventures aim to make our journeys cleaner, easier and stress-free while also contributing to a healthier way of life. In other words, they are showing some Caring *(be careful with myself and others)* for the planet, society and people by incorporating some Meaning *(live life with a meaningful purpose)* in their future business strategy.

MIXED MOBILITY SOLUTIONS

BMW and **Daimler AG** have already partnered to create such an ecosystem centred around sustainable mobility. I wrote about it in the first Healthusiasm book. Meanwhile, **Ford** wants to take things a step further. The company is currently in the process of converting an area of Michigan into a neighbourhood where they can test the future of mobility. While it will be used to test innovations, the focus is actually on building a neighbourhood where people can lead healthy and happy lives. This unique mobility testing platform prioritises the needs of the community. The district will provide sustainable homes, green open spaces, cycle paths, cafes, shuttles, scooters, shops, supermarkets, childcare and various parking options. The entire district is built on the principle that everything should be within a 15-minute walk (the 15-minute city principle). The focus of this project will be on ecological resilience, flexible mobility solutions and the health and well-being of residents. Meanwhile, **Toyota** is on its own test course to create an entire city that ensures well-being for all. The Woven City, as this project is called, is located near Mount Fuji and will trial several new mobility ideas to unlock human potential. Toyota says it is building the future fabric of life itself with the Woven City.

The Woven City by Toyota

As we have seen in this chapter, the car is a great place to make people feel good or even healthier. Many people own a vehicle and the car is closely linked to our lives and the environment around us. It is woven into the lives of many. With our homes and workplaces, the car may also be where you spend a lot of time. It can, therefore, turn into a transformational space to which your company may also be able to contribute. It is a matter of identifying which relevant Life Aspirations match the DNA of your company. If you don't see any immediate opportunities, I'm sure this chapter has amazed, informed, and inspired you somehow.

The next activity will probably also bring some amazement. We will explore another everyday activity of life: Dealing with money. We are also more aspirational when it comes to money. That does not mean we want more of it, but we deal with it differently. Let's look at some human aspirational trends in finance.

11.2 Finance is the 5th pillar of health

Money. It's something we don't talk about, or at least we didn't used to. It was one of those taboo topics relegated to the bench alongside sex, death and politics. Talking about your income was like discussing your sexual preferences or asking how someone is mourning. It was something you just didn't do. Even in religious books, a love of money is considered the root of all evil.

Money is still a sensitive topic today. It's the subject of much political debate because it is the root of inequality, for example, between people of different genders, minorities and ages. No wonder money is considered one of our society's most significant sources of stress. And recent events haven't helped matters. Money has been tight from the COVID-19 pandemic to the war in Ukraine that caused soaring fuel prices and economic recession. Plenty of articles have been written about the financial hardships people are facing. But on those websites, you can often read about the stock markets reaching new heights, people getting rich with crypto-currencies (well, there used to be a time) and celebrities paying small fortunes for luxury lifestyles.

Money is a critical cause of stress, and can literally make us sick.

As a critical cause of stress, money can literally make us sick. A report by Thriving Wallet found that financial stress can affect an individual's physical health by increasing respiratory symptoms, blood pressure, and tension or causing other physical or mental problems. A study by the UK's Money and Mental Health Institute also found that people with anxiety and depression are three times more likely to be in debt and that this can form a vicious cycle, with the debt making them more anxious and less able to work or formulate another plan to extricate themselves from their financial situation.

Nevertheless, the global movement for Healthusiasm is turning the tide. We're finally talking about those topics that used to be taboo: Sex, menstruation, death and – of course – money.

Financial health, well-being and wellness

Although discussions on health and well-being are now commonplace, there is still confusion about what financial health and financial well-being mean. Let's get that out of the way before tackling Financial Wellness. *Financial health* refers to your personal financial situation and is typically measured in income levels, savings, debt and the ability to meet your financial obligations. In short, it is how much money you have versus what you have to do with it. On the other hand, *financial well-being* is the emotion related to having to meet your current or future financial obligations. It is predicated on how comfortable you feel about your financial outlook and, therefore, impacts your life.

Financial Wellness refers to one's relationship with money. It's about the why rather than the what or the how much.

In this chapter, I'll debate Financial Wellness, a term initially used to indicate financial benefits provided by an employer. But even though this term has been around for a while, it is evolving radically. More and more, Financial Wellness refers to one's relationship with money. It's about the *why* rather than the *what* or the how much.

Financial Wellness 2.0

Financial Wellness was a bit of a buzz phrase in human resources circles and referred to the financial benefits offered by an employer, which has been and continues to be in high demand. According to a 2021 survey by Betterment, over two-thirds of Americans would prefer financial benefits to an extra week of paid holiday. Some examples of this type of financial benefits are group life insurance, disability benefits, financial education or optimised bonuses. These benefits give employees the keys to becoming financially healthy or achieving financial well-being while helping employers by boosting productivity and lowering the costs of medical treatment and absences. This is what is still primarily understood by Financial Wellness. But it has evolved in recent years.

Nowadays, Financial Wellness goes beyond mere financial benefits. It is increasingly considered integral to a person's overall health and well-being. We all understand that our health and well-being are the sum of many parts – our emotional, mental and physical health are vital for us to become the best versions of ourselves. But as we've seen, financial health is a significant cause of stress. So, we need to start considering financial wellness as another aspect of the groundwork to achieve our life aspirations.

Some employers have already started reflecting on how to meet these changing aspirations. Moving beyond the standard financial benefits, some have offered on-demand personal financial guidance and mentorship to help employees with financial literacy. These are significant initiatives because they turn existing services into transformations by focusing on **Consciousness *(being aware and comprehending)***. It can make employees feel better, healthier and happier with their financial situation.

Financial Wellness is no longer only an opportunity for employers as it goes far beyond benefits and monetary compensation.

But for some people, it might need to go one step further than literacy. Learning how to budget is a skill, but it might still cause stress and anxiety. So, how can you help people with **Calmness *(avoid stress and anxiety)*** and **Clarity *(be mindful and*** *focused)*? And that is a question directed to more than just employers. Financial Wellness is no longer only an opportunity for employers as it goes far beyond benefits and monetary compensation. It also impacts banks, insurance companies, health insurance providers, credit lenders, investment and pension funds, charities, mortgage firms, fintech start-ups, governments and even any other type of business.

FINANCIAL CARE IS THE NEW SELF-CARE

Managing finances is crucial to self-care, much like physical health. This trend is particularly pronounced among younger people, who have become more conscious of their financial health due to the pandemic. Many face stress due to limited savings and the challenge of living pay cheque to pay cheque. Effective financial management involves prudent spending and budgeting. Personal finance platforms are gaining popularity, especially among Millennials, who are keenly aware of their debts and value financial education. Platforms like **Credit Karma** *are known to be a 'one-stop-shop for financial wellness', and they are extending their reach with real-world events, such as a one-night experience at Hudson Yards, offering both entertainment and practical financial advice. These events cater to the Millennials' preference for engaging, informative experiences and transparent, solution-oriented services.*

With finance becoming the fifth pillar of good health, it is fair that both are almost organically linked now. Finance contributes to good health and well-being, but striving for good health might also be financially rewarding. At least, more initiatives are moving toward incentivising health and well-being, focusing on **Caring** *(be careful with myself and others)* or optimising **Energy** *(have vitality and stamina)* and **Strength** *(have power and resilience)*. Similarly, value-based models will aim to incentivise patients and healthcare providers to focus on better outcomes, which aligns with the human Life Aspiration for **Healing** *(recover and restore)*.

INCENTIVISING HEALTH AND WELL-BEING

Insurance companies were one of the first movers. **Oscar Health** *paid its members for walking 10.000 steps daily, while many other insurers experimented with lower premiums for active customers focused on CARING. Another insurance company,* **Prudential***, partnered with* **Virgin Pulse***, a digital wellness company, to include financial wellness in overall health management. Meanwhile,* **Alpha Bank** *experimented with higher interest rates for people who work out regularly.* **Discovery Bank***, the world's first behavioural bank, offers financial incentives to help customers develop and maintain healthier lifestyles.*

Paceline*, a company that rewards healthy behaviour with cash back for health and wellness, launched a credit card that customers can use in gyms, supermarkets, pharmacies and athletic leisure shops. And fintech start-ups are also getting involved.* **Happy Money** *evaluates 'happy' and 'sad' spending habits, while* **ZavFit** *helps people spend their money on things that make them healthy and happy.* **Honey Bee** *and* **Origin** *provide financial therapy for all.*

Another Life Aspiration that will be increasingly related to Financial Wellness is **Autonomy *(live independently and autonomously)*** or **Joy *(have amazing experiences)***. People are asking themselves how they can make money doing the things they enjoy. This was one of the questions that sparked the surge in people quitting their jobs, known as the Great Resignation, following the COVID-19 pandemic. They didn't want to work for a company that (only) paid well any more – they wanted to do what they loved and make money from that instead.

Financial Wellness has thus shifted from obtaining financial benefits to achieving Life Aspirations. Financial Wellness is transforming into a more holistic view of finances than having or not having money. It incorporates the idea of managing money effectively, understanding and making sound financial decisions. But it also envisions having a balanced approach to acquiring money and enjoying life. It's a holistic view of financial management that directly impacts one's overall health & happiness.

Financial wellness requires daily routines like other wellness practices.

People start realising that financial wellness requires daily routines like other wellness practices rooted in Life Aspirations. Dedicating time to reviewing your financial wellness, like meditation time, at-home spa sessions and healthy eating can be planned. It's an active process that involves being aware and making choices for a healthier and happier life. This may sound a bit hazy, but it's no different to financial planning for a significant life event like getting married or buying a house. That same approach to financial planning can be applied to optimising your financial wellness in your everyday life.

FINANCIAL WELLNESS PLANNING

You don't need to be in finance to help customers with their financial aspirations. **The Knot** – *a company that plans weddings – not only offers couples an opportunity to discuss mental health and relationship care before, during and after the wedding, but they also provide personal financial training to increase the newlyweds' financial wellness. What better moment than a wedding, a significant life event, to start taking a more holistic approach to your Financial Wellness?*

CASE IN POINT

Perhaps your company, too, should be thinking about what the Financial Wellness trend means for your employees. Maybe you could even think about how Financial Wellness could create customer value. How can you 'financially' support them? But this time, 'financially' does not necessarily or directly mean monetary support. It's about helping them with their Life Aspirations tied to their financial situation. It's about helping them feel better, healthier or happier.

If this sounds like music to your ears, wait until you read about the transformations in music.

11.3 The healing sound of music

My current soundtrack is made up of floaty female voices and minimal beats that sound through my earbuds and get me in the creative mood for writing. This alternative music always works for me but it wouldn't get me in the zone before going on stage or when meditating. And that's precisely what we like about music, isn't it? It can make us sad, happy, calm, excited, motivated... or anything else. Music is also my answer when people ask me why Ibiza has such a relaxing (or happy) vibe. Music transforms the place into something magical. It just has that kind of a profound transformational impact on us.

As babies, we tend to first be introduced to the soothing or even healing power of music through our mothers singing to us. This is a well-known effect of music that has been used throughout the ages. Greek physicians used flutes, Egyptian doctors chanted to heal the sick. Roman, Chinese, Indian and Arabian traditions all contain music therapy in one way or another.

Nowadays, rather than going to our mothers to be soothed, we might dig out an old vinyl record, put the radio on in the background or search for relaxing music on Spotify. The latter is one of an ever-growing selection of streaming services, which offer music as a form of **Calmness** *(avoid stress and anxiety)* for a world suffering from a mental health crisis and noise pollution. Spotify even revealed that the number of streams of mental health playlists tripled in 2020. Music is often an integral part of self-care; it's only natural that the music industry has that sense of Healthusiasm.

Music is often an integral part of self-care.

I've already talked about Lego creating a mindfulness playlist with the sound of their building blocks being shuffled around to sooth and relax listeners with this recognisable, happy sound. It was launched during the stressful period we remember as the COVID-19 Pandemic. Many socially invested artists, like Moby, Arcade Fire, or Nine Inch Nails, released a dedicated album to instil a sense of **Calmness** *(avoid stress and anxiety)* as well. Other artists like Pearl Jam's Eddie Vedder gave heart-warming concerts live on Instagram or YouTube.

But this focus on **Calmness** *(avoid stress and anxiety)* wasn't just a one-time event. Music was already shifting from purely enjoyment to relaxation. Look at how several festivals like Tomorrowland in Belgium, Wonderfruit Festival in Thailand or Kala Festival in Albania now provide wellness zones, yoga breaks and meditative sound baths as part of their line-up. Even conferences like the Global Wellness Summit or ChannelCon have integrated sound baths as a side track in their event where people can relax. Meanwhile meditation apps have become record labels, reaching up to 200 million streams of their exclusive songs annually.

I've always claimed that music is my pacemaker, but honestly, it's mostly an excuse for my emotional absence at parties with awful music. Terrible music just switches me off. That's why retailers often pay particular attention to play music that sets the right mood for shopping. Mood is also something Spotify now intends to work with. Thanks to algorithms that use my speech and background noise, it will provide the right music for one's mood, to become the soundtrack of your life. Today, artificial intelligence and smart algorithms can create music based on biofeedback. In other words, they use biometric and contextual data to generate constantly changing transformational compositions that enhance our health and happiness. This 'generative' music comes from within you with the intention to transform you.

MUSIC AS A PACEMAKER

Musical start-up **Weav** *seamlessly adapts beats per minute to the speed of someone's activity, whether they're running, skiing or having sex, aiming to boost endorphins, decrease fatigue and raise* **Energy** *(have vitality and stamina).*

Berlin-based start-up **Endel** *partnered with* **Mercedes-Benz** *to create an adaptive sound environment that serves the driver with* **Calmness** *(avoid stress and anxiety)* *and* **Clarity** *(be mindful and focused) behind the wheel. Car manufacturer* **Nissan,** *then again, wrote 'lullabies' for babies as their electric vehicle no longer made that soothing engine noise to put babies to sleep. You can find similar experiences in aeroplanes, retail stores, hotels, airports and hospitals to create those transformational spaces we discussed in the previous chapter.*

Although it may not be the first place that comes to mind, music has always been present in hospitals. The National Association for Music in Hospitals, Music in Hospitals & Care, and the Council for Music in Hospitals are associations that were founded in the early twentieth century. Even today, music is a mood booster in hospitals, with many artists visiting to cheer up patients. Medicinal music is being increasingly prescribed as well for its **Healing *(recover and restore)*** power.

MUSIC THERAPY

*Hospitals in the UK are trialling **MediMusic**, a form of 'musical drip' that can help fight pain and stress. The **NHS** is also researching whether an algorithm can curate a playlist to reduce suffering in Alzheimer's patients, intending to test it on recovering critical care patients, needle-phobic children, outpatients coping with chronic pain and patients with pre-operative stress. Soon, hospital rooms will be transformed into immersive audio spaces to create restorative and calming audio-sensory therapy for hospitalised patients.*

*The **Henry Mayo Newhall Hospital** in California is working with students from the California Institute of the Arts and audio solution **Spatial** to create restorative and calming audio-sensory experiences for hospital patients. Spatial is an audio-experience startup that empowers anyone to create audio experiences that transform the places we work, play and stay. (Transformational spaces anyone?) Sound is more than just what you hear, it's what you feel. Spatial can change the emotion of a room – and enhance everything about your space – by immersing your guests in a completely new reality. User-friendly software and apps enable creators to make living, breathing sonic worlds. Powerful audio tools drive immersive, three-dimensional sound that makes spaces feel bigger, or more intimate, or more alive... anywhere you can imagine! Spatial's soundscape spaces in the hospital are meant to promote calmness and tranquillity to those working and being treated there. The soundscape rooms will block out bustling noise from the hallways and replace them with natural sound to boost **Healing (recover and restore)**. One 'tranquillity room' is designed for families who are supporting a loved one, particularly at their end-of-life phase, with audio to help them connect through an integrative healing experience. Another 'resilience room' is meant to provide a restorative, collective environment for health providers who have recently lost a patient. Both concepts are constructed to ease the physical effects of emotional strain from end-of-life care.*

Music therapy is nothing new. Research started in the late 1800s but really gained traction with the creation of the World Federation of Music Therapy in 1985 and the International Association for Music and Medicine in 2010. It's now recognised as a profession in several countries. Pharmaceutical companies are also exploring this field as an option to support patients who are prone to avoiding or postponing taking their medicine.

MUSIC AS THERAPY

CASE IN POINT

*The **Thai government** uses music and karaoke to prevent early-onset Alzheimer's, while **Moby** wrote an entire album as therapy for anxiety, which was launched with the Institute for Music and Neurologic Function.*

***Sanofi** launched a playlist on **Spotify** to alleviate headaches. **Reckitt Benckiser**, the manufacturer of **Nurofen**, recommends certain music to help relieve pain.*

*I also really like how start-up **Sick Beats** is taking the impact of music even further by designing a vest that produces deep bass frequencies (40 Hz). What's so unique about it? The sound waves produced by the vest loosen mucus as effectively as traditional therapy. It was created with cystic fibrosis patients and is now undergoing clinical studies for future FDA approval.*

There is clearly more to music than meets the ear. You can feel music. Music makes you feel different. It can even make you (feel) healthier or happier. It transforms people. Beyond **Joy (have amazing experiences)**, music brings **Calmness (avoid stress and anxiety)**, contributes to **Clarity (be mindful and focused)**, boosts **Energy (have vitality and stamina)**, and helps with **Healing (recover and restore)**. It's intentional and even medicinal. But the question is: are you intentional about the music in your business? It may not seem applicable immediately but the Life Aspirations behind music are sure to get you off on the right foot.

Conclusion

In the Western world, our basic needs are increasingly met. People today have deeper needs closely linked to living a healthy and happy life because this is often not that easy today. We live in a world that is simultaneously experiencing a triple crisis (or are there more?), but we also live in a world where people feel empowered to influence these crises. This influence can be direct by taking specific initiatives yourself. It can also happen indirectly by motivating others to change or choosing those who stand for change. These changes are, of course, the transformations we talked about in Part One. We seek these transformations more than ever because they help fulfil our deepest human needs, the dreams and desires linked to our priorities and values. In Part Two, I coined this our Life Aspirations.

What is essential in our lives can, of course, be fulfilled at any time or in any place. It's not something that happens all at once, but it happens just about everywhere. This means that every company, from any sector or active in any part of customers' lives, can play a particular role in these Life Aspirations. What you offer to your customers must take this into account. Solving a basic need with a product or service is no longer enough. It is no longer sufficient to meet expectations with a pleasant experience. Today's customers expect you to help them achieve their Life Aspirations. Needs, expectations and Life Aspirations are the most essential ingredients of a tasty customer offer: the Customer Transformations.

Needs, expectations and Life Aspirations are the most essential ingredients of a tasty customer offer.

In Part Four, I wanted to convince you of this by bringing trends from many logical and perhaps less obvious sectors. Obviously, the places we find ourselves most often significantly impact leading a healthy and happy life. Different Life Aspirations can be fulfilled there by many other companies. How we look at and interact with our home and work has changed enormously due to this increasing focus on transformations. The same can be said of activities we do frequently, such as sports, eating and sex. We have also seen an evolution there. We no longer do it because we need it, but because it also serves a more profound need. Finally, I have highlighted several other, perhaps less obvious, sectors where Customer Transformations will also become essential very soon. The role of the car and mobility maybe brought a different view on how the automotive industry tries to be competitive in the Transformation Economy. Finance is about more than having money, while music offers more than entertainment.

Of course, it is not the purpose or even feasible to be exhaustive here. If the sector you operate in has not been mentioned in this piece, I trust the various examples still inspired you. Perhaps you have found a connection with your business, allowing you to be relevant to your customers at those places or times. Maybe the examples were enough to show that Customer Transformations are also valuable in your sector. There are many more examples of sectors, spaces and activities that play into our Life Aspirations. In fact, we haven't even touched upon the many objects near us in the different parts of our daily lives. Our watches, phones, jewellery, glasses, clothing and even shoes can all contribute to pursuing our Life Aspirations. Smartwatches bring us **Consciousness *(being aware and comprehending)*** and **Self-development *(grow and cultivate oneself)***. Clothing helps with **Looking good *(be attractive)*** or provides us with **Safeness *(feel safe and protected)*** and **Healing *(recover and restore)***. So does jewellery that gives you insights into your own recovery. Shoes ignite **Strength *(have power and resilience)*** while augmented reality glasses could spark **Creativity *(Imagine and invent)***. And there are many more examples of how objects nurture our Life Aspirations. But these objects are very technologically driven, often even standing on their own as a technology. Instead of adding yet another chapter on all these objects, I'd rather dedicate the entirety of Part Five to Transformational Technologies. Because just like objects, people wish that technologies will bring transformations. So, it fits to look at it from a broader angle as well. Let me explain to you how that works in the next chapter.

PART 5

TRANSFORMATIONAL TECHNOLOGIES

CHAPTER 12

PEOPLE WISH FOR TRANSFORMATIONS WITH TECHNOLOGY

We anticipate a lot from technology. I don't have to explain how the printing press, electricity, internet, and mobile phones transformed our world, democratised information, or made a better life possible for many. That's also why many speakers hail the arrival of new technologies as if it were a new religion. That's what the Gartner hype cycle is all about. People get excited about how it could transform their lives.

But as we have learned over the years, not all technologies are always experienced positively by everyone. There could be quite some downsides as well. The internet is considered to cause an overload of (mis)information. Many privacy concerns exist as some major players hold our identity and personal data. Meanwhile, mobile phones could add stress, addictive behaviour and impaired attention span. Not everything is all sunshine and roses. Some dangers are lurking, making the anticipation of new technology even more demanding.

Life Aspirations help to orient the intent of technology towards the values or priorities of people.

That is where the universal Life Aspirations come in. They help to orient the intent of technology towards the values or priorities of people. Life Aspirations don't change over time, but new technology offers a new way of meeting those. People always aspired to **Relationships (have meaningful connections)** or **Joy (have amazing experiences)**. Only now, with social media, has it become more accessible. Not surprisingly, Facebook's mission is to connect people, while LinkedIn wants to connect the world's professionals. YouTube wants to give everyone a voice; with Snapchat, we have fun, and TikTok intends to bring joy. But while we connect with many people, many don't feel connected anymore. It is said to have caused loneliness as one of the world's most significant health crises. Social media might give everyone a voice, but it induces more polarisation than ever seen. Perhaps it could bring joy, but addiction and social isolation are often the result. Even though these technologies play into universal Life Aspirations, the outcome might be the exact opposite or even problematic. This requires an even more intensified focus on Life Aspirations when using technology in business.

Problematic social media use

Social media is a big part of (young) people's lives, and its impact on health and mental well-being is increasingly scrutinised. Studies have linked social media use to various issues, including obesity, diabetes, social isolation, loneliness, and mental health problems like anxiety, depression, and stress. It can also contribute to sleep deficits, poor dietary habits, cognitive impairment, and symptoms akin to ADHD. Moreover, there's an association with substance-related and behavioural addictions, including gambling and even addiction to social media itself.

Jean Twenge, a psychology professor at San Diego State University, and Jonathan Haidt, a social psychologist at New York University, continuously update a freely accessible Google doc (at the time of writing: 340 pages long) with references to all published articles about social media and mental health. Meanwhile, according to the *Financial Times*, nearly 150 product liability lawsuits are filed in the U.S. against social media platforms. Some places, like Utah and Seattle, are even making laws to limit how much young people can use social media. Also, in Europe, lawmakers are increasing the pressure with the Digital Services Act (DSA) and Youth Protection Laws.

Paediatrician Michael Rich, an associate professor at Harvard Medical, views unhealthy internet use not as an addiction but as a disorder. He coins it Problematic Interactive Media Use (PIMU). This disorder encompasses symptoms where kids use video gaming, social media, pornography, and information-binging to soothe, comfort, or distract themselves uncontrollably. This is considered to be problematic if it leads to academic failure, social withdrawal, behavioural issues, family conflict, and physical or mental health problems.

Michael Rich established the Digital Wellness Lab at Boston Children's Hospital and Harvard Medical School to address these concerns. The lab engages stakeholders from academia, healthcare, and the corporate industry to understand media and technology's positive and negative effects on young people. It aims to balance the concerns of parents, doctors, and lawmakers without vilifying tech companies.

Interestingly, this lab gets support from social medical platforms like Twitch, Roblox, Snap, Discord, Meta and TikTok. Dr Rich says the focus should be on how young people behave with technology, not the technology itself. He notes that many kids use smartphones and social media without any problems. The aim is to foster a more nuanced understanding of how young people interact with digital media and the consequent effects on their health and well-being.

However, social media platforms make a profit from providing a shortcut to **Relationships *(have meaningful connections)***, while ultimately, people never felt so lonely. Porn websites and dating apps make a profit as a shortcut for **Loving *(love or be loved)*** or **Joy *(have amazing experiences)*** while more people are single, and society never had that little sex. Miracle weight loss apps and jabs promise a shortcut to losing weight, while the average weight has never been higher. It may seem odd to include parties that profit from all these shortcuts in finding a solution. But how much could they do by themselves? Instagram may have added more parental control tools, and TikTok or Pornhub have a wellness hub, but more impact will be realised by working together with the broader ecosystem, of course. Moreover, I believe that bad companies should be able to correct their wrongs to do better. In fact, they must meet people's Life Aspirations in a better way to survive in the future.

RIGHT YOUR WRONG

*Tobacco giant **Philip Morris** plans to source more than half of its revenue from smokeless products by 2025. But their 'beyond nicotine' strategy is even more radical than this. Philip Morris is actively moving into the health space: in 2022, the company acquired the Danish company **Fertin Pharma**, which produces pharmaceuticals and nutraceuticals with innovative oral and intra-oral delivery systems. Merely some months later, the company purchased **OtiTopic** which develops inhalable treatment for acute myocardial infarction and has taken a significant stake in **Vectura**, which specialises in developing inhaled medications. These acquisitions are part of PMI's strategic plan to leverage its expertise, scientific know-how, and capabilities in inhalation to grow a pipeline of inhaled therapeutics and respiratory drug delivery Beyond Nicotine. With this strategy, Philip Morris plans to build upon – what they call – world-class expertise in the research, development, and commercialisation of aerosolisation and inhalable devices to help speed the delivery of this exciting product to market.*

CASE IN POINT

The company recently hired Dr Jorge Insuasty, Sanofi's former Global Franchise Head of Immunology, Oncology, and Neurology, as its Chief Life Science Officer. He's a seasoned pharma executive who has worked for companies like Sanofi Genzyme, Novartis, and Bristol Myers Squibb. In official statements, he claimed there is no better time to plan for the future than the present. "PMI has much to offer in these new areas, and it would be inconsistent with their scientific mission not to use our knowledge and embark on new areas."

It sure feels bitterly ironic if an arsonist is selling fire damage insurance. That is why **Asthma U.K.**, *The* **British Lung Foundation**, *and about 35 other health and charitable organisations have shared their thoughts publicly. But why shouldn't tobacco companies be encouraged to reinvent themselves? How different is this from encouraging oil companies to adopt renewable energy? There is a bitter taste to companies that bring medication to people they have made sick with their products. And as long as cigarettes are the primary source of revenue for Philip Morris, the company won't have much eagerness to let go of those (unless they sell that part of the business). It also won't offer the company much credit as long as cigarettes are being sold under the same corporate brand. But as someone who is Healthusiastic about building a healthier future, I can only applaud this type of business shift. Ever since the early eighties, people have been smoking less every year. If companies selling cigarettes are shifting gears, it can only bring a healthier world faster. When I wrote the first Healthusiasm book in 2017, I envisioned that all companies would eventually focus on health. I could not even dream that tobacco giants would do the same less than four years later.*

Perhaps social media platforms are also best positioned to right their wrongs. Look at how Pinterest joined forces with the National Eating Disorders Association to ban all ads with language or imagery related to weight loss – a meaningful step to prioritise mental health over ad revenue. One year later, they are seeing a positive response from users, demonstrating the true impact such a policy can have on online behaviours and perceptions. Searches focused on healthy habits and body positivity are rising as Pinners reshape conversations around **Self-worth (*feel good about myself*)**. Meanwhile, YouTube focuses on health **Consciousness (*being aware and comprehending*)** by guiding users to actual healthcare professionals who empower users to live healthier lives and make informed decisions. The company introduced a label indicating that the info on the channel is from a certified health-care professional. They also collaborate with public healthcare organisations and providers to offer users easily understandable video content. In partnership with the World Health Summit, a YouTube health accelerator programme trains these healthcare professionals during a 10-week boot camp to optimise their channels and content.

Of course, it is better to foresee the potential downsides of new technologies up-front. And that's where an increased focus on Life Aspirations comes into play again. Sure, people wish for transformations with technology. But let's ensure its shortcut is also transformational in the long run.

In the following chapters, I'll examine how newer technologies could help people's Life Aspirations. As with previous parts and chapters, it is neither my intention nor feasible to be exhaustive here. Many innovations are launched every year. I primarily want to focus on perhaps the two most discussed since 2020: Artificial Intelligence and the Metaverse. I won't go too deep into explaining the technology behind it, but instead, focus on how they contribute to our Life Aspirations to spawn impactful Transformations.

CHAPTER 13

TWO MAJOR TRANSFORMATIONAL TECHNOLOGIES

Several usual suspects may come to mind when thinking of the most promising technologies today. Artificial Intelligence is the latest hype that generates a ton of expectations, while the Metaverse and cryptocurrencies are facing some dissolutions now. Augmented and Virtual Reality are being revived with the launch of some promising new technologies. Meanwhile, the world is being wired with 5G technology to connect all things (IoT), and robots are entering alongside autonomous cars.

I could write an entire book on emerging technologies and how they could be transformational. But compared to industries mentioned in previous chapters, technologies evolve faster. A book might not be the best medium to reflect on these technologies. But if you want to be updated regularly on these technologies, I recommend you subscribe to my newsletter at www.christophejauquet.com in which I reflect upon the transformational power of health, business and technology.

How can technologies contribute to what is essential in our lives - not the practical but the aspirational elements?

In this book segment, I will focus on how two specific technologies can become transformational for people. First, Artificial Intelligence will be approached from a longer-term perspective, and then I'll approach the Metaverse from a practical point of view. The purpose is not to elaborate on the technicalities but rather the human aspects of these innovations. How can they contribute to making people feel better, healthier and happier? What do we expect from these technologies? Not from a practical point of view but from an aspirational point of view. What do they contribute to what is essential in our lives? Or how could they potentially take away from what is vital in our lives? These are critical questions that I cannot answer in this book. But I can lay down a framework for you to use as you embark on new technologies. And, of course, The Life Aspiration Model could again be the model for you to apply in that exercise. It will help you reflect on what people aspire to because *how* technology allows the pursuit of these aspirations (or not) will be one of the critical questions for the years to come. In the following chapters, I'll try to do that mental exercise together with you.

13.1 The overabundance of Intelligence

Innovations can make almost unimaginable, incomprehensible things become real. And when they turn out to be real, they become transformational for individuals, society, and the planet as a whole. Throughout history, these breakthroughs have reshaped how we live and think. Look how humankind has produced innovations (printing press, internet, iPhone) that democratised knowledge, changed society's dynamics and impacted planet resources. Now, Generative Artificial Intelligence is poised to go one step further, giving every individual access to not only 'knowledge' but, more importantly, 'expertise' and 'creativity' as well. This latest transformational innovation is most known via the immensely popular ChatGPT, a large language model (LLM) designed for conversational interactions and trained as a tool that *generates* human-like text or images based on the input it is trained on. Popular like no other innovation before, its user base reached 100 million in just 60 days of launch. GPT, the acronym for Generative Pre-trained **Transformer**, is a remarkable, impactful step of this transformational technology.

While finishing this book, this Generative Artificial Intelligence was at its peak in the Gartner Hype Cycle. This phase is super exciting as many new applications, ideas and future prospects arise everywhere. But I'm not the typical keynote speaker who jumps on the bandwagon of mere excitement and preaches about some new technology as if it were a new religion. "Repent, or your fate will not be kind to you!" It's not my style to overhype something new like others sometimes do. After all, all articles, podcasts, YouTube videos or talks then seem to use the same examples, trying to beat one another with the latest news. That's not my game. I want to bring meaning to change. My goal is to inspire about the transformational impact some technology might have on individuals, society, the planet and – of course – your business. That's why I prefer to wait until the dust settles down, the first learnings are taken, and some disillusion sets in because that's when it gets fascinating.

Technology has the transformational power to impact individuals, society and the planet.

Hype Cycle for Artificial Intelligence, 2023

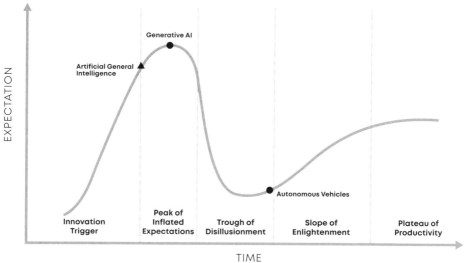

However, it's impossible to publish a new book without mentioning the transformational power of Artificial Intelligence. While my keynotes on Artificial Intelligence are more illustrative and strategically supportive for a particular business, I will omit to do so for this book as the technology is evolving at a breakneck pace. It would only make my book redundant within the shortest time. Therefore, I will instead sketch the transformational power of technology from a higher perspective, trying to shift the debate from flashy examples to the broader impact on individuals, society and the planet – something which, I believe, is not done enough during the early hype of technologies.

How it started

The term 'Artificial Intelligence' was first used in the 1950s, even though the idea of thinking machines is centuries old. Throughout legends and myths, the concept of 'thinking machines' or autonomous beings has fascinated cultures worldwide. The ancient Greeks spoke of Talos, a bronze automaton designed to protect Crete, while old Chinese tales described intricate mechanical figures that imitated human operations. Meanwhile, in the medieval Islamic world, Al-Jazari crafted automata that could mimic human actions. European legends mentioned the 'Brazen Head', a magical device reputed to answer questions and predict the future.

In 1947, Alan Turing, often considered the founder of computer science, predicted that by the end of the 20th century, the notion of 'machine thinking' would be widely accepted. History proved him right. This foresight was given substance in June 1956 when scientists and mathematicians gathered at Dartmouth College to debate the essence of a discipline so new it lacked a definitive name. These pioneers delved into the undefined domain of what would soon be known as Artificial Intelligence (AI).

Their discussions, spanning topics from cybernetics to logic theory, converged on a central theme: Creating a machine that could emulate human cognition. This 'Dartmouth workshop' marked the dawn of the relentless pursuit of AI, a journey characterised by exciting highs and discouraging lows. Over the ensuing decades, the trajectory of AI experienced fluctuating fortunes, periods of stagnation and moments of profound revelations.

Today's world sees nations and industries investing heavily in AI, with an increase of 400% in 2023 vs 2022. As a result, the pace of advancements is taking even experts by surprise. A concept from myths, legends, and science fiction swiftly became a concrete – and perhaps confusing – reality. Today, machines can 'think', mimic human intelligence and perform tasks.

MIMICKING OUR BRAIN AND CAPABILITIES

Mimicking human intelligence was achieved by training an algorithm on vast volumes of complex data sets to recognise patterns, make classifications, and predict future values. Most Artificial Intelligence today uses neural networks, computational models inspired by the biological neural network in the human brain. Like in our brain, these neural networks are composed of interconnected nodes, referred to as 'neurons', that process the information. Neurons are linked with each other by 'weights'. Every time data goes in, these weights change to make the output iteratively better and achieve the optimal result.

Neural networks at the core of Artificial Intelligence have expanded dramatically in size, boasting nearly 200 billion parameters (at the time of writing this book). Despite the extensive resources required to train these networks, Artificial Intelligence has achieved significant milestones, besting humans in games like chess and Go years ago. Today's AI technology like **ChatGPT**, **DALL-E**, **Midjourney** *and many others demonstrate AI's capability to craft stories, address complex questions, create images, translate languages, etc. Tools enable users to craft artwork in Rembrandt's style or compose hit songs without any schooling in painting or music. Similarly, individuals can design advanced websites and applications without formal IT education. Future generations of generative AI will have a comparable impact on medicine. People who never attended medical school will diagnose diseases and create a treatment plan like any clinician does today.*

What value do you want to create?

Whether during a keynote, panel discussion or podcast on the subject, I'm often asked what the impact of Artificial Intelligence will be on [said industry/business/field]. While most questions in such settings have replies that start with "That's an excellent question", I tend to say the exact opposite here. I don't think that is a good question, as Artificial Intelligence will be omnipresent and omni-impactful anyway. It's as absurd as asking 130 years ago how electricity would impact the world. Artificial Intelligence will be everywhere like electricity is today. It will permeate all aspects of life, every object and business. It will be part of the infrastructure on which the future world will be built. Like electricity, it will connect many, if not all, objects. But the infrastructure will be interconnected this time, not to send energy but to transmit data.

Artificial Intelligence will be everywhere like electricity is today. It will permeate all aspects of life, every object and business.

Today, many 'experts' would answer that previous question by replicating existing or near-future applications of Artificial Intelligence, perhaps from other industries. And then you'll hear the same examples over and over again. But the real question is the value you want to create (and that counts for every new technology). I always prefer to start with the end in mind. So, I throw the question back at whoever asked it by inviting them to answer these two additional questions: "What value do you ideally want to create in [said industry/business/field], and what data would you need for that?"

At its very core, Artificial Intelligence is transforming data into value. Knowing that we can collect any type of data today, we could create any kind of value tomorrow. Technically speaking, there is no limit to creating value from data. You need the data. That's why I believe the impact Artificial Intelligence will or should have on [said industry/business/field] depends on the concluded value 'you' can deduct from any data you want to gather, engineer and model. Often, this value will be centred around automation and efficiency, experience and convenience, accessibility and scalability, personalisation and accuracy, ... or any one of the Life Aspirations. But again, that is entirely up to the value you want to create.

What value do you want to create, and what data would you need for that?

FROM DATA TO VALUE

Collect maps and traffic data to guide people from point A to B; accumulate clicking behaviour and on-screen time to suggest preferred online content; aggregate and analyse all the objects and elements on the road and let the car drive by itself; gather DNA, RNA, protein and other relevant biometrics to design personalised cancer treatments; assemble movement, breathing and heartbeat data to analyse sleep patterns; compare a photo with an existing image database to diagnose skin cancer; identifying a particular form of linguistic degeneration as an early indicator of Alzheimer's... The list is endless. While none of the above examples are scientifically or technically correct and complete, they showcase how to think when creating value from data with Artificial Intelligence. You can easily see from these examples how it might help with life aspirations like, for instance, **Consciousness (being aware and comprehending)**, **Safeness (feel safe and protected)** *and* **Healing (recover and restore)** *just to name a few.*

Another misconception about the impact of Artificial Intelligence is that we tend to start from the data we know or have. Many start-ups in the AI sphere today are doing good but not great things. And that's not necessarily their fault. One can only work with what you have, but it limits the creativity (of others) to see its real potential. This is most obvious in healthcare, I believe. It's one of the sectors most reliant on but least equipped with data. Artificial Intelligence is only scratching the surface of what it could mean there. Better use of Electronic Patient Dossiers, widespread understanding of genomics data, interoperability between technologies and exploitation of more biometrical data will materialise a massive jump forward in health and self-care. But the same can be said for many other industries. We don't have the proper data yet to create the best value.

Healthcare is one of the sectors most reliant on but least equipped with data.

That also counts for algorithms that treat the data. It's hard to fully grasp the impact of Artificial Intelligence by looking at the current standalone solutions. As with other technologies, it's the combination of different algorithms into one string that will make the most impressive impact. The potential of this 'String Strategy' is complex to grasp fully. It becomes even more complex and powerful when Multi-Model solutions are *stringed*, which can then process, interpret, and understand multiple types of data inputs such as text, image, sound, or numerical data. In a sense, everything is possible. So again, the impact on [said industry/business/field] really depends on the value you want to create. Afterwards, you probe for the data (and the algorithms) that could support you.

STRING STRATEGY

Companies that string various technologies can easily outperform existing competitors. Take a drone as an example: by itself, it's a sophisticated remote-controlled helicopter, essentially a toy. However, if you equip a drone with a camera, it transforms into a tool for surveillance that provides **Safeness *(feel safe and protected)***. Add depth sensors, a robotic arm, and artificial intelligence to the mix, and you have a self-operating device capable of revolutionising warehouse management and delivery systems by optimising transportation routes. Meanwhile, traditional businesses might still rely on slower, less efficient manual forklifts. The coming decade is poised for a surge in transformational breakthroughs as cutting-edge technologies mature and an increasing number of companies combine current and newer innovations. This convergence will lead to novel business opportunities.*

In the field of Artificial Intelligence, it is no different. You can combine speech-to-text intelligence with machine translation. But some real magic happens if you then string this with text-to-speech intelligence, voice synthesis technology, and lip-syncing AI. The string of those technologies allows you to record a short clip of yourself speaking and having it transformed into you saying this in another language. That is how HeyGen amazed the world in 2023. The AI company, known for its AI-generated avatars, took social media by storm with this. Many people shared videos of themselves online speaking in many languages while the tone and timbre of their voices remained recognisably the same. It requires, of course, the perfect technical alignment between all these algorithms. And each algorithm must gather the appropriate 'data'.

What makes it even more challenging to answer that 'impact question' is the rapid advancement of Artificial Intelligence. Some suggest that AI applications could become at least 30 times more potent in the next five years. Jensen Huang, NVIDIA's CEO, has gone further to predict AI models will be a million times more advanced than ChatGPT within a decade. Meanwhile, Shane Legg, co-founder of Google's DeepMind, argues that by 2028, AI will reach a level of proficiency in intellectual tasks comparable to humans, hinting at a milestone known as Artificial General Intelligence (AGI). But in November 2023, leaked information by OpenAI engineers started rumours that a project named Q* had already achieved a significant breakthrough towards this AGI. Rapid advancements have never been so 'rapid'.

But what does this Artificial General Intelligence (AGI) mean? It means that technology will match humans' intellectual capabilities. This AGI is anticipated to cause a seismic transformation across individual lives, societal functions, and global systems. In the healthcare sector, for instance, professionals' exclusive domain of medical expertise is expected to be disrupted. Advanced Large Language Models, including versions of ChatGPT, will democratise this expertise, potentially altering the roles of caregivers into careguides sooner than my predictions in Chapter 8.2 might suggest. Sure, healthcare providers will remain important but I wonder whether they will be in front or behind the scenes.

Healthcare providers will remain important, but I wonder whether they will still be in front or behind the scenes.

It's very challenging to know where we are, where we are going or how fast we will get there. DeepMind researchers are working to refine these concepts, suggesting that AGI should be viewed not as a final destination but rather as a continuum of capabilities. They aim to set up a framework similar to the one used for autonomous vehicles, which is divided into six levels of autonomy based on a specific quantification of the performance. This framework could provide a clearer understanding of AI's progression and allow for more precise discussions about the milestones within the field of AI. It also might help to answer the question better: What will be the impact of AI?

But again, providing a simple answer to that particular question remains diffi-cult. No more than five years ago, it was said that creativity would keep humans relevant in a world filled with AI. Today, Artificial Intelligence already sparks an overabundance of creativity that trumps human spontaneous creativity. In fact, I constantly interact with large language models to spark my imagination, going back and forth on specific topics. What I used to do as an internal dialogue now has become an external exchange with a machine that can recite a ton of inspirations. I also find it hard to believe that emotions will keep us as 'relevant' as humans, either. The narrative has now become that humans have the unique and exclusive ability to have and show emotions. But we don't hold a monopoly on emotions. When machines can mimic emotions as if they are humans, they'll probably be better at it because they don't get tired or distracted.

Integrating emotions in software, also known as Emotion AI, emotive AI, affec-tive AI, or Artificial Empathy, will be the main topic in the next couple of years. This will surely spark another significant leap forward. This technology, which is focused on processing and replicating human emotions, has the potential to transition from mere measurement to genuinely valuable applications. One of the utopian advantages of Emotion AI is its ability to make human-machine inter-actions more authentic and natural. It will yield exciting opportunities for per-sonalising the user experience with emotions, which can strengthen customer or patient engagement. This is particularly intriguing in health and self-care, where understanding and responding to emotional cues can significantly enhance pa-tient care and support.

THE CHALLENGES WITH EMOTIVE AI

CASE IN POINT

Despite the potential of Emotive AI to enhance interactions between humans and ma-chines, significant challenges remain concerning its accuracy and usability. It remains challenging to label the emotions based on specific data points correctly. For example, in vocal tones, both anger and excitement might be expressed with high pitch, while facial expressions for anger and disgust can appear similar. Emotions are inherently subjective and can be interpreted differently from person to person, adding another layer of complexity to accurately identifying them through AI.

The scientific community is also at odds over the definition of emotions and how they are formed or shown. In 2020, this lack of consensus led researchers at the AI Now Institute in New York to call for a ban on using sentiment recognition in critical decision-making areas like recruitment, citing the lack of solid scientific backing. Moreover, In June 2022, **Microsoft** *announced it would stop selling and investing in emotion recognition software because of the lack of consensus on a definition of 'emotions' and the inability to generalise the linkage between facial expression and emotional state across uses, regions, and demographics.*

Despite these concerns, the future relationship with emotion-sensing machines is set. They could fulfil a need for empathy that is sometimes lacking in (some) human interactions. In healthcare, emotive AI could assist in diagnosing mental health conditions, understanding the emotions of people with dementia who may struggle to express themselves, and gauging the resilience of cancer patients. Emotive AI could increase the empathy of caregivers or health coaches (regardless of whether these caregivers or coaches are human, software, robots, or digital beings). In fact, I believe it will be the biggest driver of success in Digital Health and healthcare more broadly because Emotive AI guarantees a crucial element (often absent in health and self-care sectors): Empathy. In Chapter 14 we dive deeper into this use case.

Emotive AI will be the biggest driver of success for Digital Health and healthcare in general.

It's not easy to provide a simple answer to the question, "What will be the impact of AI on [said industry/business/field]?" In this section, I've tried to argue why this is the wrong question, as Artificial Intelligence is a structural part of the infrastructure upon which another world will be built. In other words, it will be everywhere. Another reason for this being the wrong question is the exceptional speed at which it evolves. Nevertheless, reflecting on its impact on humans, society and the planet is worthwhile. In the following paragraphs, I'll sketch different scenarios often part of more extensive discussions around Artificial Intelligence. These are vital reflections if we want to create the value people wish to have with these transformational technologies. We will go from utopian to dystopian futures and revert to more realistic scenarios in which humanity might be simultaneously enhanced and challenged. Finally, we will consider the impact on Life Aspirations with Artificial Intelligence.

The ultimate intelligence for health and happiness

The transformational value of Artificial Intelligence could be endlessly good for humanity. After all, intelligence has evolved society from primitive subsistence to the modern world. Artificial Intelligence presents a profound opportunity to enhance this evolution even more. It promises to enhance potentially everything from medicine to climate change solutions, from personal growth to scientific and economic advancement. It could be considered a moral imperative, paving the way to a superior world for current and future generations. Artificial Intelligence is defined by unparalleled progress and enhanced human experience. Each individual, whether a child, professional, or leader, stands to gain from it.

ONCE-IN-A-LIFETIME DISCOVERIES

DeepMind's *AlphaFold (Google) has dramatically transformed life sciences by predicting the 3D structures of proteins in seconds – a process that once took months or years. Protein structures are fundamental to life sciences because they perform essential functions within our cells. The configuration of a protein directly influences its role, and comprehending its structure permits scientists to predict its behaviour and interaction with other molecules, mainly when mutations occur. With over 200 million protein structures identified, AlphaFold's database now aids research in many fields, from sustainability to disease understanding. This dataset that illuminates nearly the entire protein universe is one of the most significant since mapping the human genome. Deepmind's AlphaMissense, then again, uses that structural information, among other data, to assess genetic variations of protein function and predict how it causes specific genetic diseases. Together, they accelerate our ability to understand and intervene in biological processes at a molecular level like never before.*

CASE IN POINT

A new age of biological research has been initiated that is already concentrated on beating antibiotic resistance, stopping malaria, creating plastic-eating enzymes, and fighting osteoporosis, cancer, or autism with new drug discoveries. I wouldn't be surprised if either AlphaFold or AlphaMissense will be the first Nobel prize that goes to an AI machine. These are once-in-a-lifetime discoveries that happened within a span of 12 months. On a side note, most protein structures are freely available in bulk via Google Cloud for researchers to work with.

The famous historian and philosopher Yuval Noah Harari states that AI marks the end of human history, or at least history as (solely) written by humans. In that quote lies the core of today: We are partnering up with machines to build the future. With the help of AI, we augment our capabilities. Faster data analysis supports our human judgement. Efficiency improvement for repetitive tasks allows us to concentrate on complex work. Automated support contributes to having more nuanced interactions between humans. Emotional intelligence empowers humans with more empathy. Human creativity is extended with new forms of expression, while ethical strategies for complex problems are steered by leveraging large amounts of data.

Artificial Intelligence will not replace humans. Artificial Intelligence will replace the humans who don't work with it. You might have heard this before. But the challenge remains to discover (in a timely way) the right ways to integrate this Artificial Intelligence in our work, because this will be a good thing. Research by McKenzie & Company (2023) indicated that developers who use AI reported feeling more than two times happier and more satisfied than others. They felt this way because these tools did the tedious work for them and provided them with information faster. They bring **Calmness (*avoid stress and anxiety*)** and spark **Creativity (*imagine and invent*)**.

It's not hard to envision a near future where everybody has such a personal digital assistant powered by Artificial Intelligence. Think of it as voice-activated devices like Alexa or Siri, but fully competent to autonomously manage various tasks that make our lives significantly more convenient. It suggests responses to emails, transcribes voicemails, organises meetings, acts as a personal tutor that teaches you new skills, books reservations, heats your home before arrival at home, etc... Our life experience will be entirely different. But what if these digital assistants could make you feel better, healthier and happier? It would be transformational if digital assistants could, for example, help me maintain my **Energy (have vitality and stamina)** by suggesting a menu based on my nutritional needs or strengthen my **Relationships (have meaningful connections)** by helping me plan enough social time. Such transformations will be more valuable than convenient experiences as we will see in Chapter 14.

CASE IN POINT

DIGITAL HEALTH ASSISTANTS IN THE WORLD'S HEALTHIEST CITY

The **LINE***, part of Saudi Arabia's NEOM project, envisions a mirrored linear city stretching 170km across the desert. This horizontal cityscape is intended to catalyse progress and become one of the world's healthiest cities. It will be prioritising health by leveraging digital technology and Artificial Intelligence. The LINE will have only one hospital, but it will be a place of very last resort. Instead, their aim is to foster an environment where health is continuously managed as a personal responsibility. Therefore, residents can access innovative health technologies like personal digital health assistants. A digital twin will use wearable devices for continuous, individual health assessments. 'Doctor NEOM', an AI virtual doctor, will provide preventive care advice based on these health assessments.*

It's easy to imagine every workplace foreseeing a digital companion for their employees and perhaps for their customers. This companion could provide the aforementioned support where the actual needs or bottlenecks in the company exist. Artificial Intelligence can easily solve some of the needs, and considering the quick, broad uptake of large language models like ChatGPT, many people might expect such an experience pretty soon. But it would definitely help to feed your digital business companion with the correct values and priorities to differentiate from other employers or competitors. Indeed, integrating valuable Life Aspirations will make a difference and engage people even more. Because it's more transformational and that's what people aspire to.

Pseudocognition, human agency and consciousness

Copernicus made us understand that the world is not at the centre of the universe, while Darwin explained how we are hardly different from other animals. Freud argued that humans are not infallible, sometimes even irrational. But today, humanity starts to understand it is not the smartest one on the planet. We are being humbled again.

Artificial Intelligence would achieve higher scores on high school exams than humans today. It does not mean it is as competent as humans yet. But it possesses more information over a broader spectrum of topics. In fact, the estimated IQ of Artificial Intelligence by the end of 2023 was 155, which is higher than 99% of the population. This intelligence is very intimidating for humans as our superior intelligence helped us to survive for millennia. Tigers are stronger animals than humans, but we can outsmart them. Being 'outsmarted' by machines will feel convenient initially but destabilising at some point. AI machines will soon even become more knowledgeable about us than we are about ourselves. Convenient but destabilising for sure. It changes what or how we believe.

Tigers are stronger animals than humans, but we can outsmart them. Being 'outsmarted' by machines will feel convenient initially but destabilising at some point.

Sam Altman, Open AI's CEO, rightfully said that AI systems don't need to achieve full AGI to persuade people about something easily. And there lurks a considerable danger. People have fought wars because of what they believed in. They are willing to kill others or be killed because of that belief. We have already seen how social media generated echo chambers, reinforcing people's opinions and polarising the world. But the supply of misinformation can soon be infinite. It's not difficult to imagine how AI-driven personal assistants can alter or strengthen one's beliefs, which I often call 'Echo Personas'.

Hence, we are entering an era of pseudocognition. Algorithms are replacing rational human thinking and deep critical analysis with a superficial or thoughtless rehashing of information. This is challenging, perhaps even scary, and brings many questions. How much can we consciously trust these algorithms that are (currently still) black boxes? Are we conscious that we put all of our data in that box? Is it safe enough? Can everybody consciously keep up with this speed of technological change? Are we still conscious of our choices? These are critical questions. In history, humans learned how to survive by making conscious decisions based on the myriad of impulses. But what are the consequences of renouncing this consciousness and (too) often relying on algorithms?

IS CHATGPT TAKING OUR CONSCIOUSNESS AWAY?

The process of writing is a crucial way humans share and think deeply. We write to share our views on life, better understand our thoughts or let our feelings out. But writing also helps us reflect carefully, use reason, and create ideas that we can return to and think about more. A famous thinker, Eric Havelock, said that when people in ancient Greece started to write, it helped them contemplate better and even develop new ideas. This all comes from our human ability to think and feel. If we let Artificial Intelligence do our writing, how much might we lose of our ability to think? How well will we be able to express ourselves? How conscious will we still be? After all, **Consciousness (being aware and comprehending)** *and* **Creativity (imagine and invent)** *are both important Life Aspirations that cannot be taken away entirely from us.*

The algorithm behind dominant AI systems will therefore have considerable power over its users. And the profit-making business or the regulating political regime behind those algorithms will control what people believe, say or do. Before you assume that would not happen to you, how often do you 'unconsciously' follow the instructions of your GPS? Human agency will be a hot topic for debate for years to come because humans easily tend to pick convenience over complexity. But what would be the incentive for companies or governments to honour human agency anyway? Within 10 years, we might not be asking if humans are in control, but which humans are in control. This will put our **Autonomy** *(live independently and autonomously)* to a significant test.

NON-ALIGNED GOALS

Even in the best-case scenario that algorithms are programmed to do something benefi-cial, they could still apply a destructive method for achieving their goal. The **YouTube** *algorithm automatically pushed conspiracy theory videos forward when asked to keep people on the platform longer. Likewise, you might be careful to ask a self-driving, intel-ligent car to bring you to the airport as fast as possible. You might be chased by a police helicopter if not all the values of the AI system are aligned with (y)ours. But when, how and by whom can these autonomous machines be stopped from achieving 'their goal'? I don't think I have to paint doomsday scenarios you might have seen in late '90s movies to make my point.*

While regulation is on its way, I firmly believe every company continues to have an enormous responsibility to consider these consequences. The Artificial Intel-ligence you will implement or offer to your customers will answer a clear need and meet the expected convenience. I don't doubt that. But it will be vital to think about the universal Life Aspirations that those AI systems need to meet as well. I'll elaborate on this in the following paragraphs.

Making AI transformational

Copernicus, Darwin and Freud might have lowered human self-esteem, but Ar-tificial Intelligence feels like diminishing humans. After all, intelligence used to be an essential part of how we identify ourselves. Humans are more intelligent animals, and more intelligent humans are (generally speaking) more successful than others. Today, intelligence goes from being an individual characteristic to becoming a commodity, like electricity. Its value will decrease. But it will become an essential part of the infrastructure on which the future will be built, whether we are ready for that future or not. This future might hold tremendous opportunities to better our lives, but it also has severe consequences for humanity. Therefore, it will remain vital to carefully balance out the upsides against the downsides of this transformational technology. I even believe we should rethink what it means to be human.

I know this last sentence is exceptionally philosophical to be mentioned in a business book. I wouldn't be surprised if some frowned or raised their eyebrows after reading it. But if your company or organisation plans to deploy Artificial Intelligence, it is a pertinent question. What do people value in this world with an overabundance of intelligence, creativity (and soon emotions)? What are people still good at? How do we want to make them feel? How do they still relate to each other?

Intelligence goes from being an individual characteristic to becoming a commodity on which the future world will be built. It's time to rethink what is means to be human.

If your company or organisation plans to roll out solutions with Artificial Intelligence, please don't only employ engineers. It will be critical to include colleagues who are focused on humans (your customers or patients) and what is valuable for them in life. Because yes, I am confident you will easily design products and services that meet your customers' needs. And it will not be too hard to create convenient experiences for them either. But in this new, unsettling AI world, it will be vital to think about the Life Aspirations of your customers and build experiences that make them feel better, healthier or happier.

THE IMPORTANCE OF LIFE ASPIRATIONS

*It would be best to ask yourself, for example, questions about the **Autonomy (live independently and autonomously)** you want to provide. I imagine that human agency will be part of many debates in your company: Where do we provide decision support, and how do we deliver decision-making? Perhaps you want to reflect upon **Spontaneity (act spontaneously)**. The new AI world will be (too?) predictable.*

Spotify may suggest artists that match the music you often listen to, but sometimes, it might be nice to discover something new accidentally. Could we appreciate serendipity again? Perhaps decisions based on intuition will make us feel valuable as humans again? How can we provide **Nothingness (do, feel, see or hear nothing)**. *If Artificial Intelligence is omnipresent to guide us, wouldn't you want to be left alone occasionally? How do we make people feel* **Safeness (feel safe and protected)**? *Should we think about what type of* **Relationships (have meaningful connections)** *people are looking for? And what about* **Realness (be genuine and true to myself and others)**? *Authenticity was Merriam-Webster's word of the year 2023. This highlights a growing authenticity crisis we are seeing today. Are people still authentic today (on social media)? Can companies be authentic (enough)? Is that picture, music or social media post authentic? And is information authentic when it is made with Artificial Intelligence? We have never questioned authenticity that much. One could even argue whether the word 'authenticity' is not already overused or overpolitised. In fact, it is the reason why I prefer the word* **Realness (be genuine and true to myself and others)**. *Because more and more, we want something that feels or is real. And I don't expect that to change in a world full of Artificial Intelligence.*

It's challenging to list all the ways Artificial Intelligence can support people in pursuing their Life Aspirations. But with the Life Aspirational Model in this book, you can reflect upon these universal values and priorities anytime. It will help turn Artificial Intelligence into the transformational technology people want. And the same approach can be applied to other technologies as well. In the next chapter, we'll use it for the once-hyped Metaverse.

13.2 The Life Aspirations in virtual worlds

When I first heard about the Metaverse, I was perhaps more excited than I'd been since 2001, when I researched the future of mobile internet for my thesis at the

University of Leuven in Belgium. Many critical factors that would make mobile internet successful were missing back then, but I still felt intense excitement about what lay ahead. I concluded my research by saying that mobile internet would take off once a 'mobile internet application store' had been created. This happened six years later when Apple launched the first App Store. By now, you must be used to using mobile internet on your phone. Maybe that's how you ordered this book, on the same device you use to order groceries, watch television, book a tennis court, take and share pictures and read newspapers. In 2001, it was already clear to me that mobile internet would be that kind of game changer.

I've been similarly excited about the Metaverse for a few years, but I wondered whether I should include something about it in this book. It still feels like such a wild, far-fetched idea. How can we create a virtual alternative universe? And even if we did, why would people even use it? Then again, like the chapter on Artificial Intelligence, the purpose is never to 'convert' you to the idea of the Metaverse as if it were a religion. Nor would I aim to delve into the technicalities or all other potential aspects of the Metaverse. But then again, the Metaverse is a perfect example to explain the importance of Life Aspirations when innovating with technology. So, here I go again.

But first, what is the Metaverse?

The Metaverse has slightly different definitions, but you can think of it as a 'more immersive' internet experience. In the Metaverse, you can do the same things you would do on the internet but in a virtual, three-dimensional environment. It can be the result of combining AR (augmented reality), VR (virtual reality), XR (extended reality), AI (artificial intelligence), online gaming, social media, cryptocurrencies and Web 3.0 features in one place. But that is a more advanced state of the Metaverse. I believe there are different levels of 'the Metaverse'. Navigating a 3D world on a flat computer screen is already a basic immersive Metaverse. Ultimately, it might even involve brain implants that create brain-computer interfaces and fully virtual experiences, as we know from the Matrix movies. We can then experience all kinds of amazing bodily experiences, whether or not they actually happen with one's physical body. That's why it excites some people while it scares others.

But because the Metaverse is supposed to be an immersive experience, it will allow you to do even more than just internet things. In the Metaverse, you can also efficiently do the things you otherwise would do in the physical world. It's an environment where physical and virtual reality coexist and interact. It is a hybrid mix between physical reality and virtual reality. It represents a more integrated and interactive approach to technology, where the boundaries between real and virtual become blurred.

The Metaverse will blur the boundaries between real and virtual.

While this may sound confusing for some, this is already slowly seeping into the behaviour of young people. When my 11-year-old son is at a family party, he knows he isn't allowed any screen time during the day. "We are here together now" is the main argument for that decision. But it does not resonate with him. The digital world is part of their reality. It's where they are together as much as in the real world, if not more. You also might have noticed that many of the conversations between children or cousins are about virtual worlds: the worlds they've built in Minecraft, the clothes they bought for their avatar in Fortnite or the games they've created in Roblox. Children don't see these worlds as separate from the real world as much as grown-ups do. When they are allowed some screen time at the end of the day, they play as well together in the virtual world as in the real one. The boundaries between the real and virtual worlds are already blurred.

PHYSICAL AND VIRTUAL REALITY COEXIST

What we do in the physical world can be done virtually as well, thus further blurring the barrier between real and virtual. We saw this take off during the COVID-19 pandemic, with all the physical places (like the ones mentioned in Part Four) being recreated in a virtual space so people could celebrate their graduations and enjoy after-work drinks. Virtual concerts attracted 33 million people on **Fortnite** *or* **Roblox**.

CASE IN POINT

We saw consumer electronics brand **LG** launch virtual products, while **H&M** offered virtual clothes in the digital world of Animal Crossing. De **Efteling**, a theme park in the Netherlands, recreated its attractions in Minecraft. Even the earliest virtual worlds allow us to do almost everything we would do in the real world.

There is no clear distinction between what we (can) do in the real world and the virtual one. They coexist side by side, providing similar opportunities. **Upland** and **Decentraland** are perhaps the strangest examples of them all. These virtual worlds let you buy, sell, and trade properties mapped to real addresses virtually. Someone in the Metaverse can now own your piece of land (the one you own in the real world), build a new virtual house, and sell it to make money.

Now that you understand what is meant by the Metaverse, let me tell you that I wouldn't be surprised if that word might lose some of its relevancy in the short term. The enormous recent backlash could deter companies from referring to their ambitions as Metaverse projects. Also, watch how Apple launched their long-awaited Mixed Reality glasses, Apple Vision Pro, without mentioning the Metaverse (or Virtual Reality). They introduced the era of 'spatial computing', a word that Meta then also used at the launch of their Oculus Quest 3.

Spatial computing is the technology that integrates the digital and physical worlds into an interactive, three-dimensional simulation of a physical world. In this Mixed Reality, digital objects can exist alongside and interact with the elements from the real world. It allows users to manipulate and interact with these digital objects to mimic real-life spatial awareness and physical interaction. In other words, virtual objects are anchored to the real world. You can even manipulate them.

Whether you are a fan of the Apple Vision Pro or not, it is interesting to place it within other technological innovations that are increasingly emerging. I am thinking of the many objects around us that collect data on which we can unleash an intelligent algorithm: Our wearables collect information about our bodies; electric cars with self-driving ambitions collect data about the objects they pass; heating systems try to capture the environment; and so forth. The entire world (and ourselves) is thus converted into data that Artificial Intelligence can use. But the more data we collect, the easier it becomes to build a virtual version of reality in parallel (metaverse) or as a virtual layer on top of the real world (Augmented reality) with which we can interact. Technologies such as OpenAI's video generator, called SORA, can also help in (re)creating that virtual world. It was not without reason that it was referred to at launch as "a simulation creator of the real world". The emerging wave of robots is another example based on collecting data and mapping our environment. Are you doubting the importance of these innovations? Well, look at the success of Nvidia's stock market value. They bring the necessary computing power (GPUs) and a textbook example of a digitised world (the Omniverse).

But in this new technological world, we will need devices to use or control these various technological innovations. And that is precisely what (a device like) the Apple Vision Pro will bring. It is a new way of computer-human interface. To interact with technology, we've evolved from stationary (desktop) to wearable (laptop) and then handheld computers (smartphones). Headsets, like the Apple Vision Pro, will facilitate Spatial Computing as the necessary means of interacting with these new AI-powered technologies like the metaverse, robots and augmented reality. In that way, the device will be our new operating system for AI-driven digital components mixed with the real world around us.

But first, back to the Metaverse. In this Chapter, I'll mostly speak about examples in the Metaverse as a full-on virtual world. Recent successes and disappointments with the Metaverse will help me to explain the use of Customer Transformations and Life Aspirations. However, a similar reasoning could be applied to the Spatial world with a mixed reality. Similar Life Aspirations will apply to this Spatial world as well. Even the Metaverse examples in this chapter could – and probably will – one day become a mixed reality. I advise using this chapter as an exercise to include Life Aspirations when innovating with technology.

Expecting virtual experiences

The Metaverse had a massive moment in 2021 when Facebook changed its company name to Meta as part of a new strategic direction primarily focused on the Metaverse. It has received a lot of backlash ever since. Facebook and the entire tech and entertainment industry had to tune down their Metaverse ambitions. Meta pivoted towards generative AI in its 'year of efficiency' after the Metaverse division racked up over 46 billion dollars in losses. Meanwhile, Microsoft, Disney, Walmart and many others shut down their Metaverse departments.

Where did it go so wrong? That's where the theory of Customer Transformation comes in handy. In Chapter 3, I explained how you can create value by meeting the customer's needs, expectations and Life Aspirations. It is obvious how the Metaverse can meet specific *needs* like buying products, facilitating conversations and providing entertainment. But is this the experience that people really *expect* today? How many people have had virtual or 3D experiences? And in how many of those cases were these experiences sufficiently better than today's best practices? We would have to look at youngsters that meet daily on Roblox, Minecraft, Gorilla Tag, Rec Room or Fortnight to find those in favour. For others, meeting people in real life still trumps meeting them in a virtual world today. But even gamers haven't fully interchanged console gaming with VR gaming. Technology is not widespread enough nor capable of improving the current experience. So, in many situations, people won't *expect* a virtual experience to satisfy their needs (yet).

We are weaving a layer of sensors through our physical environment to collect data that will allow us to build highly sophisticated virtual versions of that physical world as if they were real.

However, in some situations, the Metaverse is already providing a better experience. The technological fundamentals are in place, and the recent spur in Artificial Intelligence mentioned in the previous chapter will also accelerate this. Look at how we are weaving a layer of sensors through our physical environment to collect data and feed the neural networks of Artificial Intelligence. From the sensors in our cars to the ones on our arms and in automated manufacturing plants, we are digitising the physical aspects of the world around us. The data from these sensors will allow us to build highly sophisticated virtual versions of that physical world as if they were real. These virtual twins provide a better experience to the existing need for testing environments, making it possible to conduct tests before applying them to the real world.

VIRTUAL TWIN WORLDS

BMW and **NVIDIA** have collaborated to create the BMW Group's Omniverse, a virtual factory planning tool. This platform uses NVIDIA's Omniverse technology, allowing BMW to simulate its production processes in a highly detailed and realistic virtual environment. This virtual world enables BMW to experiment with factory layouts and workflows in ways that are not feasible in the real world, such as testing different production scenarios without needing physical alterations. It allows for efficient planning, optimisation, and flexibility in manufacturing processes, saving time and resources. This virtual simulation provides insights and allows for adjustments that would be costly or impractical to test in a real-world setting. Cities, ports and power stations are all developing virtual twins today. But this is not the first time NVIDIA has been involved in creating virtual twins. An even more ambitious initiative is the Earth-2 initiative, which focuses on developing digital twins of Earth to enhance weather prediction accuracy, forecast climate change more effectively, and develop strategies for mitigation and adaptation. The **European Union** is also involved in an ambitious 'digital twin' of planet Earth. The DestinE project, previously known as Destination Earth, will simulate the atmosphere, ocean, ice, and land with unrivalled precision, providing forecasts of floods, droughts, and fires from days to years in advance.

The earth or manufacturing sites are complex ecosystems that don't allow for much live experimentation, testing or simulations without harm. Virtual twins serve a great need there. The same can be said for humans. That's why, in 2016, Bill Ruh, then-CEO of GE Digital, predicted we would have a virtual twin at birth. This virtual twin would take data from diverse health sensors, provide real-time insights and predict the future of one's health. It would not just fix us when something is wrong but reduce the risk with health-related recommendations. The following examples show how these virtual twins deliver a better experience than before. In those use cases, the Metaverse will continue to grow in popularity significantly.

VIRTUAL TWIN HUMANS

In 2014, **Dassault Systems** *launched its Living Heart Project to build a virtual twin of the human heart. Several projects later, the company launched a remarkable marketing campaign with a virtual twin, Emma Twin, to promote the role of virtual twins in healthcare. She is made as a scientifically accurate virtual representation of a woman based on anonymous women's medical data and characteristics. Thanks to her 3D-modelled body, doctors and researchers can analyse the effects of diseases and test hundreds of treatments virtually without risk to real people. Emma is presented as a crash test dummy for healthcare and you can follow Emma on LinkedIn for updates on clinical studies that include virtual twins.*

The **FDA** *is actively supporting the development of virtual twins in the medical field. It intensified a collaboration with Siemens by providing them with nearly $2 million for a pilot program to show how virtual twins could improve product quality, development, and commercialisation. Meanwhile,* **Siemens Healthineers** *is developing a virtual twin of the heart to enhance drug treatments and simulate cardiac procedures, contributing to safer and more effective pharmaceutical research. Similarly,* **Unlearn** *and* **Merck KGaA**'s *partnership focuses on using digital twins to streamline drug testing processes in clinical trials.*

Several other activities could be experienced in the Metaverse as well, from working out to having sex or educating oneself. But before being popular in the Metaverse, these virtual experiences must first meet the basic expectations of the real world. They will only succeed if the Metaverse experience is better than the real world. For example, medical education with virtual 3D models is more impactful than learning anatomy from a book. Attending a patient's ongoing operation virtually can be more educational than hearing the story afterwards. These experiences are better than the current ones and will, therefore, be popular 'in the Metaverse'.

Another way to popularise specific activities in the Metaverse is to appeal to that target group that already has had enjoyable virtual experiences. Because they will *expect* the added value of a virtual experience. That is why many Metaverse initiatives focus on youngsters first, who have the most satisfying experience with virtual worlds through gaming. These experiences are exceptionally interesting for them, and therefore, they might expect similar expectations in other parts of their lives. Not surprisingly, educating those youngsters within the Metaverse might engage them a lot. And that's what several organisations are already experimenting with.

VIRTUALLY EDUCATING YOUNGSTERS

In 2017, **Pfizer** *created an educational game for children with haemophilia in* **Minecraft**. *The game, called Hemocraft, focuses on the importance of being prepared and sticking to their treatment plan.* **JDRF**, *the global organisation for type-1 diabetes research, created One World in* **Roblox**. *Their virtual world allows for education, celebration and play while allowing people to connect with family members, friends and classmates.*

If you want to find a use case for the Metaverse, it is critical to look beyond what is possible and search for the experiences people *expect* to happen in a virtual world. Does it answer the need better when the experience is virtual? It won't immediately be successful if they don't need or *expect* it yet. But there are other opportunities in the Metaverse. Opportunities could arise from the pursuit of Life Aspirations. Let's look at how the Metaverse can be a Transformational Technology.

Virtual transformations

In previous chapters, we discussed how different spaces are becoming transformational. Cars become transformational because they give people **Energy (have vitality and stamina)** during a long ride. Houses are transformational when they help people feel **Calmness (avoid stress and anxiety)**. We want to feel **Safeness (feel safe and protected)** at work, while we exercise for **Strength (have power and resilience)** in gyms. We travel to another place to come back transformed. The Metaverse is also a place where people can go or retreat to. And yes, it can also be transformational.

When the experience isn't transformational, it won't attract enough interest.

Aside from gaming, Meta's focus of its Metaverse was directed towards the workspace. Chapter 10.2 mentioned that the workplace needs to be a transformational environment and that is also why the Meta Horizon Workrooms are sold as 'Zoom meetings' in a three-dimensional environment to improve collaboration and **Relationships (*have meaningful connections*)**. But from a leaked internal memo, the world learned that Meta's staff does not even use Workrooms themselves. When the experience is not sufficiently better than the experience in the real world, it does not bring enough value. When the experience isn't transformational either, it won't attract enough interest. I also don't immediately expect many successful Metaverse-like applications in telehealth for those same reasons. Virtual clinics will continue to operate through video conferencing or messaging until the three-dimensional space becomes more transformational.

EARLY VIRTUAL HOSPITALS

*Nevertheless, early experiments are being set up to introduce people to this new experience and change their expectations. **Aimedis Avalon** is perhaps the world's first medical Metaverse, a 3D world dedicated to health, wellness, and science. Integrated with the Aimedis ecosystem, it connects to health IT systems and includes full AI integration with interactive avatars and IoT APIs for device connectivity. Avalon is accessible on various platforms, including PC, Mac, gaming consoles, and mobile devices, and will eventually support VR and AR technologies. It's designed for many users, from healthcare professionals and patients to students and insurance companies, offering therapies, consultations, education, and fitness experiences. Based on Unreal Engine, the system operates smoothly across devices, adapting to different hardware capabilities. Aimedis Avalon allows users to buy, rent, or offer healthcare services and experiences, creating an expansive healthcare universe.*

CASE IN POINT

In the United Arab Emirates, Dubai inaugurated its first hospital in the Metaverse, allowing patients to experience services virtually. The Emirates Health Service introduced the world's first Healthcare Metaverse platform, **MetaHealth**, *and the* **Thumbay Group** *announced plans for another Metaverse hospital. Similarly, Saudi Arabia's* **Seha Virtual Hospital** *supports 170 hospitals. NEOM is also at the forefront of the metaverse evolution, and its flagship healthcare system will be underpinned by the latest in state-of-the-art digital innovation and emerging technology, including the Metaverse. By 2030, the Kingdom is expected to contribute significantly to the Metaverse economy. But for now these are early experiments that don't meet the expectations of desirable health experiences.*

But in some areas, virtual spaces are already transformational today. Mental health is an excellent example because it can help with relevant Life Aspirations, as discussed in chapter 7.2 on Mental Health. In the coming years, developing a 'mental-verse' could be one of the most anticipated benefits of this virtual world. Most people might prefer personal care today. Still, many patients argue that the quality of mental therapy can vary due to the day of the week of the appointment, the weather outside or other recent events. This difference in quality may be true for other therapeutic areas as well, but it is even more felt and thus impactful in mental healthcare. Therefore, the Metaverse model of care, which could make such dependencies abstract, has the potential to revolutionise the way mental health therapy is delivered.

First, the stigma that surrounds mental health very often requires some **Safeness** *(feel safe and protected)* before people feel comfortable to open up about it. That is even more the case for people who suffer from mental health conditions like social anxiety that make it difficult to interact with others in the real world. However, virtual spaces have increased the likelihood of help-seeking behaviour because, in the Metaverse, patients and their mentors can anonymously meet. Creating a confidential and safer environment offers equal opportunities to different people.

VIRTUAL MENTAL HEALTH SPACES

Bump Galaxy is a community for mental health in the virtual world of Minecraft. It gathers together mental health coaches, psychiatrists and patients from around the world to work together on collaborative game-specific care programmes. Members of Bump Galaxy can spend time in a virtual forest for meditation, reflect on their dreams at the top of sand dunes, uncover trauma in underwater temples or participate in a collective sound bath in the rainforest with one of their favourite DJs. This is just one exciting example of the power the Metaverse could have in mental healthcare. For example, imagine a joint therapy session with a relationship counsellor from Sweden and a hypnotherapist from Japan. The Metaverse is easily accessible, rich in valuable experiences, very diverse and always available. It brings people together across national borders, care practices and knowledge worlds. It goes beyond the borders (and regulations) of a country or healthcare system. That's why solutions like Bump Galaxy might have the power to deinstitutionalise and decentralise healthcare as mentioned in Chapter 8.3.

Bump Galaxy, Game World Therapy created by Bianca Carague

Mind-Easy, *a digital mental health start-up, created the first virtual mental health clinic in Decentraland, a 3D virtual world browser-based platform where users can buy virtual plots of land. The clinic aims to provide accessible mental health resources to address therapist shortages and long waitlists, transforming mental healthcare into a more sustainable, equitable, and effective system. The virtual clinic provides therapy spaces, sensory immersion experiences, consciousness exploration spaces, peer support, and exercise areas. The Tokyo-based start-up* **Mind Palette**, *then again, has developed a virtual reality platform that allows patients to receive cognitive behavioural therapy (CBT) treatment in a virtual environment. SK Telecom, one of South Korea's largest telecommunications companies, developed a virtual Mental Health Clinic where patients receive counselling and therapy from licensed mental health professionals. Meanwhile,* **Virtual Ukraine** *is a virtual experience set in a virtual replica of Kyiv's House with Chimaeras, a fortress just across the street from Zelensky's office in the Ukrainian capital. It provides a peaceful environment for displaced Ukrainians to connect and heal from war-related traumas. Through talk therapy and peer support, they share the stories and challenges of their relocation and PTSD. The initiative aims to facilitate psychological recovery through virtual community support and discussion.*

Researchers found in 2022 that people who socialised in virtual worlds – as opposed to 2D online platforms – felt transported to that physical space. During periods of loneliness, disconnection and social rejection, virtual spaces can then provide **Relationships (*have meaningful connections*)** or create a sense of **Belonging (*feel accepted and included*)**. This feeling even feeds their **Self-worth (*feel good about myself*)**. The mental-verse then becomes a transformational space that would not have been possible in the physical world.

Finally, simulated experiences can be a valuable treatment in itself and even an alternative to the increasingly popular psychedelic drugs that can often still have quite a few side effects and dangers related to them. A recent study found that participants who experienced simulations (or hallucinations) generated greater cognitive **Spontaneity (*act spontaneously*)** afterwards. This field is, of course, still in its infancy, but it can also impact the future of the mental-verse.

How the Metaverse serves Life Aspirations

Life Aspirations are universal human dreams and desires that reflect their values and priorities at a specific moment. People will always want to pursue those Life Aspirations, and every new technology will provide them new ways of fulfilling these. The better a new technology helps achieve certain Life Aspirations, the more relevant technology will become for humans. That is also true for your business strategy. The more you apply new technologies to rightfully meet these universal human values, the more your strategy and solutions will be welcomed. You could conduct specific customer research on the Life Aspirations to define the best strategy. But you can also use Large Language Models, like ChatGPT or Gemini, for this exercise. Ask how a technology like the Metaverse, for example, could help humans pursue specific Life Aspirations that *prevent* things from becoming worse. Below, you can see an output generated by ChatGPT when that question is asked. Most answers are obvious and remain superficial, but you can then go back and forth on specific answers to dig deeper and make it more tangible.

CASE IN POINT

HOW CAN THE METAVERSE HELP PURSUE THE FOLLOWING LIFE ASPIRATIONS [...]

1. Solidarity (feel stronger united): *Community Building – the Metaverse allows for the creation of communities based on shared interests, causes, or backgrounds. Joining or forming such groups can foster a sense of unity and collective strength.*

2. Caring (be careful with myself and others): *Empathy and Support Groups – virtual spaces can be safe havens for expressing empathy and supporting others. Engaging in activities or groups focused on mental health, well-being, and peer support can cultivate a caring attitude.*

3. Safeness (feel safe and protected): *Controlled Environments – the Metaverse provides controlled environments where users can engage without the physical risks of the real world. This can create a sense of safety, especially for those exploring new experiences or interactions.*

4. Calmness (avoid stress and anxiety): *Relaxation Spaces – the Metaverse can offer virtual environments designed for relaxation and stress relief, such as virtual nature reserves, meditation rooms, and calming soundscapes.*

5. Clarity (be mindful and focused): *Mindfulness and Concentration Tools – virtual tools or games designed to enhance concentration and mindfulness can be utilised to improve mental clarity.*

6. Consciousness (being aware and comprehending): *Educational Platforms – the Metaverse can host a variety of educational platforms and experiences that offer deep insights into different subjects, enhancing awareness and understanding.*

By leveraging the unique capabilities of the Metaverse, individuals can explore and fulfil these aspirations in innovative and meaningful ways.

Every Life Aspiration from the real world can apply to the virtual one. Some are even essential for humans to be themselves. People want to be **Looking good (be attractive)** in real life? They aspire as much in the Metaverse. An avatar is a digital extension of their personality. Therefore, they will purchase the necessary 'clothing' to create that image. It's no different than dressing up to go out, and has spurred a business valued at 70 billion dollars while growing at 20% annually. But their personality doesn't stop with the clothes they wear. 'Emotes' are even so important. These avatar movements, a particular way of waving or dancing, for example, make them unique. These purchases made Fortnite a game giant valued at $50 billion. In the future, these digital expressions will be complemented with individual facial expressions. All of which will increase their **Self-worth (feel good about myself)** in the virtual spaces. Even online school platforms have understood the importance of these Life Aspirations. They reward students for their grades with online coins they can spend on virtual clothing, accessories, expressions or companion animals for their personal avatar. Some claim that these Life Aspirations are so vital for humans, that 'Freedom of Form' will soon be part of our (virtual) future. In this variant of Freedom of Speech, people will demand the freedom to look like they want to (and be addressed as such). They will aspire to **Belonging (feel accepted and included)**, just like in the real world. It is clear that the social aspect of these virtual worlds is super valuable for people. People will build **Relationships (have meaningful connections)**, form groups that provide **Solidarity (feel stronger united)**, or gather together to find some **Meaning (live life with a meaningful purpose)**. That's when technologies, like the Metaverse (or spatial worlds), become transformational.

People will always want to pursue Life Aspirations, and every new technology will provide them new ways of fulfilling these.

CHAPTER 14

FUTURES OF TRANSFORMATIONAL TECHNOLOGIES

14.1 Digital humans as healthcare providers

Every technology can be transformational. It always comes down to the same thing: how does a technological innovation help pursue particular Life Aspirations? I want to explore one specific future in this chapter that is as stunning as it is eye-opening: Digital Humans. It is meant as an example, a mental exercise you could apply to other technologies. And I'd like to take you back to more than 100 years ago for that exercise.

At the time, the village physician was among the local community's most respected and noteworthy people. It was convenient to have this person nearby, sometimes even directly in people's homes if necessary. He knew the people he treated personally, and he considered their personal reality with empathy and **Kindness** *(be kind to myself and others)*. It was a meaningful **Relationship** *(have meaningful connections)*. The physician was part of the same community people felt **Belonging** *(feel accepted and included)*, which generated trust, authenticity and **Realness** *(be genuine and true to myself and others)*.

But thanks to medical knowledge and technological advances, more physicians started working together and adding nurses to their care teams. Later, clinical laboratories and more medical tools required even more organisation among healthcare professionals. Small collaborations were turned into clinics and, eventually, small hospitals to become the go-to place for people with serious illnesses or those needing surgery. As cities grew and more factories were built, more people started to use hospitals, not just for illness and surgery but also for childbirth and taking care of babies. Birth and death, formerly events that occurred in the home, now took place in a hospital. Hospitals became the institutions of first rather than last resort.

The respect for physicians, which used to come from their kindness and caring, suddenly came from their ability to use science to treat diseases.

As hospital routines became increasingly technical and standardised, patients came to be seen as mere embodiments of diseases that needed to be researched and treated. This approach changed the doctor-patient relationship, as professionals focused primarily on successfully diagnosing and treating pathologies. The respect for physicians, which used to come from their **Kindness** *(be kind to myself and others)* and **Caring** *(be careful with myself and others)*, now came from their ability to use science to treat diseases. Meanwhile, hospitals tilted even more towards treating acute episodes of physical illness and conducting complex technological interventions. Financial constraints and the ever present instrumentation characterised it. As a result, prolonged hospital stays became too expensive and were shortened. In merely 100 years, healthcare shifted from personal care to impersonal bureaucratisation, workflows, governance and heavy processes. I called this *the system-based approach* in Chapter 6.

I may sketch the reality a bit harshly in this brief history of healthcare. But I'm sure you can confirm that it's hard to have personal contact with a physician, as was the case with the village physician. It's even hard to simply see a physician. When it comes to healthcare, we are used to patiently waiting (pun intended). We wait for an appointment, in the waiting room, for referrals, lab results, a diagnosis, feedback, treatment and getting better. Along this journey, it has become rare to feel **Kindness** *(be kind to myself and others)*, **Belonging** *(feel accepted and included)*, **Realness** *(be genuine and true to myself and others)* or **Relationships** *(have meaningful connections)*, like we use to have with the village physician.

It's often said that healthcare is a human business. It's supposed to be primarily based on human interactions. But I often feel we've lost much of the human factor when healthcare became bureaucratised in processes and workflows. We need to bring back that aspect in healthcare and Digital Humans might be one valuable solution. So, let me introduce you to different Digital Humans and then stretch our imagination to use them for this challenge.

Digital Humans

Digital humans sound unreal. Well of course they do; they are not real. Something about digital humans always makes you say to yourself: this isn't really happening, is it? But it is happening. In fact, I anticipate you'll be talking to a Digital Human sooner rather than later. You may be stunned by some of the examples I give in this

Part of the book, but that's the idea. I want to show you how some innovations can soon be transformational.

There's not yet any set definition for **Digital Humans**. Technology is changing and growing so fast that it's challenging to establish a description before the technological boundaries change again. For the moment, digital humans are often defined as "computer-generated moving images of a human being, used mainly in games or movies (as an extra in large crowd scenes)". That's a very shallow definition and I'll try to be more precise.

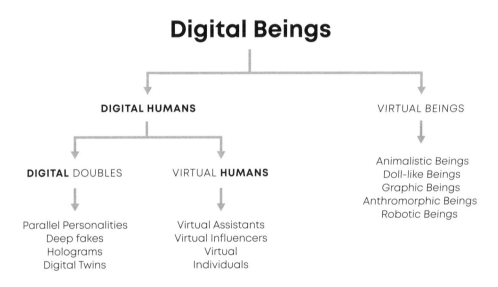

First of all, not all computer-generated moving images depict human beings. Looking around the virtual world, you quickly realise that many avatars don't look human. Some are animalistic, doll-like, graphic, while others are anthropomorphic or robotic beings. I refer to these as **Virtual Beings**. Together with Digital Humans, these Virtual Beings make up all types of avatars, or **Digital Beings**, in the current virtual world.

In this chapter, I won't elaborate on these non-human-like avatars. It's not that they aren't relevant, but for simplicity (and recognisability), I'll be talking about human-like beings, the **Digital Humans**. In the following paragraphs, you'll learn that there are two types of Digital Humans, each with its own subcategories. One type is called Digital Doubles because they are digital versions of real human beings, while Virtual Humans, on the other hand, are unique to the virtual world. Now, let's explore the different Life Aspirations they offer.

Digital Doubles

As the world becomes increasingly digital and even virtual, people have been exploring and experimenting with different depictions of themselves. Along the way, I've noticed that there are now four different ways people present themselves in a digital environment. Each offers specific advantages to make expectations or aspirations.

Personal avatars are by far the most popular Digital Humans. They have gained plenty of traction with the popularity of Fortnite and Roblox – free online games that make billions of dollars every year from avatar personalisation. The previous chapter mentioned that gamers consider these personalised avatars as essential as their real-life personality. You could consider them to have personalities parallel to our real-life person. Today, you'll even find such **parallel personalities** outside the games themselves. Live streamers, such as MelodyProjekt and CodeMiko, are only known as avatars by their hundreds of thousands of Twitch followers. They carefully crafted an online personality and, through various hardware and software, can move and interact in real-time with their followers. Such personal avatars or parallel personalities are easily, or at least more often, accessible online. They are nearby. Now, imagine if physicians would be that nearby. I'll get to that in a minute.

Personalised avatars or parallel personalities in Roblox

Somewhere between scarily dangerous and genuinely funny are **deep fakes**. These digital doubles of real people look so real they're hard to distinguish from the real ones. You've probably seen videos of Barack Obama and Tom Cruise saying some bizarre stuff. It's confusing. The internet has created so much fake news and misinformation, which is already profoundly troubling. Now, deep fakes make you question everything and everyone. Of course, this technology can be truly dangerous. When Russia invaded Ukraine in February 2022, deep fake videos with President Zelensky and President Putin were used to confuse people on both sides of the war. It was the first use of deep fake technology for armed causes. However, there are also tremendous opportunities, as South Korean politician Yoon Suk-Yeol can confirm. Thanks to his deep fake digital double, he could talk to multiple people simultaneously, allowing his digital double to answer questions from an audience. At the same time, he did something else in reality. His reach became much more extensive. Several million people spoke with the politician's double in just a few weeks. Although people knew about the digital double, it gave the audience the feeling that they were important as they genuinely interacted with the political candidate. It makes people feel some **Belonging (feel accepted and included)** because they are listened to at any time.

Yoon AI, the Deep fake of Korean politician Yoon Suk-Yeol

Meanwhile, **holograms** are being used to bring the dead back to life, at least to a certain extent. Deceased artists like Tupac Shakur, Whitney Houston, Roy Orbison and Frank Zappa are still doing world tours as if they were teletransported as holograms from the past. In a certain way, holograms made teletransportation a reality. That is also what the company Proto was thinking. They produce holograms in a range of sizes that are so lifelike it feels like the person has been transported to another place and time. It feels like **Realness** *(be genuine and true to myself and others)* because it is real. It's just teletransported. Now, imagine being medically educated by a hologram medical professional.

The last Digital Double is the Digital or Virtual twin and was already treated in the previous chapter. Technology will allow us to build a digital replica of ourselves. iCarbonX is a Chinese tech company with such ambitions. It is already developing digital twins that enable users to experiment with lifestyle choices and help defeat disease. Digital twins can serve us well in our lives. Have you ever wanted to ask someone a question about your health? Well, why not ask yourself? It provides **Consciousness** *(being aware and comprehend)* and **Self-development** *(grow & cultivate oneself)*. Both are essential to optimise your health or prevent health risks. And it's a role that the village physician previously took upon himself. He was always there to make people aware and teach them about their health.

Virtual Humans

Digital doubles are a digital representation of existing humans. Virtual Humans, on the other hand, are unique, human-like people that only exist virtually. Here's my definition of a virtual human that explains the concept in more detail: a computer-generated moving image of a unique, human-like being capable of engaging in conversations with humans whilst seemingly living "life" according to its personal human-like preferences interests and values.

It's debatable whether or not virtual humans already exist today, at least in line with the above definition. But what's certain is that different parts of this definition are already present in our lives. We can have conversations with Digital Humans who are not a multiplied or parallel version of existing humans. So, let's explore a bit further.

The most popular virtual humans are known to us as automated chatbots that serve as **virtual assistants**. They guide us or answer our most urgent questions on websites, in applications, during conferences or at entrances. Most of you have had personal encounters with conversational bots already. They may be the best human-like solution between a helpdesk and FAQ page today, definitely when they speak and look like a human. That used to be hard. Many looked clunky or could only answer pre-defined questions. But that is what they did. They are there when you need it, like the village physician. It helps people with **Autonomy *(live independently and autonomously)*** as well.

Today, Artificial Intelligence has changed the game. Large Language Models make conversations feel more human and new video generators solved many challenging aspects of designing human-like virtual assistance: the skin, the hair, the look in their eyes, the inside of the mouth. Disney materialised the creation of photo-realistic eyes and inner mouths through the neural rendering of faces. And Unreal Engine, a 3D creation company, made it incredibly easy to design hyper-realistic human faces within no more than a couple of minutes with their MetaHuman Creator. How Unreal Engine creates virtual humans so real is... well... unreal... However, what makes these virtual assistants most human is their unique personality. A personality that does not exist in the real world. It's a vital aspect of virtual humans.

VIRTUAL ASSISTANTS

Nestlé *created a cookie coach named Ruth who answers the most frequently asked questions about making cookies (even how to make them gluten-free). In 2020, the* **New Zealand police** *force enlisted their newest officer, Ella, a conversational bot interacting with citizens daily. What's important to note here is that both examples are 'new' individuals with their own personalities, character traits, facial features and (so-called) backgrounds. This type of virtual assistant, which answers quickly and with a human touch, is also invaluable in healthcare. There are already plenty of examples around today. The* **NHS** *uses virtual assistant Olivia to schedule flu vaccines, while the WHO employ virtual health worker Florence to provide digital counselling services to people trying to quit smoking. In the Netherlands,* **Pharmi** *helps patients with arthritis who have questions about their treatment.*

NHS assistant **Olivia**   WHO worker **Florence**   Pharmacist **Pharmi**

A unique personality is what **virtual influencers** need to have as well. I was stunned when I realised in 2017 that Lil Miquela, a person I've been following on Instagram, was not real. Her life seemed real. But the 19-year-old was nothing but the first Virtual Influencer, a fictional computer-generated person who has human-like characteristics, features and life events. With over 7 million followers on socials, she is the perfect brand ambassador. But it doesn't stop here: she also features on the covers of fashion magazines, in television advertisements, and on Spotify. Her collaborations generate an annual revenue of about 12 million euros. Not bad for a Virtual Human. Throughout the years, I've followed all her travels, her break-ups and friendships (with real human beings), the parties, her jokes, and so forth... Her socials are a documentation of the 'real' life of a virtual person. A life that spans 6 years (while she remains 19, of course). Some virtual influencers even look so real that they cause turmoil for not being real. That was the case for Knox Frost, a 21-year-old Virtual Human from Atlanta in the USA. His social media posts talk about how he processes the internet's mixed reactions to his existence and struggles to fit in. Despite all this, Knox Frost has become the most popular male virtual influencer, so much so that he even collaborated with WHO to inform his million followers about COVID health guidelines. Yes, an international organisation enlisted a virtual influencer to help tackle a very real challenge. Virtual influencers blur the lines between real and unreal, but they can educate people on **Safeness** *(feel safe and protected)* like the village physician once did.

Lil Miquela, the most popular Virtual Influencer on social media

Today, we are familiar with Virtual Assistants and Influencers – two separate use cases with different features. But you can expect both to be growing to each other feature-wise. It's not difficult to imagine the value of Virtual Influencers having conversational features. On the other hand, it could also make sense to add more individual personality traits and 'life events' to Virtual Assistants. But what if those Virtual Humans would grow 'with you' into a **Virtual Individual** unique to you? This may sound like the movie HER. The film talks about how the protagonist falls in love with a Virtual Assistant with a sensitive, playful personality who starts to know him. The movie was launched in 2012 but was made a reality a couple of years later by Microsoft: Xiaoice. What began as a side project from its Cortana Chatbot quickly became valued at more than $ 1 billion. Today, over 660 million people are holding life-like, empathetic conversations with Xiaoice to satisfy their emotional needs that in real-life communication (unfortunately) are not met. Xiaoice is also expected to be one of the first virtual individuals who can listen and talk simultaneously. Being interrupted while you talk. How human-like can it be? How much more **Realness *(be genuine and true to myself and others)*** can we expect?

VIRTUAL INDIVIDUALS

*Virtual Individuals have already proven to be in demand. Today, more than 7 million people use Replika, 'an AI companion who cares'. He or she will make you laugh, discuss emotions, debate psychology and provide you with insights about yourself. It's important to understand that this virtual individual is never a finished product. Like other artificial intelligence, it grows with the number of conversations you have. Your Replika will turn into a virtual human who knows you and can call you for a chat. Replika also has a Not Safe For Work (NSFW) feature, which facilitates explicit and erotic text-based interactions, enabling users to engage in adult-themed conversations and role-playing scenarios. In February 2023, Replika removed the NSFW features to avoid scrutiny regarding the explicit role-playing interactions. It was part of a rebranding effort to position itself as a platform for platonic friendship and mental wellness. But this change was not welcomed by its users, who claimed to have a **Loving (love or be loved)** relationship with the virtual individual.*

Samsung is another key player in the virtual individual landscape. The company presented their virtual humans, called NEONs, at CES in 2020. They were thoughtfully introduced as 'a new kind of life' and 'a believably real being'. And they're right – a NEON looks and behaves like a human and will soon become intelligent enough to be fully autonomous, show emotions, learn skills and create memories. A virtual individual made by one of the most powerful consumer tech companies in the world is definitely something to keep an eye on, especially because one of its future applications is that of a virtual healthcare provider. Yes, your doctor might one day be a virtual individual.

The Digital Village Physician

In chapter 13.1 on Artificial Intelligence, I mentioned how the LINE would provide all citizens with Doctor NEOM, a virtual physician who's always near and helps pursue Life Aspirations. It's a transformational experience that does not differ so much from what the village physician offered a hundred years ago. It approaches people personally and considers their reality with empathy and **Kindness** *(be kind to myself and others)*. It builds a **Relationships** *(have meaningful connections)* that makes them feel **Belonging** *(feel accepted and included)*, which generates trust, authenticity and **Realness** *(be genuine and true to myself and others)*. Health and self-care requires human interaction. And if workflows and processes don't allow humans to cater to the necessary Life Aspirations, a digital village physician might be the closest thing available.

It feels unsettling to bring back human interaction and empathy with digital humans. However, I said before that we must rethink what it will mean to be human. I also believe that, in today's reality, it will be vital to think about the Life Aspirations of your customers and build experiences that make people feel better, healthier or happier. People wish for transformations with technology. In fact, 82% of people believe a Digital Human as a therapist can already support their mental health better than a human, according to a global study by Oracle (2022). And how world-shocking this may sound, you can already notice where these Digital (Humans) will make their impact first. As advisors, they will be helping people navigate through the complexities of the world; they will act as personal life coaches, offering motivation and focus; they are personalised to understand and empathise with the user's specific circumstances, providing conversation and support when needed. And yes, that is exactly what the village physician used to do.

14.2 Other technologies

Technology, in one form or another, has had a significant impact on our lives for millennia. But in recent decades, perhaps every aspect of our lives, of what we do in life, has been subject to some form of technological change. This offers opportunities and perspectives; it solves existing challenges and brings new challenges. But what is certain is that it completely changes who we are, what we want and what we can do. Our needs are being met entirely differently by new, practical technological solutions. Unfortunately, this doesn't necessarily make us feel better, nor does it make us healthier or happier.

Every need can be met, yet it will not necessarily make us healthier and happier.

But let's take it one step further. Within 10 years, absolutely everything will be possible thanks to technological innovations. Every need can be met, yet (still) it will not necessarily make us healthier and happier. This question will become increasingly important to consider: What is really important in people's lives? Therefore, the Life Aspirations in Part Two of this book will only become more valuable. If technology is not used to fulfil these universal values and priorities, our health and well-being risk being pressured.

But even if we think a technology helps pursue specific Life Aspirations, even then, we will have to be skeptical. Is the technology really fulfilling the Life Aspirations, or not? For example, social media may offer you connections, but you don't feel really connected to people. Social media seems like an answer to the aspiration for **Relationships *(have meaningful connections)***, but does it do this in a way that makes us happy? I wouldn't dare to give an outright positive answer to that question. This is exactly the challenge at hand in the coming years.

Conclusion

I have tried to get you thinking about these challenges in Part Five of this book. I wanted to do this based on probably the two most talked about technological innovations of the last three years and how they could be transformational. This is not an obvious exercise; several relevant elements have probably not been discussed yet. But I wanted to show you how technology can be transformational and why transformational technology can be (more) successful. The future vision of Digital Humans in healthcare was a perfect example of how technology may be able to fulfil some Life Aspirations that have received less attention in recent years. But at the same time, you may also have felt that Digital Humans might not be the 'perfect' solution, just like social media is not the perfect solution for maintaining meaningful relationships. And that is precisely the challenge of transformational technologies.

The coming together of these technologies will profoundly change our society, especially our interactions with the world around us (including people). Considering what is important to people in this new world will be vital. Because as technology changes faster than humans can adapt (emotionally, socially, culturally), this leads to mini/macro moments of human crisis. Social media has indeed led to the greatest loneliness crisis in human existence even though it intended to connect people with each other. Such human shock is also expected with the new wave of technologies. Therefore, it will be essential for any creator or distributor always to consider what really matters to people: Life Aspirations.

EPILOGUE

What is your intention?

As this book comes to a close, I don't like ending it by presenting you with the same angles again. I have already sufficiently explained the importance of Transformations and the usefulness of Life Aspirations. Before you close the book and put it aside, I would like to reduce all the theories and trends to their essence. An essence that you can take with you in your daily life as a business manager, healthcare professional or simply as a human being. And I believe this essence can be expressed with a single question: **"What is your intention?".** Herein lies the underlying message or the soul of this book.

Let me unpack that for you.

Today, it is not just about the actions themselves but the fundamental intention of doing something. Intention begins with our dreams and desires and considers our values and priorities. These 'Life Aspirations' - as we have called them in this book - drive the decisions we make every day. They are intentional.

We are thus thinking intentionally about our actions. And this comes as no surprise. We are forced to be more intentional: Disastrous climate disasters, unjust wars, shameful scandals, ubiquitous loneliness, geopolitical tensions, and sudden health scares form the daily information we absorb. We can make this better, right? We have to do something about this!

Hence, we increasingly intend to do better for ourselves, society or the planet (See: Part One). We also feel strengthened because compared to 25 years ago, we have more opportunities to 'do something' ourselves. So, it no longer only remains intentional. Today's social, cultural and technological developments give us more control over our intentions. As a result, we take things into our own hands and undertake intentional actions.

But we also make intentional choices as we often can't do it alone. Sometimes, we seek help from others with the same intentions. When choosing brands or companies, we imagine asking them, "What is your intention?" (see Part 4). In discussions with healthcare professionals, we determine how their recommendations match our intentions (see Part 3). Finally, the usefulness of technology is balanced with its actual intention (see Part 5). Today, the value presented to us in healthcare, by companies or with technology must be aligned with our own values, our Life Aspirations. Those are the intentions people are looking for.

In the Transformation Economy, your customers will value products, services and experiences based on authentic, valuable intentions that meet theirs. Asking yourself, "What's my intention?" might be the most relevant takeaway from this book.

But maybe you are asking the same question about me (or this book): "What is your intention?".

Well, I intend to create awareness and provide solutions for what matters most: our health, well-being and happiness. Nothing is more important than being healthy and happy, right? I want to help build a healthier future. I aspire to make healthcare, consumers, or technology companies think about their intentions: How can they keep or make their customers healthy and happy? How can they help their customers pursue their Life Aspirations? With this book, I want to demonstrate that the time has come for this. Because yes, deliberate actions with good intentions are the common denominator for all the trends in the Transformation Economy.

As you read this book's last sentences, I invite you to share your thoughts, questions and, of course, intentions via my website.

Thanks for reading.

-Christophe-
www.christophejauquet.com

THANK YOU

The process of writing a book is lonely. I often call myself a hermit or say that I am living under a rock. This has been a lonely reality, especially in recent months. And yet, you need help to write a book. It's been a years-long process fueled by numerous conversations with people smarter than me. Those conversations are necessary for a book. If I had to rely on the ideas in my own head, the soup would be bland. "I keep stirring my own soup that I can no longer taste it." So, thanks where thanks are due. However, it is impossible to recall the faces of the many conversations over the past 42 months. Still, your messages certainly resonate in this book.

A new book is triggered by a persistent question and/or a new insight. In the case of this book, there were three moments that sparked it. First, many customers challenged me after the first book with the question, "What is healthy and happy really?" This had to be answered. There was no escape. In fact, it urged the need for a second book.

A second trigger came from an intrigued reader and fan of the 'Customer Transformation' ideas of Joseph Pine II and James H. Gilmore. Alain Thys, a Transformation Architect, asked me how I saw the realisation of Customer Transformations in reality. I wasn't quite sure, and yet my answer led me to the word "Aspirations." Because it made sense. But that's all I knew yet.

The last trigger was an insight given to me by pharmacist Luc Kleynjans. In some of the conversations with him about the launch and positioning of his start-up, Yoboo, he told me that the most frequently asked question in his pharmacy is linked to the desire to have more energy. So, energy was the first aspiration I discovered. Seth Godin then provided insight into many other universal human desires, and conversations with psychologists confirmed the path I was walking on.

However, it took me more than 3 years to test this out, shape it and write it down in a digestible form. This required time, but especially a second brain to let my often heavy, complex thoughts come down in a soft, straightforward way. Alanah Reynor was the one who repeatedly urged me to speak clear, concrete language. The people from Lannoo Campus, Niels Janssens and Marije Roefs, also managed to untangle the twists and turns in my head again and again. Karl Demoen, a visual mastermind, succeeded in converting words into powerful images (see cover).

This is how this new book came about with my own ideas, models and visions. And, to be frank, launching such new ideas and models into the world is nerve-wracking. I would therefore like to thank all my customers who served as a 'testing ground' for this thinking. Thanks to them, I felt where things were going well and where things could be improved. However, I only felt really confident about this book thanks to the additions and improvements made by the proofreaders. I was fortunate to learn from many brilliant people who picked up on my writing. Jane Sarasohn-Kahn, LinkedIn's top voice in healthcare with the same Healthusiasm as myself, supplemented my ideas where necessary. Mo Zouina, my Healthusiasm Podcast panellist and good friend, pointed out the missing human tone. Kris Michiels, CEO of the Belgian Marketing Association, challenged me to go even further. After her invaluable input for the first book, Nathalie Bloom, an experienced patient engagement and innovation lead, was again an inspiring sounding board for this second book. Geert Reyniers, a digital health pioneer with amp healthcare and pharma experience, found the missing pieces in the healthcare component. Frank Eijsink, a Board Member of an insurance company that emphasises the human factor within insurance helped me increase the credibility of my ideas. I hope I have taken all your feedback to heart. In any case, you have contributed to the quality and readability of my written ideas.

The panellists of the Healthusiasm Podcast also contributed a lot to this. Every month, we discussed several topics that made it into this book. Thank you for your smartness, Aline Noizet, Dr. Aditi U. Joshi, Dr. Keith Grimes, Krupa Suthar, Mo Zouina, and the many guests we had the pleasure of exchanging ideas with.

I am deeply grateful to my girlfriend Micheline D'hooge and my son Elouan Jauquet for their unwavering support and understanding during the writing process. Your patience and tolerance of my demanding need for silence in the house were instrumental in making this feat possible. I also want to thank my parents, Philippe Jauquet and Linda Dewulf, for always being there to listen during the challenging moments. Your presence and support have been my source of strength and perseverance.

Sadly enough, in the final stages of writing this book, I lost two dear figures: my cousin Olivier Jauquet and my best friend at university, Antoine Van den Bogaert. Their passing, after a long battle with a terrible disease, underscored the importance of Life Aspirations for all of us. I dedicate this book to their Lust For Life, which continues to inspire me and is reflected in the pages of this book.

Thank also you, the reader, for making it all worth it.

-Christophe-